WELFARE ECONOMICS AND
SOCIAL CHOICE THEORY

Welfare Economics and Social Choice Theory

Allan Feldman
Brown University

Martinus Nijhoff Publishing, Boston
Boston/The Hague/London

Distributors for North America:
Martinus Nijhoff Publishing
Kluwer Boston Inc.
160 Old Derby Street
Hingham, Massachusetts 02043

Distributors outside North America:
Kluwer Academic Publishers Group
Distribution Centre
P.O. Box 322
3300AH Dordrecht, The Netherlands

Library of Congress Cataloging in Publication Data

Feldman, Allan, 1943–
  Welfare economics and social choice theory.

  Bibliography: p.
  Includes index.
  1. Welfare economics. 2. Social choice. I. Title.
HB99.3.F45   330.15'5   79-25744
ISBN 0-89838-033-2

Printed in the United States of America

CONTENTS

PREFACE

This book covers the main topics of welfare economics — general equilibrium models of exchange and production, Pareto optimality, externalities and public goods — and some of the major topic of social choice theory — compensation criteria, fairness, voting, Arrow's Theorem, and strategic behavior. The underlying question is this: "Is a particular economic or voting mechanism good or bad for society?" Welfare economics is mainly about whether the market mechanism is good or bad; social choice is largely about whether voting mechanisms can improve upon the results of the market.

The book grew out of my undergraduate welfare economics course at Brown University, and it is intended for the undergraduate student who has some prior familiarity with microeconomics. However the book is also useful for graduate students and professionals, economists and non-economists, who want an overview of welfare and social choice results unburdened by detail and mathematical complexity.

Welfare economics and social choice both suffer, I think, from excessively technical treatments in professional journals and monographs. One purpose of this book is to present these fields in a way that reduces mathematical technicalities. Knowledge of calculus and linear algebra is not a prerequisite for reading this. However, the results are presented rigorously; there are theorems and proofs (occasionally relegated to appendices), and the reader should be familiar enough with logic to know when A implies B and when it doesn't. What mathematical notation is used is defined and explained as it is introduced. Each analytical chapter contains examples to illustrate the concepts and the theorems, and most of the chapters provide exercises for the reader.

At the ends of most chapters are lists of selected references. These references sections are not meant to be scholarly bibliographies; rather, they should be used by the reader who wants to dig a little deeper into a subject, or who wants to find out a little about the source of a possibly ancient idea.

I would like to thank all my past students of welfare economics and social choice for helping me distill this material. I would like to thank the editors of *Economic Inquiry* and *The American Economic Review,* in whose journals parts of Chapters 8, 10, and 11 were previously published. My wife Barbara patiently read much of the manuscript while it was being prepared, and Mrs. Marion Wathey heroically typed it.

Providence, Rhode Island   *A. F.*

INTRODUCTION

THE CONCERNS OF WELFARE ECONOMICS

Welfare economics is the normative branch of economics: it is concerned with *what is good and what is bad,* rather than *what is.* This distinguishes it from the positive branches of economics, such as labor economics, health economics, economic history, the theory of financial markets, development and international trade, monetary and macroeconomics. Each of the positive branches is largely devoted to explaining why things are the way they are: e.g., why doctors are paid more than nurses, why some countries export agricultural commodities and some export machinery, and why business fluctuations occur. Many positive economists make policy prescriptions; some say we ought to have no minimum wage, or we ought to have a higher minimum wage, or we ought to have lower tariffs, or we ought to have a 3 percent annual growth in the money supply. These prescriptions are all based partly on positive economics (the prescribers have information that indicates the likely consequences of actions that might be taken) and partly on normative economics (the prescribers have some ideas about which consequences are *good* and which are *bad*).

1

Welfare economics is not the Boy Scout Code of Honor of economics. It is obviously more than that: it is very analytical, very deductive, very much a collection of theorems, or statements of the form "If A, then B." In fact, it might be viewed as a branch of symbolic logic, and you could strip it entirely of its normative content by simply saying it is a collection of theorems — all of which are logically true, but none of which is connected to everyday affairs or to values. None of the theorems says "The United States Government ought to do X, Y, and Z." But when welfare economics is viewed this way it's not as exciting as it can be. To see why welfare economics is concerned with what is good or what isn't good, rather than whether or not A implies B, we turn to the contents of some of those theorems.

The first basic idea we use is the notion of a competitive economy. In the United States the economy is a complicated mixture of firms and people, tens of thousands of wheat and corn farmers, dozens of oil refiners, a handful of car manufacturers, thousands of actors and actresses, hundreds of thousands of builders, and millions of consumers. Some of the markets for goods and services are extremely competitive, in the sense that no one person or firm has a significant influence on prices, such as the market for soybean meal; while some of the markets are extremely concentrated, in the sense that a few firms or people have a major influence on prices, such as the auto market. The question of concentration and its effects are beyond the scope of this book, and we will assume for simplicity in most of what we do that people and firms take prices as given. Moreover, the properties of particular markets for particular goods, special problems like the state of the soybean market in 1978, will not concern us here. We will deal instead with a model, an abstraction, a concept of a competitive economy, which we think does relatively little violence to the reality. To be specific, a competitive economy for us is a system of profit-maximizing firms and rational, or utility-maximizing individuals. What can be said about such a system? In particular, is there anything normative to say about it? Can we say it's good or bad?

The question leads to our next basic notion, the idea of Pareto optimality. According to the dictionary, the word *optimal* means most favorable or best. But we have a special idea of optimality, which can be illustrated with two examples of economic situations that are not Pareto optimal. First, suppose that three boys can earn $5, $5 and $7 respectively (that is, $5 for boy 1, $5 for boy 2, and $7 for boy 3) by doing a certain chore X for their mother. Suppose that there is a different chore Y which would earn them $6, $6 and $7, respectively. Also, suppose that the chores are equally onerous, and suppose that their mother doesn't care whether they do X (and she pays $17) or they do Y (and she pays $19). If all of this is true, we can say that X is not Pareto optimal because there exists an alternative Y which could make some people better off than X (boys 1 and 2) and no one worse off.

Second, suppose three men own three trucks. Man 1 has a Ford, man 2 has a Chevy, and man 3 has a Dodge. Suppose also that man 1 prefers Fords to Chevys to Dodges; that man 2 prefers Fords to Dodges to Chevys; and man 3 prefers Fords to Chevys to Dodges. Also, suppose they are free to swap, if they want to. Then this distribution of trucks among the three is not Pareto optimal because there is an alternative distribution, in which man 1 still has his Ford, man 2 has the Dodge, and man 3 has the Chevy, that makes some people better off (men 2 and 3) and no one worse off.

In short, a situation is not Pareto optimal if there is an alternative situation available that makes some people better off and no one worse off. A situation, a state of affairs, or an economy *is* Pareto optimal if there is *no* alternative available that makes some people better off and no one worse off.

With the ideas of a competitive economy and of Pareto optimality in hand, we can turn to the first basic theorem of welfare economics: It says that, barring externality and public goods problem, a competitive economy guarantees a Pareto optimal economic outcome. And the normative idea here is that a competitive economy is "good," in the sense that it produces an optimal outcome. Any economic system that didn't produce an optimal outcome would be obviously "bad," because there would exist an alternative which some people would prefer and everyone would like as well.

The reader might note that our notion of Pareto optimality is a weak notion of goodness because it is very inclusive. It is certainly the case that if something is not optimal than it ought to be overruled, but just become something is optimal doesn't mean it's really best. For instance, in our three-boy example, if they were paid $1, $1 and $17 respectively for chore Y, Y might well be optimal, although awfully hard on boys 1 and 2. Or, in the three-man example, there are many distributions of the trucks among the men that are optimal, such as the distribution that assigns all three trucks to man 1. But this is awful for men 2 and 3. So the theorem that says a competitive economy guarantees a Pareto optimal outcome is fine so far as it goes — but it might not go far enough. There are too many Pareto optima, some of them palatable and some not.

This observation, that the market mechanisms might produce a good (Pareto optimal) result, but not the very best result, motivates the second basic theorem of welfare economics. Suppose someone or something concludes that of all the Pareto optimal distributions of goods possible in an economy, distribution X is the very best, the ideal of the optimal. The second basic theorem says that, with minor modifications involving transfers of cash among various people, the competitive mechanism can be used to reach X. That is, X can be achieved via the interplay of profit-maximizing firms and/or utility-maximizing individuals. Consequently, it is unnecessary to have a huge bureaucracy to decide who gets what in the economy.

In short, the first theorem says that a competitive market economy produces a Pareto optimal result (and that's good), and the second says that any Pareto optimal distribution of goods can be achieved via a slightly modified competitive mechanism. These two theorems link together the competitive market mechanism and Pareto optimality. This is the essence of classical welfare economics.

THE CONCERNS OF SOCIAL CHOICE THEORY

Where do we draw the line between welfare economics and social choice theory? The two basic theorems of welfare economics link competition and optimality. But neither one answers these questions: How should we choose among Pareto optimal situations? How do we distinguish among the good? Or, in general, under what circumstances is it reasonable to say that alternative A is better for society than alternative B? The most important results in welfare economics indicate that competitive market mechanisms are good in the sense that they are Pareto optimal. The most important results in social choice theory are connected with attempts to answer this general question: When is A socially better than B?

Most economists assume that people have preferences. When faced with any two alternatives A and B a person can say whether he prefers A to B or prefers B to A, or likes them equally well. Is it conceivable that a society — a collection of individuals — has social preferences that are similar to an individuals preferences? If it makes sense to say that society does have preferences, then there is a way to judge among the many Pareto optimal allocations, to find the very best from among the good. And there is a way to decide whether alternative A is better for society than alternative B. In short, there is a way to answer the questions left unanswered by the theorems that link the competitive market mechanisms and Pareto optimality. Social choice theory is, therefore, largely about social preferences, and how they might be found.

Social preferences might be defined by a charismatic religious leader (like Ayatollah Khomeni in Iran in 1979) or a charismatic political leader (like Lenin or Mao Tse-Tung). This is clearly an important possibility, but we won't analyze it seriously since we are interested in the theory of democratic institutions in this book. Social preferences might be defined by "experts," by "leaders," by "opinion makers," or by movie stars like Marlon Brando and Jane Fonda. This is again a serious possibility that we won't take very seriously. Social preferences might be determined by economic criteria, by market criteria, or by things like cost-benefit analysis. This possibility we do take seriously. Perhaps A should be considered better for society than B if A represents more dollars than B. Social preferences might be determined by egalitarian criteria, by fairness criteria, or by notions like Rawls' maximin criterion. Perhaps A should be considered better for society than B if A creates more equality than B. Again, this is an important possibility, and we do analyze it here.

But we have not yet touched on the most interesting way to discover social preferences, most interesting at least for citizens of a democratic society. We have noted that the competitive market mechanisms and the connected idea of Pareto optimality tell us something about what's good and what's not, but don't distinguish very fully among the good. The major alternative to the market mechanisms, at least for us, is the political process, and the political process ultimately depends on voting mechanisms. Voting mechanisms are in fact widely used to judge among good, (or Pareto optimal) alternatives, and voting processes are extensively used to decide when alternative A is socially better than alternative B. Voting is an exceptionally important way to define or reveal social preferences, and we shall analyze it carefully here. (Incidentally, another way to distinguish between welfare economics and social choice theory is to say that the former is about market mechanisms and the latter is about voting mechanisms, while both are about what's good and what's not good.)

There are many ways to try to find social preferences — market-related procedures and voting procedures being most important for our purposes. There are many ways to approach the problem: Is A socially better than B?

What then are the basic results of social choice theory? What general statements can we make about whether alternative A is better than alternative B? Does social choice theory provide a rule that always answers that question satisfactorily?

First, we should note that there are positive results in social choice theory — results that says things like "majority voting has properties X, Y, and Z, or plurality voting has properties W, U, and V." For instance, a theorem of Duncan Black says that if people's preferences satisfy a certain requirement, then majority voting produces social preferences that are as reasonable and as rational as any person's preferences. And if this is the case, it's easy to determine (at least conceptually) when A is better for society than B, to determine which of the Pareto optimal (or good) situations are really best for society. Majority voting becomes a source of sensible social preferences, and can be used as the ultimate test of what's better for society than what.

But it has been known, at least since the late eighteenth century, that majority voting has one very serious logical flaw. If A, B, and C are three alternatives, it is possible that majority voting will indicate that (1) A is socially better than B, (2) B is socially better than C, and (3) C is socially better than A. That is, there might be a voting paradox, a voting cycle, and the social preferences derived by majority vote might be irrational. For instance, a country's legislature might be contemplating these alternatives: (A) to increase expenditures on national defense, leaving expenditures on other budget items constant; (B) to increase expenditures on welfare programs, leaving expenditures on other budget items constant; or (C) to decrease expenditures on all budget items. It is quite possible that the legislature might conclude, through majority voting, that (1) is better to increase defense expenditures than welfare expenditures, (2) it is better to increase welfare expenditures than to decrease all expenditures, and (3) it is better to decrease all expenditures than to increase defense expenditures. But this is irrational, and leaves no acceptable course of action!

Also, as we shall see, there are serious objections that can be made against other procedures for determining when A is socially better than B. For instance, many of the market-related procedures, the procedures that provide the theoretical foundation for important everyday tests like cost-benefit tests, reduce in the end to a question of Pareto optimality vs. non-Pareto optimality, to statements like "A is socially better than B if A is Pareto optimal and B isn't." This surely isn't very helpful, because the goal is to find a way to judge among the many Pareto optima.

In fact, much of the analysis of social choice theory produces negative conclusions, conclusions of the type: Procedure X for determining when A is socially better than B has such-and-such a nasty characteristic. And all of these negative conclusions are drawn together in one important negative theorem, the most important single result of social choice theory, the Impossibility Theorem of Kenneth Arrow.

What does it say? The essence of Arrow's result is that any procedure for finding social preferences — whether it is based on the market, on voting, on expert opinion, or whatever — any procedure must have some serious flaw. So the search for a procedure to find social preferences, the search for a general answer to the question "when is A better for society than B," has to be inconclusive.

But it is such an important search that it must be made, even though it can't have a happy ending. And much of social choice theory, much of the second half of this book, is about that search.

PRACTICAL CONCERNS OF WELFARE ECONOMICS
AND SOCIAL CHOICE THEORY

So far we've indicated that welfare economics tells what is good (the Pareto optimal situations) and what isn't (the non-optimal situations), and that, barring externality and public goods problems, there is a crucial link between the competitive market mechanism and Pareto optimality. We've also indicated that general answers to the question of "Is A socially better than B?" are hard to come by. These are both fairly abstract results, but there is a practical welfare economics issue that we haven't touched: What happens to that crucial link between competition and optimality when there are externalities, when there are public goods?

When one person's decisions affect another person's welfare in a way that is not reflected by market prices, we have an externality. For instance, suppose person A smokes cigars in the same room with person B, a non-smoker. Then A's decisions affect B's welfare, they impose a cost upon B that A does not pay. And in a case like this, the market doesn't provide the proper signals to A, and the resulting situation is not Pareto optimal. The link between the competitive market and optimality is destroyed.

What is a public good? It is a good whose consumption is non-exclusive: when A has it, so must B. For instance, a public park is a public good: if it is there for one person to enjoy, it's there for everyone to enjoy. National defense is a public good: if the armed forces are protecting the person and property of A, then they are doing so for A's compatriot B. A police and judicial system is a public good: if there are police officers and judges and jails which protect A from mayhem, theft and fraud, then they are also protecting B from mayhem, theft and fraud. Now when there are public goods present, the private market mechanism, in which consumers are buying goods to maximize their own utilities, again doesn't provide people with the right signals. People could (and do) hire armed guards. But who would have his own court and jail system, if it weren't provided by the state? Who would have his own army? Who would buy his own Yellowstone Park? When there are public goods like these around, private markets won't accomplish the right results, and the link between the competitive market mechanism and optimality is again destroyed.

What then should be done to establish a Pareto optimal outcome when there are externalities or public goods on the scene? These are the practical problem of welfare economics.

There are several solutions explored in this book. To solve externality problems, there are Pigouvian taxes and subsidies, which internalize the externalities. For instance, if the cigar smoker is causing 10¢ worth of damage to others with each cigar he smokes, tax him 10¢ per cigar. This will give him the right signal, and optimality will be reestablished.

To solve the problem of producing and financing a public good, there are several tax expenditure systems available. In all these systems, individuals pay taxes to a government, which decides on how much of the public good ought to be produced, and pays for its production out of tax revenues. In the Wicksell-Lindahl system, a person's marginal benefit from public expenditure is linked to the tax he pays. This system leads to optimal expenditures on the public good — providing people don't try to avoid taxes by misrepresenting their desires for the public good. In the demand revealing system, people have no incentives to misrepresent their demands for the public good. We shall discuss these tax-expenditure systems at some length, as well as the Groves-Ledyard system and a majority voting tax system.

In short, welfare economics establishes a link between competitive markets and optimality. So competitive markets are good. Social choice theory points out all the pitfalls in answers to the general question: "When is A socially better than B?" And the practical side of welfare economics patches up some of the gaps between the theory of perfect private markets, and the reality of externality and public goods problems.

1 PREFERENCES AND UTILITY

FUNDAMENTAL ASSUMPTIONS

We suppose that there is a set of states, or alternatives, or bundles of goods, or "things" in the world. At various times we'll use various symbols to denote those things, but for now, we use the letters $x, y, z, \ldots$ Later on we will be more explicit about the nature of our set of things.

The first fundamental assumption that we make about people is that they know what they like: they know their preferences among the set of things. If a person is given a choice between x and y, he can say (one and only one sentence is true):

1. He prefers x to y
2. He prefers y to x
3. He is indifferent between the two.

This is the axiom of *completeness*. It seems reasonable enough.

But some objections could be made to it. For a variety of reasons, a reasonable person might not be able to choose. If you are given the choice between shooting your dog and shooting your cat, you will balk. If you don't

9

know what x and y really are; if, for example, both are complicated machines like cars and you don't know much about them, you may be unwilling to choose. If you are used to having your choices made for you; if you are dependent on your parents, your doctor, your religious guide, your government, you may be incapable of making choices yourself. Moreover, it may be painful, time consuming, distasteful, and nerve-wracking to make choices, and we will more or less ignore these costs of decision making. In spite of these objections, we make the assumption.

The second fundamental assumption is the axiom of *transitivity*. The assumption has four parts:

1. If a person prefers x to y and prefers y to z, then he prefers x to z.
2. If a person prefers x to y, and is indifferent between y and z, then he prefers x to z.
3. If a person is indifferent between x and y, and prefers y to z, then he prefers x to z.
4. If a person is indifferent between x and y, and is indifferent between y and z, then he is indifferent between x and z.

There are several possible objections to the transitivity assumption. Parts (1), (2), and (3) may simply not be true for some people under some circumstances. It might be the case that you prefer apple to cherry pie, and cherry to peach pie, while you prefer peach to apple. In fact, experiments with real subjects sometimes do reveal intransitivities of this sort, although when they are brought to the subjects' attentions, they typically change their minds. Part (4) is the least realistic, since it can be applied repeatedly to get nonsense results: Let x_1 be a cup of coffee with one grain of sugar in it; let x_2 be a cup of coffee with two grains of sugar in it; and so on. Now it's almost certainly the case that you can't taste the difference between x_k and x_{k+1}, for any whole number k, and so you must be indifferent between them. Therefore, by repeated applications of (4), you must be indifferent between x_0 and $x_{1,000,000}$, which is probably false. The problem here is evidently the existence of psychological thresholds. It can be escaped by assuming those thresholds away, or by assuming away the existence of finely divisible states of the world.

It is possible for some purposes to do without parts (2)–(4) of the transitivity assumption, in which case we say preferences are *quasi-transitive*. And quasi-transitivity itself can be further weakened, by assuming:

If a person prefers x_1 to x_2, and prefers x_2 to x_3, . . ., and prefers x_{k-1} to x_k, then he does *not* prefer x_k to x_1.

If preferences satisfy this assumption we say they are *acyclic*. In most of what follows, however, we assume all of transitivity for individuals' preferences.

The third and last fundamental assumption is that people always choose an alternative which is preferred or indifferent to every alternative available to them. They choose "best" alternatives for themselves. In short, they are rational.

BEST ALTERNATIVES AND UTILITY FUNCTIONS

In the middle and late nineteenth century it was popular in some philosophical circles to assume that pleasure and pain could be numerically measured. The measurement was in terms of *utils* or *utility units,* which were considered as scientifically real as units of length, mass, or temperature. Now a unit of length is scientifically real for several reasons: first, there is a standard object which everyone agrees represents one unit (e.g., a platinum rod in a vault in Paris); second, there is a natural zero for length; third, units of length can be added, subtracted, and multiplied by numbers according to the rules of arithmetic, and the results make sense: 2 meters + 2 meters = 4 meters.

Some of the nineteenth century advocates of utility calculus thought utility could be standardized and measured, like length; they thought the units could be used to measure everyone's happiness; they thought there was a natural zero between pleasure and pain; and they thought units of utility could be added and subtracted in a reasonable way.

But no one has yet succeeded in defining an objective unit of utility. Is it a level of electrical activity somewhere in the brain? Is it an index constructed from pulse, blood pressure, glandular activity data? Is it a rate of salivation, a degree of pupil dialication, or perspiration? We don't know. There is now no way of comparing levels of satisfaction among different people. For that matter, there is no objective way of measuring utility at two different times for the same individual.

But there is a subjective way: Ask him. (If you don't believe what a person says, you might choose instead to observe him. See what he chooses when he has what opportunities. If he chooses x when he might have chosen y, he reveals his preference for x.)

The problem with asking about utility is this. If you ask "How many units of happiness would you now get if I give you a banana?" you will be laughed at. The question must be more subtly put. Ask instead, "Would you prefer a banana or an apple?" This is our fundamental question.

Asking "Would you prefer x to y" will never get you a measure of utility with well defined units, a zero, and other nice mathematical properties. But it will allow you to find alternatives that are at least as good as all others, and, remarkably, it will allow you to construct a numerical measure to reflect tastes. The determination of best alternatives and the construction of a measure of satisfaction are both made possible by the completeness and transitivity assumptions on preferences. Therefore, the theory of preferences, with those two assumptions, is connected to, and is a generalization of, the old-fashioned nineteenth century theory of utility.

THE FORMAL MODEL OF PREFERENCES

Before we can proceed, we need to introduce some notation. Let x and y be two alternatives. We consider a group of people who are numbered 1, 2, 3, and so on. To symbolize the preferences of the ith person we write xR_iy for "i thinks x is at least as good as y"; xP_iy for "i prefers x to y"; and xI_iy for "i is indifferent between x and y."

The relation R_i should be viewed as the logical primitive, the "given." The relations P_i and I_i can be derived from R_i with these definitions:

xP_iy if xR_iy and not yR_ix
xI_iy if xR_iy and yR_ix

In words: Person i prefers x to y if he thinks x is at least as good as y but he does not think y is at least as good as x. And i is indifferent between x and y if he thinks x is at least as good as y and he thinks y is at least as good as x.

Now our fundamental axioms of completeness and transitivity are formally put this way:

Completeness. For any pair of alternatives x and y, either xR_iy or yR_ix.

Transitivity. For any three alternatives x, y, and z, if xR_iy and yR_iz, then xR_iz.

Notice that these definitions are in terms of the primary relation R_i, rather than in terms of the derived relations P_i and I_i. The verbal definitions in the section above were in terms of P_i and I_i. The reader can check that the verbal and the formal definitions are in fact logically equivalent. That is, if R_i is transitive in the sense that, for all x, y, and z, xR_iy and yR_ix implies xR_iz, then the following must also be true:

1. xP_iy and yP_iz implies xP_iz. (See Proposition 1 below.)
2. xP_iy and yI_iz implies xP_iz.

3. xI_iy and yP_iz implies xP_iz.
4. xI_iy and yI_iz implies xI_iz.

The less fundamental (and weaker) assumptions of quasi-transitivity and acyclicity are formally put this way:

Quasi-transitivity. For any three alternatives x, y, and z, if xP_iy and yP_iz, then xP_iz.

Acyclicity. For any list of alternatives x_1, x_2, . . ., x_k, if $x_1P_ix_2$, $x_2P_ix_3$, . . ., and $x_{k-1}P_ix_k$, then not $x_kP_ix_1$.

Let us now prove that if a preference relation R_i is transitive, it must be quasi-transitive, and if it is quasi-transitive, it must be acyclic:

Proposition 1. If R_i is transitive, then it is quasi-transitive. If R_i is quasi-transitive, then it is acyclic.

Proof. Suppose first that R_i is transitive. We want to show it is quasi-transitive. Suppose xP_iy and yP_iz. We need to show xP_iz, that is, xR_iz and not zR_ix. Now xP_iy means xR_iy and not yR_ix, and yP_iz means yR_iz and not zR_iy. Since xR_iy and yR_iz, xR_iz follows by R_i's transitivity. If zR_ix were also true, then we would have zR_ix, xR_iy, and, by R_i's transitivity, zR_iy, which contradicts not zR_iy. Consequently, zR_ix cannot be true; that is, not zR_ix. But xR_iz and not zR_ix means xP_iz, and R_i is quasi-transitive.

Next suppose R_i is quasi-transitive. We want to show it is acyclic. Suppose $x_1P_ix_2$, $x_2P_ix_3$, . . ., $x_{k-1}P_ix_k$. We need to show not $x_kP_ix_1$. Since $x_1P_ix_2$ and $x_2P_ix_3$, $x_1P_ix_3$ by quasi-transitivity. Similarly, since $x_1P_ix_3$ and $x_3P_ix_4$, $x_1P_ix_4$ by quasi-transitivity. Repeated applications of this argument gives $x_1P_ix_k$, and not $x_kP_ix_1$ follows immediately.

Q.E.D.

We have already noted that preferences can be quasi-transitive without being transitive: the grains-of-sugar-in-coffee example shows this. Preferences can also be acyclic without being quasi-transitive or transitive. Suppose someone likes apples (A) better than bananas (B), and bananas better than cherries (C), but is indifferent between apples and cherries. Then his preferences relation is AP_iB, BP_iC, and AI_iC. This doesn't violate acyclicity since there is no preference cycle. (If CP_iA holds, there is a cycle.) But the preference relation is not quasi-transitive, since quasi-transitivity would require AP_iC.

With the necessary tools in hand, we proceed to define what is meant by an individual's "best" choices. Suppose S is some collection of alternatives. Let x be an element of S. Then x is said to be best for person i if i thinks it is at least as good as every other element of S.

Formally, i's *best set in S* or i's *choice set in S*, denoted $C(R_i,S)$, is defined as follows:

$$C(R_i,S) = \{x \text{ in } S | x \, R_i y \text{ for all } y \text{ in } S\}$$

This is read: "$C(R_i,S)$ is the set of all x's in S, such that $x \, R_i y$ for all y's in S." (Note that braces { } means "the set" and a slash | means "such that.")

Now to the next result. Proposition 2 answers the question "When can we be sure best things exist?" One answer is: Whenever a preference relation (defined on a finite set) is complete and transitive.

Proposition 2. Let S be a finite set of alternatives available to person i. Suppose R_i is complete and transitive. The $C(R_i,S)$ is nonempty. That is, best choices exist.

Proof. Choose one alternative, say x_1, from S. If it is best, we are done. If not, there is an alternative, say x_2, for which

$$x_1 R_i x_2$$

does not hold. By completeness $x_2 R_i x_1$ must hold, and therefore, by definition

$$x_2 P_i x_1$$

If x_2 is best, we are done. If not, we can choose an x_3 such that

$$x_3 P_i x_2$$

by the same argument as above.

This process can either terminate at a best choice (in which case we are done), or it can go on indefinitely. Since S has only a finite number of elements, if the choice process goes on forever, it must repeat. Therefore, there must be a cycle:

$$x_1 P_i x_k P_i x_{k-1} P_i \ldots x_3 P_i x_2 P_i x_1$$

Repeated applications of the transitivity assumption implies $x_k P_i x_1$. But this contradicts $x_1 P_i x_k$. Hence, the process cannot continue indefinitely and the choice set is nonempty. Q.E.D.

But Proposition 2 could clearly be strengthened by substituting the assumption of quasi-transitivity, or of acyclicity, for our fundamental assumption of transitivity, since the key to the proof is the possible existence of a cycle in the individual's preferences. In fact, the following proposition is also true. The proof is virtually the same as for Proposition 2, and is left to the reader.

Proposition 3.   Let S be a finite set of alternatives available to person i. Suppose R_i is complete and acyclic. Then $C(R_i,S)$ is nonempty. That is, best choices exist.

Proposition 3 can itself be strengthened to more clearly indicate the connection between the existence of best or choice sets, and acyclicity of the preference relation. The following proposition says that when R_i is complete, best sets are always nonempty if *and only if R_i is acyclic:*

Proposition 4.   Suppose R_i is complete. Then $C(R_i,S)$ is nonempty for every finite set of alternatives S available to person i, if and only if R_i is acyclic.

Proof: The "if" part of the proof follows from Proposition 3. To prove the "only if" part, we assume $C(R_i,S)$ is nonempty for every finite set of alternative S. We want to show R_i is acyclic.

Suppose to the contrary that R_i is not acyclic. Then there exist alternatives $x_1, x_2, \ldots, x_k$ such that $x_1 P_i x_2, x_2 P_i x_3, \ldots, x_{k-1} P_i x_k$, and $x_k P_i x_1$. Let $S = \{x_1, x_2, x_3, \ldots, x_k\}$. Then $C(R_i,S)$ is empty, since every alternative in S is inferior to some other alternative in S. But this is a contradiction. Consequently R_i must be acyclic.   Q.E.D.

The propositions above answer this question: Given particular assumptions about a person's preferences, can he always identify best alternatives? The next proposition answers a different question: Is there a numerical function, a utility function, which represents a person's preferences? If the answer is yes, then familiar mathematical tools can be applied to the problem of identifying best alternatives, since the search for a best alternative reduces to the problem of maximizing a utility function. If the answer is no, the use of utility functions, indifference curves, and all the other common tools of economics, is very likely illegitimate. It turns out that the answer is yes if preferences are complete and transitive. (And in this case, acyclicity cannot substitute for transitivity.)

Proposition 5.   Let S be a finite set of alternatives available to person i. Suppose R_i is complete and transitive.

Then we can assign numerical values $u_i(x)$, $u_i(y)$, $u_i(z)$, etc., to the alternatives in S so that

$$u_i(x) \geq u_i(y) \text{ if and only if } x R_i y$$

In other words, there is a utility function u_i which places values on the alternatives that exactly reflect i's preferences. The proof is in the appendix to this chapter.

We should note that u_i could be transformed without altering its preference representation property. For instance, if we define $v_i = u_i + C$, where C is any constant, then $v_i(x) \geq v_i(y)$ if and only if $u_i(x) \geq u_i(y)$, if and only if xR_iy. Therefore, v_i represents R_i as well as u_i does. And if $u_i(x) \geq 0$ for all x's, u_i^2 would represent R_i as well as u_i. In fact, any transformation of u_i that does not change relative values leaves the representation property intact. For this reason, u_i is called an ordinal utility function, and, unlike the hypothesized utility functions of nineteenth century philosophers, it does not behave like a cardinal measure such as length: For our utility function, there exist no standard units, there are no natural zeros, and it makes no sense to add $u_i(x)$ to $u_i(y)$. Nor does it make any sense to add $u_i(x) + u_j(y)$, if u_j is another person's utility function.

What then is the use of an ordinal utility function? In fact, it transmits exactly the same information as the preference relation it represents: neither more, nor less. But a utility function allows us to analyze, in a compact and easy way, the behavior of an individual in an economic environment. It is quite correct to say that a consumer chooses a bundle of goods that is preferred or indifferent to every other bundle available to him. But it also correct to say that he choose a bundle of goods to maximize his utility, and the utility approach is mathematically and graphically convenient. It allows us to use the standard tools of the economist's trade.

Under certain mathematical assumptions too complex to be made explicit here, Proposition 5 can be extended as follows:

Proposition 6. Let S be a (possibly infinite) set of bundles of goods. Suppose R_i is complete and transitive over S. Then there exists a utility function u_i defined on S which exactly reflects i's preference relation R_i.

This proposition will be used extensively in the following chapters.

INTRODUCTION TO SOCIAL PREFERENCES

Interest in quasi-transitivity and acyclicity arises largely from the analysis of social preferences, rather than of individual preferences. It is hard to imagine, for instance, that a person could have preferences which are acyclic but not quasi-transitive. But society's preferences are not, as we shall explain at length in later chapters, nearly so sensible as a person's.

A few examples will clarify the idea of social preferences, and the possibilities of nontransitivities for them. Suppose a group is making choices between alternatives, by using some voting rule. If x defeats y in a vote, let us say x is socially preferred to y, which we now write xPy. If x and y tie, let us say x and y are socially indifferent, which we now write xIy. If x is socially preferred to y or socially indifferent to y, we now write xRy. Where we had R_i, P_i, and I_i for individual 2's preference, strict preference, and indifference relations, we now have R, P, and I for society's preference, strict preference, and indifference relations.

Let us be more specific about the voting rules. Assume for simplicity that there are only three people in the group that is making the choices, and assume there are only three alternatives, x, y, and z.

Our first example is an instance of Condorcet's voting paradox, to which we shall return in Chapter 9 below. The voting rule is simple majority rule: a vote is taken between a pair of alternatives, and if alternative A gets more votes than alternative B, then A wins. Suppose the individuals' preferences are as follows: Person 1 prefers x to y to z. Person 2 prefers y to z to x. Person 3 prefers z to x to y. Each individual has sensible transitive preferences, but they evidently disagree on the relative merits of the three alternatives. We can indicate these preferences diagramatically by listing the alternatives from top to bottom in the order of each person's preferences:

1	2	3
x	y	z
y	z	x
z	x	y.

Consider a vote between x and y. Evidently, if the individuals vote according to their preferences, which we assume they do, person 1 votes for x; person 2 votes for y; and person 3 votes for x. Consequently, xPy. Next, consider a vote between y and z. Now person 1 votes for y; person 2 votes for y; and person 3 votes for z. Consequently, yPz. Finally, consider a vote between x and z. Now person 1 votes for x; person 2 votes for z; and person 3 votes for z. Consequently, zPx. We have a cycle here, since xPy, yPz, and zPx. These social preferences are not even acyclic.

The moral is social preferences might be very odd indeed — they need not share the sensible rational qualities of individual preferences. What about best sets in this example? We do have $C(R, \{x,y\}) = \{x\}$: x is best if the choice is limited to x and y. Similarly, $C(R, \{y,z\}) = \{y\}$, and $C(R, \{x,z\}) = \{z\}$. But R has a cycle. So Proposition 4 warns us that there is some set of available alternatives S for which $C(R,S)$ is empty. And, in fact, $C(R, \{x,y,z\})$ is empty: if all three alternatives are available, none is best according to majority rule. Each alternative is worse than one of the others.

Now we turn to a slightly different example. Suppose the people, alternatives, and preferences are as above, but the majority rule mechanism is modified as follows: A vote is taken between a pair of alternatives, and if alternative A gets more votes than alternative B, then A wins — unless person 1 prefers B to A. If 1 prefers B to A, and A wins a majority over B, then A and B are declared tied, or socially indifferent. We call this rule simple majority rule with a vetoer. Person 1 has a veto, in the sense that he can prevent any alternative from actually beating another alternative he prefers. What are the voting results for this rule? Consider a vote between x and y. Alternative x gets two votes to one for y, and person 1, who prefers x anyway, does not exercise his veto. Consequently, xPy. Next, consider a vote between y and z. Alternative y gets two votes to one for z, and person 1 again does not exercise his veto. Consequently, yPz. Finally, consider a vote between x and z. Alternative z gets two votes to one for x, but now person 1 does exercise his veto, since he prefers x to z. Consequently, xIz. In sum, xPy, yPz and xIz. These social preferences are acyclic, although they are not quasi-transitive. Since they are acyclic, Proposition 4 tells us that best sets are always nonempty. In fact, $C(R, \{x,y,z\}) = \{x\}$ in this case; the alternative x is socially best. (It is no accident, of course, that x is also person 1's favorite.)

For the third example, we again continue with the people, alternatives and preferences above, but majority rule is now discarded. The new rule is an oligarchy of persons 1 and 2, and it works like this: A is socially preferred to B if and only if both persons 1 and 2 prefer A to B. Otherwise, A and B are socially indifferent. Now consider a "vote" between x and y. Person 1 prefers x to y, but 2 prefers y to x. Consequently, xIy. Next, consider a vote between y and z. Person 1 prefers y to z and person 2 prefers y to z. Consequently, yPz. Finally, consider a vote between x and z. Person 1 prefers x to z but person 2 prefers z to x. Consequently, xIz. In sum, xIy, yPz, and xIz. Here there are no cycles, so the social preference relation is acyclic. Moreover, the definition of quasi-transitivity is (vacuously) satisfied. (It would not be satisfied if xPy and yPz, and xIz, as in the former example.) But the social preference relation is not transitive, because transitivity requires that if xIy and yPz, then xPz must follow. So this is an example of a quasi-transitive, but not transitive, social preference relation. Note that $C(R, \{x,y,z\}) = \{x,y\}$, the favorite alternatives of the two oligarchs.

The next examples are not hypothetical as the three preceding ones. They were first discussed, in the 1970s, by Donald Brown:

We now consider two voting rules used by the United Nations Security Council. The first was in force prior to August 31, 1965. At that time there were five permanent and six nonpermanent members of the Security Council. To be passed, a motion needed seven affirmative votes, and the concurrence of all five permanent members. That is, each permanent member had to vote aye on a motion, or to abstain, or that motion would be defeated. Each permanent member had a veto. Now, assuming that each nation's Ambassador had transitive (i.e., sensible) preferences, the procedure could not cycle. To see this, suppose there were a series of motions, or amendments to motions, or amendments to amendments, such that x_1 defeated

x_2, x_2 defeated x_3, x_3 defeated x_4, . . ., and x_{k-1} defeated x_k. Since x_1 defeated x_2, x_1 got seven affirmative votes from the eleven members of the Council. Consequently, one of the permanent members must have voted affirmatively for x_1 over x_2. Say the United States voted affirmatively for x_1. Then the United States presumably preferred x_1 to x_2. Now x_2 was passed over x_3. Consequently, x_2 had seven affirmative votes over x_3, and the concurrence of all five permanent members. That means every permanent member either preferred x_2, to x_3, or was indifferent between the two. In particular, the United States either preferred x_2 to x_3, or was indifferent between the two. Similar reasoning shows the United States either preferred x_n to x_{n+1}, or was indifferent between the two, for $n = 3, 4, . . ., k-1$. Consequently, by repeated applications of transitivity, the United States preferred x_1 to x_k. Therefore, the United States would have used its veto power to prevent x_k's winning over x_1: so x_k could not possibly defeat x_1. A cycle could not occur: the voting rule was acyclic. From Proposition 4 we know that no matter what set of alternatives was available, the voting procedure would sensibly identify at least one best alternative.

The second United Nations Security Council voting rule was put in force on September 1, 1965. At that time, the nonpermanent membership of the Council was increased from six to ten. The permanent membership remained at five. To be passed, a motion now needs nine affirmative votes, and the concurrence of all five permanent members. This procedure can cycle. To see this, we construct an example. There are ten alternatives, labelled x_1, x_2, . . ., x_{10}. Assume for the sake of argument that the five permanent members are all indifferent about all these alternatives: None feels strongly enough about any of the alternatives to veto it. Assume that the preferences of the nonpermanent members are as follows: (Under member 1, we list the alternatives, from top to bottom, in that Ambassador's order of preference; similarly for 2, 3, and so on.)

1	2	3	4	5	6	7	8	9	10
x_1	x_{10}	x_9	x_8	x_7	x_6	x_5	x_4	x_3	x_2
x_2	x_1	x_{10}	x_9	x_8	x_7	x_6	x_5	x_4	x_3
x_3	x_2	x_1	x_{10}	x_9	x_8	x_7	x_6	x_5	x_4
x_4	x_3	x_2	x_1	x_{10}	x_9	x_8	x_7	x_6	x_5
x_5	x_4	x_3	x_2	x_1	x_{10}	x_9	x_8	x_7	x_6
x_6	x_5	x_4	x_3	x_2	x_1	x_{10}	x_9	x_8	x_7
x_7	x_6	x_5	x_4	x_3	x_2	x_1	x_{10}	x_9	x_8
x_8	x_7	x_6	x_5	x_4	x_3	x_2	x_1	x_{10}	x_9
x_9	x_8	x_7	x_6	x_5	x_4	x_3	x_2	x_1	x_{10}
x_{10}	x_9	x_8	x_7	x_6	x_5	x_4	x_3	x_2	x_1

The table is formidable, but the analysis is perfectly simple: Consider a vote between x_1 and x_2. Everyone except the Ambassador from Country 10 prefers x_1 to x_2. (The permanent members are indifferent.) Consequently, x_1 defeats x_2. Consider a vote between x_2 and x_3. Everyone except the Ambassador from Country 9 prefers x_2 to x_3. (The permanent members are indifferent.) Consequently, x_2 defeats x_3. Similarly, x_3 defeats x_4, x_4 defeats x_5, x_5 defeats x_6, x_6 defeats x_7, x_7 defeats x_8, x_8 defeats x_9, and x_9 defeats x_{10}. Now consider a vote between x_1 and x_{10}. Everyone except the Ambassador from Country 1 prefers x_{10} to x_1. (The permanent members are indifferent.) Consequently, x_{10} defeats x_1, and there is a voting cycle!

To briefly summarize the observations of this section, the question of transitivity for a preference ordering, which hardly arises for an individual's ordering, does arise with a vengeance for a social preference ordering. In our discussion of individuals, where it is comfortable to assume completeness and transitivity for preferences, we shall largely use Proposition 5 and the utility functions that proposition guarantees exist. But when we return to social preferences, we shall have return to the concepts of this chapter, and pay careful attention to ideas like completeness, transitivity, and transitivity's weaker cousins, quasi-transitivity and acyclicity.

EXERCISES

1. Show that if a preference relation R_i is transitive in the sense that xR_iy and yR_iz for all x, y, and z, then (i) xP_iy and yI_iz implies xP_iz, and (ii) xI_iy and yI_iz implies xI_iz.
2. Hockey team A defeats hockey team B. Hockey team B defeats hockey team C. Hockey team A ties hockey team C.
    a. Is this preference order complete? Is it transitive? Quasi-transitive? Acyclic?
    b. Can you identify a best hockey team?
    c. Can you construct a "quality" function u for hockey teams, with the property that $u(x)>u(y)$ if and only if x defeats y? Show with numbers why you can or cannot do this.
    d. Can you construct a pseudo quality function v for hockey teams, which only satisfies this property: if x defeats y then $v(x) > v(y)$?
3. Suppose a committee has five rational members, and, for motion x to defeat motion y, x needs four affirmative votes out of the five.
    a. Show that if there are five alternatives available, there can be a voting cycle.
    b. Show that if there are only four alternatives available, there cannot be a voting cycle.

APPENDIX

Proof of Proposition 5.   For notational convenience in this proof, we will drop the subscript *i* wherever it appears.

Suppose S is finite and R is complete and transitive. We want to show that there exists a utility function u such that

$u(x) \geq u(y)$ if and only if xRy

First, we subdivide S into "indifference classes."

Let $C_1 = C(R,S)$. C_1 is nonempty by Proposition 2.

The alternatives in S which are not in C_1 we call $S - C_1$.

Let $C_2 = C(R,S - C_1)$. C_2 is nonempty by Proposition 2.

The alternatives in S which are not in C_1 or in C_2 we call $S - C_1 - C_2$.

Let $C_3 = C(R,S - C_1 - C_2)$. C_3 is nonempty by Proposition 2.

We continue in this fashion until we have exhausted S. This we must be able to do because S is finite. Let C_h be the last class so constructed.

Now define $u(x) = \begin{cases} h \text{ if } x \text{ is in } C_1 \\ h - 1 \text{ if } x \text{ is in } C_2 \\ \cdot \\ \cdot \\ \cdot \\ 1 \text{ if } x \text{ is in } C_h \end{cases}$

Next we show that $u(x) \geq u(y)$ implies xRy. Suppose $u(x) \geq u(y)$. Then x is in the same class as y, or in a class constructed before the class containing y. Let C_k be the class containing x. Then x is in $C(R, S - C_1 - C_2 - \ldots - C_{k-1})$ while y is in $S - C_1 - C_2 - \ldots - C_{k-1}$. Therefore, xRy.

Finally, we will establish that xRy implies $u(x) \geq u(y)$. We will argue that $u(x) < u(y)$ implies not xRy. Suppose $u(x) < u(y)$. Let C_k be the indifference class containing x, and C_j be the indifference class containing y.

Since $u(x) < u(y)$, x's class C_k was constructed after y's class C_j. Therefore, y is in $C(R,S - C_1 - \ldots - C_{j-1})$, x is in $S - C_1 - \ldots - C_{j-1}$, but x is not in $C(R,S - C_1 - \ldots - C_{j-1})$. Therefore, yRx and there is some alternative z in $S - C_1 - \ldots - C_{j-1}$ such that yRz (because y is in the best set $C(R,S - C_1 - \ldots - C_{j-1})$) but not xRz (because x is not). By completeness, if not xRz, then zPx.

Now by transitivity, if yRz and zPx, then yPx. Hence, not xRy, which is what we wanted to establish.   Q.E.D.

SELECTED REFERENCES

(Items marked with an asterisk (*) are mathematically difficult.)

1. K. Arrow, *Social Choice and Individual Values,* 2nd Edition, John Wiley and Sons, Inc., New York, 1963, Chapter II.

   This is an easy to read chapter of the classic monograph by Kenneth Arrow. It has short but useful observations on older literature. Arrow's notation and formalization of preferences and best or choice sets are the ones followed in this book.

2. D. J. Brown, "Aggregation of Preferences," *Quarterly Journal of Economics,* V. 89, 1975, pp. 456–469.

   This relatively nontechnical piece by Donald Brown is meant to introduce the nonspecialist to modern variants of Arrow's Impossibility Theorem. In these variants *oligarchies* and what Brown calls *collegial polities* take the place of dictators in Arrow's original theorem. Our example above of a majority rule mechanism with a vetoer is a Brown collegial polity. Our observations about the Security Council of the United Nations are taken from this Brown article.

*3. G. Debreu, *Theory of Value,* John Wiley and Sons, Inc., New York, 1959, Chapter 4.

   Chapter 4 of Gerard Debreu's classic monograph has a rigorous proof for existence of continuous utility functions. The mathematics is rather sophisticated.

*4. R. D. Luce, "Semiorders and a Theory of Utility Discrimination," *Econometrica,* V. 24, 1956, pp. 178–191.

   This article deals with individual preferences that are complete, but not transitive. Instead of transitivity, quasi-transitivity, or acyclicity, Luce assumes the following intuitive property: It is possible to "string out all the elements of S [the set of available alternatives] on a line in such a fashion that an indifference interval never spans a preference interval." For such preferences, there is a theorem similar to, but slightly different than our Proposition 5.

5. A. K. Sen, *Collective Choice and Social Welfare,* Holden-Day, Inc., San Francisco, 1970, Chapter 1*.

   Amaryta Sen's book provides an extremely clear treatment of most topics in social choice. Chapter 1*, on preferences relations, is formal but not difficult. Sen's Lemma 1*1 is the original version of our Proposition 4 above.

2 BARTER EXCHANGE

INTRODUCTION

In the previous chapter we analyzed preferences and developed, in Propositions 5 and 6, the connections between preferences and utility functions. In that chapter the set of alternatives was abstract; it might have been interpreted as virtually anything: The alternative might have been consumption bundles, political candidates, meals in a restaurant, careers. In fact, the alternatives might have been potential dates, or potential spouses. People have analyzed the system of choice of spouses in terms of completeness and transitivity of preferences, and so on.

In this chapter and several that follow, we shall focus on a particular set of alternatives, the alternatives of primary concern to a microeconomist. A microeconomist analyzes the economic behavior of consumers and producers of goods and services. Now a consumer is someone who buys, or gets in trade, quantities of goods, or things, like food, housing, cars, clothes, medical care, haircuts, and so on. He acquires these things because he wants them, because he likes them, because he needs them, or, in our language, because he prefers them to what he gives up in exchange for them, or because they give him a higher level of utility than the things he gives up in exchange. If A swaps B a 1969 Oldsmobile and a dog for a 1970 Ford, A does it because he prefers the 1970 Ford to the 1969 Olds/dog combination, or because the Ford gives him more utility. B does it because the 1969 Olds/dog combination gives him more utility.

This chapter will be about such swapping, or barter exchange. In order to analyze barter exchange, we will construct a model in which a group of people exchange bundles of goods among themselves. The story goes roughly like this: Each trader starts with some given initial bundle of goods. A new distribution of goods, or allocation, is proposed by someone. The traders discuss the proposal among themselves. If some group of traders decides that it can do better on its own, with its given initial resources, it objects to the proposal, and the proposal is rescinded or blocked. Then a new proposal is made by someone. The process continues until an allocation is found to which no group of traders objects. The traders then accept that new distribution of goods.

This is basically the model of barter exchange developed by Francis Y. Edgeworth in 1881. It will hopefully provide us with certain insights about how an economic system of exchange works, or ought to work, and what a system of exchange might accomplish for the people who comprise it.

ALLOCATIONS

The set of alternatives is now a set of distributions or allocations of goods in an economy.

Let's suppose that there are n people, numbered 1, 2, . . ., n. Usually a person is indexed with the letter i. Often we'll let $n = 2$, in which case we are talking about what happens when there are only two people (like Adam and Eve exchanging fruit in the Garden of Eden).

We assume there are m different goods. Typically we index a good with the letter j, so the goods are numbered $j = 1, 2, . . ., m$. This is the entire list of goods. In some contexts, there might be only one ($m = 1$) or two ($m = 2$) goods. In others, there might be tens of thousands of goods.

A good is something that a consumer might want to consume. It might be apples, or fruit. But if one good is apples, another good cannot be fruit without producing boundless confusion. The goods are distinct, non-overlapping. Housing might obviously be a good. Happiness probably isn't a good, since you can't easily buy it or trade it. We don't like to think of a consumer going to a store to buy happiness. But services can be goods in our list. A shoeshine is a plausible good; a visit to a dentist is another.

We will assume for mathematical simplicity that every good is perfectly homogeneous and perfectly divisible, like water, gasoline, or natural gas.

Obviously pianos aren't divisible. But the divisibility assumption is very convenient in economic analysis since it allows us to use continuity arguments, and, anyway, it does not produce misleading conclusions. That is, the results we derive using divisibility are, in the main, true when indivisibility is explicitly allowed.

Now let's turn to some more notation. We let x_{ij} be person i's quantity of good j. The first subscript identifies the person, the second identifies the good. If good 3 is bananas, then x_{13} is the number of bananas for person 1. Obviously, x_{ij} must always be nonnegative: a person cannot possess a negative quality of a good.

We let x_i be person i's bundle or vector of goods. Thus $x_i = (x_{i1}, x_{i2}, x_{i3}, \ldots, x_{im})$; so x_i shows m things: i's quantity of good 1, i's quantity of good 2, i's quantity of good 3, $\ldots$, i's quantity of good m. For example, if $m = 3$, good 1 is apples, good 2 is peaches, and good 3 is bananas, and if $x_1 = (8,2,0)$, then person 1 has 8 apples, 2 peaches, and no bananas.

Next, we define $x = (x_1, x_2, \ldots, x_n)$. Now x show person 1's bundle of goods, person 2's bundle of goods, $\ldots$, person n's bundle of goods. It is a list of bundles of goods. To say the same thing, it is a vector of vectors.

In the theory of exchange there is no production; what goods are available are there in the beginning. We let ω_{ij} be person i's starting or initial quantity of good j. Similarly, ω_i is his initial bundle, and ω is the initial list of bundles of goods. The total of good j available must be

$$\omega_{1j} + \omega_{2j} + \omega_{3j} + \ldots + \omega_{nj} = \sum_{i=1}^{n} \omega_{ij}$$

The symbol

$$\text{``} \sum_{i=1}^{n} \omega_{ij} \text{''}$$

is short-hand for "summation of the ω_{ij}'s, where i ranges from 1 to n."

An *allocation* is a list of bundles of goods x with totals of goods consistent with the totals initially available. This means

$$\sum_{i=1}^{n} x_{ij} \text{ must equal } \sum_{i=1}^{n} \omega_{ij}$$

for every j, that is, every good. We call the set of allocations a, and a is formally written as follows:

$$a = \{x \mid x_{ij} \geq 0 \text{ for all } i, j \text{ and } \sum_{i=1}^{n} x_{ij} = \sum_{i=1}^{n} \omega_{ij} \text{ for all } j\}$$

The set of alternatives in the theory of exchange is a.

One of the simplest examples of an exchange economy involves only two people and one good; so $n = 2$ and $m = 1$. Let the total quantity of the good initially available, $\omega_{11} + \omega_{21}$, be equal to 1. Then α is the set of all pairs (x_{11}, x_{21}) such that $x_{11}, x_{21} \geq 0$ and $x_{11} + x_{21} = 1$. The set of allocations in this economy can be easily diagrammed. To picture α, draw a line segment one unit long. Choose a point x on the line segment, and let the distance from the lefthand end of the line to x represent person 1's quantity of good x_{11}, and let the distance from the righthand end of the line to x represent person 2's quantity of the good x_{21}. Now x_{11}, $x_{21} \geq 0$, and $x_{11} + x_{21} = 1$, so every such point represents an allocation, and, conversely, every allocation can be represented by such a point, or division of the line.

THE EDGEWORTH BOX DIAGRAM

The most useful example of an exchange economy is one in which there are two people and two goods. This economy's set of allocations can be illustrated in an Edgeworth box diagram, which is constructed in the following manner:

Again suppose that the total quantity of each good available is one unit. Instead of a line segment one unit long, we draw a square, each of whose sides is one unit long. Good 1 will be measured horizontally, and good 2 will be measured vertically. A division of the horizontal side(s) of the box represents a division of the first good between the two people, that is, the quantities x_{11} and x_{21}. A division of the vertical side(s) of the box represents a division of the second good between the two people, that is, the quantities x_{12} and x_{22}. Dividing the horizontal and vertical sides is equivalent to choosing a single point in the box, and therefore, any point in the Edgeworth box diagram represents an allocation, and conversely, any allocation is represented by a point in the Edgeworth box.

In Figure 2-1, person 1's bundle x_1 can be read off by measuring x's coordinates from the origin in the lower lefthand corner, and person 2's bundle x_2 can be read off by measuring x's coordinates from the upper righthand corner.

The next step is to represent the preferences of the two people. We will always assume that person i has a utility function $u_i(x)$, defined for any allocation x. A locus of allocations for which the function u_i is constant is called an *indifference curve*. This is analogous to an elevation line on topographical map, or an isobar on a weather map. In Figure 2-2 we have drawn a few indifference curves for person 1 (the solid lines) and for person 2 (the

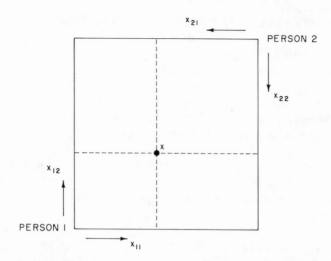

FIGURE 2-1

dashed lines). It is typically assumed that people's utilities rise as the quantities of goods they possess increase, so indifference curves further from person 1's origin (the lower lefthand corner) represent higher levels of u_1; and 2's indifference curves further from his origin (the upper righthand corner) represent higher levels of u_2. The point ω represents an initial allocation.

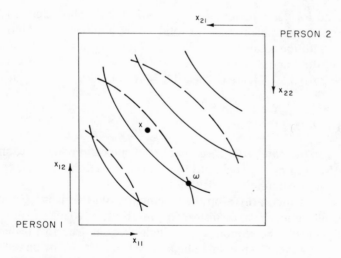

FIGURE 2-2

PARETO OPTIMAL ALLOCATIONS AND THE CORE

Some allocations are unambiguously inferior to others. For example, in Figure 2-2 x is preferred by both people to the initial allocation ω. Moreover, x is feasible for them: 1 and 2 can join together, trade, and reach x — given that they have ω in the beginning. If an arbitrary group of people can join together and better a proposed allocation, with their initial resources, we say they block the proposal. This notion is formalized as follows:

First, individual i is said to be *selfish* if u_i is a function of x_i alone: $u_i(x) = u_i(x_i)$. This means i is neither helped nor harmed by any other person's consumption of any good. Now let us assume that all individuals are selfish.

Consider a group of traders, called S. S might be one person, it might be several persons, or it might be all. Let $\{s_i\}_{i \text{ in } S}$ represent a set of bundles of goods, one bundle for each member of S. We say that $\{s_i\}_{i \text{ in } S}$ is *feasible* for S if

$$\sum_{i \text{ in } S} s_{ij} = \sum_{i \text{ in } S} \omega_{ij} \text{ for every good } j$$

The symbol

$$\text{``} \sum_{i \text{ in } S} s_{ij} \text{''}$$

is shorthand for "summation of the s_{ij}'s over the i's who belong to S." A set of bundles is feasible for S if the totals of the goods in those bundles are consistent with the totals the members of S initially possess. If x is a proposed allocation and S is a coalition, we will say that S can *block* x, (or S can *block x from* ω) if there is a feasible set of bundles $\{s_i\}_{i \text{ in } s}$, such that:

$$u_i(s_i) \geq u_i(x_i) \text{ for all } i \text{ in } S$$
$$u_i(s_i) > u_i(x_i) \text{ for at least one } i \text{ in } S$$

The *core* (or the *core from* ω) is that set of allocations which cannot be blocked (from ω) by any coalitions. Note that the definition of the core depends on our assumption of selfishness.

Now let us temporarily drop the assumption of selfishness. Consider a proposed allocation x, and, instead of an arbitrary coalition, the whole group of people in the economy. The whole group objects to x if there is a feasible alternative which is unambiguously better. A set of bundles $y = (y_1, \ldots, y_n)$ is feasible for the whole group if it is an allocation. We therefore make the following definition: An allocation x is not Pareto optimal if there is another allocation y such that

$$u_i(y) \geq u_i(x) \text{ for all } i = 1, 2, \ldots, n$$
$$u_i(y) > u_i(x) \text{ for at least one } i$$

If there is no such alternative, x is a *Pareto optimal,* or *efficient* allocation.

When the selfishness assumption holds and the core is therefore well defined, Pareto optimality is implied by inclusion in the core: An allocation is in the core if no group, including the whole set of traders, blocks it. An allocation is Pareto optimal if the whole set of traders does not block it. In what follows we will assume selfishness unless we say otherwise.

Let's pause to consider the significance of the three crucial ideas here: blocking, the core, and Pareto optimality. All have been defined in the context of a simple exchange-economy model. But the ideas are clearly generalizable. The notion of Pareto optimality is especially ubiquitous. It can be used as a test of the adequacy of any arrangement that is meant to satisfy people's preferences, economic or not. For suppose a situation — economic, political, or whatever — has the property that it can be changed so as to make everyone as well off ($u_i(y) \geq u_i(x)$ for all i) and some people better off ($u_i(y) > u_i(x)$ for at least one i). Then the situation has the potential for unambiguous improvement. Since it has the potential for unambiguous improvement, it is unambiguously imperfect. The ideas of blocking and the core are most easily applied to an exchange economy with selfish traders; so suppose an allocation has the property that some group of people can unambiguously improve upon it. Then the allocation is clearly objectionable for that group, and is therefore unambiguously imperfect. On the other hand, if an allocation is in the core, then no group can raise a clear objection to it.

Of course, a group's blocking or objecting to a proposed allocation depends on that group's initial resources. Consequently, the core depends on the initial distribution of goods or allocation ω. If ω makes A rich and B poor, that fact is reflected in the core. Whether or not a group can clearly object to a proposed allocation depends on what the group initially has.

The set of Pareto optimal allocation, on the other hand, does not depend on the initial distribution of goods among people, although it obviously does depend on the initial totals of the various goods.

Let's consider an illustration in an Edgeworth box diagram. When there are just two traders and two goods, and both traders have convex-shaped smooth indifference curves like the curves in Figure 2–3, the Pareto optimal allocations are the points, like x, y, and z, at which indifference curves of the two people are tangent. At these points it is impossible to make one

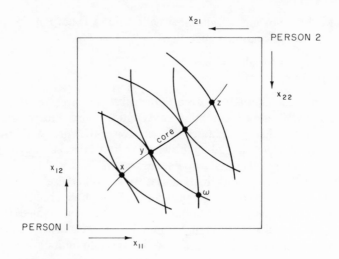

FIGURE 2-3

party better off without hurting the other. Point x, however, is blocked by person 1, since $u_1(\omega_1) > u_1(x_1)$. Similarly, z is blocked by 2. The core is the locus of Pareto optimal points, such as y, lying on or within the lens shaped area bounded by the indifference curves passing through ω.

ALGEBRAIC EXAMPLES

It will be useful at this point to work through a few algebraic examples, to see how to calculate the Pareto optimal and core allocations in an exchange economy.

As a first example, suppose there are two people and two goods, and suppose the people have these utility functions:

$$u_1 = x_{11}x_{12}$$
$$u_2 = x_{21} + 2x_{22}$$

In other words, person 1's utility level is the product of the quantities of the two goods he has, person 2's utility level is equal to the amount of good 1 he has plus twice the amount of good 2 he has. Let the initial allocation be $\omega_1 = (\frac{1}{2}, \frac{1}{2})$, $\omega_2 = (\frac{1}{2}, \frac{1}{2})$. Each starts with $\frac{1}{2}$ unit of each good.

In this case, person 1's indifference curves are hyperbolic (because $x_{11}x_{12} = $ constant is the formula for a hyperbola) and person 2's indifference curves are straight lines. In order to proceed, we need to find expres-

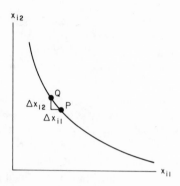

FIGURE 2-4

sions for the marginal rates of substitution, or the absolute values of the slopes of the two people's indifference curves.

An arbitrary indifference curve is drawn in Figure 2-4. The absolute value of the slope of the indifference curve at the point P is $|\Delta x_{i2}/\Delta x_{i1}|$. (This is an approximation for other than infinitely small Δ's.) Now $|\Delta x_{i2}/\Delta x_{i1}|$ is person i's *marginal rate of substitution* of good 2 for good 1, which we can abbreviate MRS for person i. To calculate an MRS it is most convenient to consider the marginal utilities of goods 1 and 2 for person i. The *marginal utility* of good 1 for i, which we abbreviate MU of good 1 for person i, is the rate at which his utility changes as his consumption of good 1 changes, or $\Delta u_i/\Delta x_{i1}$. The marginal utility of good 2 for i, or MU of good 2 for person i, is defined analogously. Now if person i loses Δx_{i1} units of good 1, his loss of utility is $\Delta u_i = \Delta x_{i1} \cdot$ MU of good 1 for i, by the definition of marginal utility. Similarly, if he acquires Δx_{i2} units of good 2, his gain in utility is $\Delta u_i = \Delta x_{i2} \cdot$ MU of good 2 for i, again by definition. If person i starts at the point P in Figure 2-4 and goes to the point Q, he loses Δx_{i1} units of good 1 and gains Δx_{i2} units of good 2. But he ends up on the same indifference curve, so the net change in his utility is zero. Consequently, the loss in utility equals the gain in utility, in absolute value, or

$$|\Delta x_{i1} \cdot \text{MU of good 1 for } i| = |\Delta x_{i2} \cdot \text{MU of good 2 for } i|,$$

from which it follows that

$$\text{MRS for person } i = \left| \frac{\Delta x_{i2}}{\Delta x_{i1}} \right| = \frac{\text{MU of good 1 for } i}{\text{MU of good 2 for } i}.$$

We can use this formula in our example.

Person 1's utility function is $u_1 = x_{11}x_{12}$. The marginal utility of good 1 for him is the rate at which $x_{11}x_{12}$ grows as his consumption of good 1, or x_{11}, grows. Now if x_{11} rises by Δx_{11} units, then u_1 rises by $\Delta x_{11} \cdot x_{12}$ units. Consequently, MU of good 1 for person $1 = x_{12}$. Similarly, MU of good 2 for person $1 = x_{11}$. Thus MRS for person $1 = x_{12}/x_{11}$.

Person 2's utility function is $u_2 = x_{21} + 2x_{22}$. The marginal utility of good 1 for him is the rate at which $x_{21} + 2x_{22}$ grows as his consumption of good 1, or x_{21}, grows. Now if x_{21} rises by Δx_{21} units, then u_2 rises by $\Delta x_{21} \cdot 1$ units. Consequently, MU of good 1 for person $2 = 1$. Similarly, MU of good 2 for person $2 = 2$. Thus MRS for person $2 = \frac{1}{2}$. (Note that there are no approximation complexities in this example, that is, no Δx_{ij} terms in the expressions for marginal utilities. If such terms appear, it is necessary to take the limits of the expressions involved as the Δx_{ij}'s approach zero.)

We are ready at this point to illustrate our little exchange economy in an Edgeworth box diagram, in Figure 2-5. The box is one unit on each side. We have sketched in four (hyperbolic) indifference curves for person 1, and four (straight line) indifference curves (with $|\text{slope}| = \frac{1}{2}$) for person 2. The two individual's indifference curves are tangent where their slopes are equal, or where

MRS person 1 = MRS person 2.

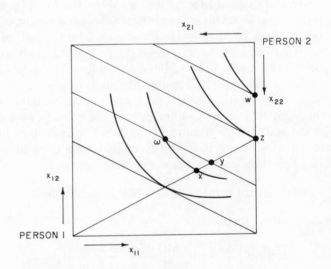

FIGURE 2-5

This gives

$$\frac{x_{12}}{x_{11}} = \frac{1}{2}, \text{ or } x_{12} = \frac{1}{2}x_{11}$$

Graphically, this is the straight line from person 1's origin to the point z. This straight line segment gives part of the set of Pareto optimal allocations, since any move from a point on it (like x or y) must take someone worse off.

But there are Pareto optimal allocations other than these tangency points. Consider, for instance, the point w. In order to make person 1 better off, starting at w, we would have to move above the hyperbolic indifference curve for person 1 going to w. This would make person 2 worse off. That is, there is no way to make everyone as well off and at least one better off. In fact, all the points on the righthand side of the box above point z are non-tangency Pareto optimal allocations.

Where are the core allocations in this example? Any core allocation must also be Pareto optimal, so the core allocations lie somewhere on the lines we've already identified as Pareto optimal. But a core allocation must not be blocked by person 1, or by person 2. Person 1 would block any allocation that gives him less utility than ω_1, or any allocation below his hyperbolic indifference curve through ω. Similarly, person 2 would block any allocation that gives him less utility than ω_2, or any allocation below (with respect to his origin) his straight line indifference curves through ω. Consequently, the core is the locus of points on the straight line between points x and y, including the endpoints x and y.

In this example, then, we would expect barter exchange between persons 1 and 2 to move the economy from ω to a point on the line segment from x to y.

Our next example has three people and two goods. We suppose the three traders have the following utility functions and initial bundles:

Person 1: $u_1(x_1) = x_{11}x_{12}$ $\qquad \omega_1 = (1,9)$
Person 2: $u_2(x_2) = x_{21}x_{22}$ $\qquad \omega_2 = (5,5)$
Person 3: $u_3(x_3) = x_{31}x_{32}$ $\qquad \omega_3 = (9,1)$

Instead of explicitly calculating the Pareto optimal and core allocations, let us simply consider one proposed allocation. Let x be given by:

$x_1 = (3,3)$
$x_2 = (5,5)$
$x_3 = (7,7)$

Clearly, no single individual will want to block x, because $u_i(x_i)$ is greater than or equal to $u_i(\omega_i)$ in every case. Moreover, the allocation x is Pareto optimal: If you draw Edgeworth boxes for all the pairs of traders, you will find each pair's indifference curves just touch at the points which correspond to x. Yet x will be blocked. This is so because the move from ω to x is a bad deal for 1 and 2. If they acted on their own, and ignored 3, they could rearrange their resources as follows:

For 1: $s_1 = (2,5)$
For 2: $s_2 = (4,9)$

This is a feasible set of bundles for them because

$2 + 4 = 1 + 5 \,(= \omega_{11} + \omega_{21})$
$5 + 9 = 9 + 5 \,(= \omega_{12} + \omega_{22})$

Moreover, both traders would be better off with (s_1,s_2) than they would under the proposed allocation x, since $u_1(s_1) = 10 > 9 = u_1(x_1)$, and $u_2(s_2) = 36 > 25 = u_2(x_2)$. In short, we would not expect barter exchange to lead this economy to the allocation x.

Our final example has two parts. Consider first a two-person, two-good economy in which the traders have utility functions

$u_1(x_1) = x_{11}x_{12}$
$u_2(x_2) = x_{21}x_{22}$

and in which the initial bundles are $\omega_1 = (9,1)$, $\omega_2 = (1,9)$. An Edgeworth box diagram for this economy would be ten units on each side, the initial allocation would be close to the lower righthand corner, and both people would have nice hyperbolic indifference curves. Reasoning like that used in the first example shows person 1's MU of good $1 = x_{12}$, person 1's MU of good $2 = x_{11}$, and consequently, the MRS for person $1 = x_{12}/x_{11}$. Similarly, MRS for person $2 = x_{22}/x_{21}$. Now consider the particular allocation x given by:

$x_1 = (3,3)$
$x_2 = (7,7)$

At this allocation, MRS for person $1 = \frac{3}{3} = 1$; MRS for person $2 = \frac{7}{7} = 1$; so the indifference curves of the two are tangent, and it follows that x is a Pareto optimal allocation. Moreover, each person likes x at least as much as he likes ω:

$u_1(x_1) = 3 \cdot 3 = 9 \geq u_1(\omega_1) = 9 \cdot 1 = 9$
$u_2(x_2) = 7 \cdot 7 = 49 \geq u_2(\omega_2) = 1 \cdot 9 = 9$

Therefore, neither individual would block x. (Obviously person 1 is getting the short end of the stick here, but he cannot block unless he is actually worse off than he is initially.) Since x is Pareto optimal and since x would not be blocked by either person, x is in the core of this economy.

Next let's "replicate" the economy by creating an identical twin for each of our traders. Person 1's twin is person 3. Person 2's twin is person 4. The utility functions for the two newcomers are:

$$u_3(x_3) = x_{31} x_{32}$$
$$u_4(x_4) = x_{41} x_{42}$$

The initial bundles are $\omega_3 = (9,1)$, and $\omega_4 = (1,9)$. Now consider the particular allocation x given by:

$$x_1 = (3,3)$$
$$x_2 = (7,7)$$
$$x_3 = (3,3)$$
$$x_4 = (7,7)$$

The new twinned x allocation is clearly analogous to the old one. Now the old x allocation was in the core. What of the new one?

Suppose x is proposed, or on the table, and persons 1, 2, and 3 get together. Under x, their utilities are $u_1(x_1) = 9$, $u_2(x_2) = 49$ and $u_3(x_3) = 9$. The total quantities of the two goods they are endowed with are given by sums of their initial bundles $\omega_1 = (9,1)$, $\omega_2 = (1,9)$ and $\omega_3 = (9,1)$. Consequently, they start with 19 units of good 1 and 11 units of good 2. Consider this set of bundles:

$$s_1 = (4,3)$$
$$s_2 = (11,5)$$
$$s_3 = (4,3)$$

Note that the sums of the goods in the s_i bundles are nineteen units of good 1 and 11 units of good 2. Moreover, $u_1(s_1) = 12 > u_1(x_1) = 9$; $u_2(s_2) = 55 > u_2(x_2) = 49$, and $u_3(s_3) = 12 > u_3(x_3) = 9$. Therefore, the group of people $S = \{1,2,3\}$ blocks x. The x of the replicated economy is not in the core.

The implication of this example is that as an economy gets large (at least via replication), the core in some way shrinks. This shrinkage was first analyzed in 1881 by Edgeworth. He reasoned that a large core is associated with a small number of traders; when there are few people there is lots of room for bargaining. But a small core is associated with a large number of traders; when there are lots of people there a well established market prices, and there is little room for bargaining.

FINAL NOTES ON THE CORE:
THE NUMBER OF COALITIONS

In a move to the core every group of traders, no matter how small, mid-dling, or large, must be satisfied — satisfied in the sense that it could not withdraw from the negotiations and do better on its own. Moving to the core is perfect free trading and perfect free trading is moving to the core. Of course, the core depends on the initial allocation, while the set of Pareto optimal allocations does not. But given the initial allocation, the core is a good set of outcomes for society.

Unfortunately, we have up till now overlooked a potentially disastrous problem. When there are two traders, it is computationally simple to decide whether or not a particular allocation is in the core. One must answer yes or no to these questions: Would trader 1 block it? Would trader 2 block it? Would traders 1 and 2 acting together block it? When there are three traders, it is still not too difficult to decide whether or not a particular allo-cation is in the core. One must answer yes or no to each of these questions: Would trader 1 block it? Would trader 2 block it? Would trader 3 block it? Would traders 1 and 2 acting together block it? Would traders 1 and 3 act-ing together block it? Would traders 2 and 3 acting together block it? Would traders 1, 2, and 3 acting together block it?

But what if there are, say, fifty people? Is it computationally possible to decide whether or not an allocation x is in the core? Is it possibly in our life-times to examine each possible group or coalition in the set of fifty people, to determine whether that group would block? Unfortunately, it is not. When there are fifty people, there are $2^{50} - 1$ different groups that might block. And $2^{50} - 1$ is approximately equal to 1,125,900,000,000,000.

When there are reasonably large numbers of people in the economy do there exist ways to find allocations in the core? Or is the idea of the core generally useless because the number of coalitions is astronomical? We'll see in the next chapter that we can in fact reach core allocations.

EXERCISES

1. In an economy with two people and two goods, suppose

$$u_1(x_1) = 3x_{11} + 2x_{12}$$
$$u_2(x_2) = x_{21}x_{22}$$
$$\omega_1 = (10,9)$$
$$\omega_2 = (0,1)$$

    a. Carefully draw an Edgeworth box diagram to represent the economy. Include a few indifference curves and the point ω.

    b. Solve for the Pareto optimal allocations. Illustrate them graphically. Illustrate the core graphically.

2. Consider an economy with three people, who have the following utility functions and initial bundles:

$$u_1(x_1) = 3x_{11} + 2x_{12} + x_{13} \qquad \omega_1 = (0,1,0)$$
$$u_2(x_2) = 2x_{21} + x_{22} + 3x_{23} \qquad \omega_2 = (1,0,0)$$
$$u_3(x_3) = x_{31} + 3x_{32} + 2x \qquad \omega_3 = (0,0,1)$$

    a. Could any pair of people block ω?

    b. Could any single person block ω?

    c. Is ω Pareto optimal?

3. There are three people and two goods in an economy. The utility functions and initial bundles are given below:

$$u_1 = x_{11}x_{12} \qquad \omega_1 = (0,8)$$
$$u_2 = 2x_{21} + x_{22} \qquad \omega_2 = (2,2)$$
$$u_3 = x_{31}x_{32} + x_{32} \qquad \omega_3 = (8,0)$$

Suppose it is suggested that the three traders move to the allocation x given by $x_1 = (1,2)$, $x_2 = (8,4)$, $x_3 = (1,4)$.

    a. Calculate the marginal rates of substitution for the three at the allocation x. (Note: If the MRS's are all equal, then x will be Pareto optimal.)

    b. Show that x makes no one worse off than the original allocation.

    c. Show that x is not in the core.

SELECTED REFERENCES

(Items marked with an asterisk (*) are mathematically difficult.)

*1. G. Debreu and H. Scarf, "A Limit Theorem on the Core of an Economy," *International Economic Review*, V. 4, 1963, pp. 235–246.

    This was the first rigorous treatment of the Edgeworth conjecture that the core shrinks to the set of competitive equilibrium allocations as the economy grows large. Debreu and Scarf formalized the replication argument and proved Edgeworth's conjecture.

2. F. Y. Edgeworth, *Mathematical Psychics,* London, Kegan Paul, 1881. See especially pages 16–42.

    In addition to laying the foundation for the Edgeworth box diagram (which he did not actually use in the form later popularized), Edgeworth develops the idea of the core in this readable book. He also develops the notion of a "recontracting process," which works as follows. An allocation is proposed by someone. Then each group of traders or coalition in the economy meets, and decides whether or not the allocation is acceptable. If not, some coalition blocks it, and another proposal is put forward. If no coalition blocks, the proposal is in the core, and the process terminates.

*3. A. M. Feldman, "Recontracting Stability," *Econometrica,* V. 42, 1974, pp. 35–44.

*4. J. Green, "The Stability of Edgeworth's Recontracting Process," *Econometrica,* V. 42, 1974, pp. 21–34.

This paper has a proof of stability for a recontracting process. That is, Green provides a theorem that says under certain assumptions a recontracting process will be dynamically stable. It will eventually reach the core and stop. Also see reference 3 above.

*5. H. Scarf, "The Core of an N-Person Game," *Econometrica,* V. 35, 1967, pp. 50–69.

It is possible to construct examples of economics in which the core is empty, and any allocation is blocked. For such examples, perfect bargaining might go on until all the participants die of exhaustion. But these examples are special. In this paper Scarf shows that the crucial ingredient is convex indifference curves — with a convexity assumption core allocations do in fact exist. Economists normally assume that indifference curves are convex, so Scarf's result is reassuring.

3 MARKET EXCHANGE AND OPTIMALITY

INTRODUCTION

In chapter 2 we analyzed barter exchange — that is, exchange without prices. In the Edgeworth model of that chapter, the traders start at some given initial allocation, and a proposal is made for a new allocation. Each group of traders decides whether or not it can, by itself, better the proposal. If no group can better it, the proposal is in the core, and is accepted.

In this chapter we analyze a more familiar type of economic exchange — exchange governed by prices. However, the model remains rather abstract, since there are no stores, cash registers, checks, or dollar bills in our description of price exchange.

The story goes roughly like this. Each trader starts with some given initial bundle of goods. But now there is a market at which people buy and sell according to given prices. Someone in the market announces a list of prices. Each trader decides, on the basis of those prices, how much of each good he wants to buy and sell. The things he buys are always payed for with the things he sells (since there are no bank accounts, no loans, no accumulations of cash). Consequently the value of what he wants to buy (at the announced market prices) must equal the value of what he wants to sell (at the announced market prices). Or, equivalently, the value of the bundle of goods he wants to consume must equal the value of the bundle of goods he starts with.

But what people can consume is limited by what actually exists in the exchange economy. If we start with ten units of food distributed between two people, and there is no production, then the total amount of food that those two can consume is, in the end, ten units. That is, for each good, total supply must equal total demand, for there to be an equilibrium. The first announced list of prices might not yield an equilibrium. If it does not, there is no actual exchange made, and the person who announces the prices changes them. Eventually a list of prices is found which does have the equilibrium property that supply equals demand for each good. When this list is found, the transactions are actually made, and the equilibrium allocation of goods is established.

This is essentially the model of price-governed exchange first analyzed by Leon Walras in 1874. The subtle part of the Walrasian model is its characterization of the behavior of the person who announces prices; fortunately, we won't dwell on that. What is important for us in the model is the characterization of the equilibrium in a competitive price-governed economy: In a Walrasian equilibrium, each person is buying the best bundle (for him) that he can afford, and all the individual decisions are consistent, in the sense that total demand equals total supply for each good. In spite of its level of abstraction, this is a good description of a smoothly running economic machine. What we can learn about the Walrasian model therefore should give us some insight into real competitive economies.

THE TWO-PERSON, TWO-GOODS MODEL

The simplest price-governed exchange model is a two-person, two-goods model. Suppose persons 1 and 2 have selfish utility functions u_1 and u_2, respectively, and initial bundles ω_1 and ω_2, respectively.

Now suppose 1 and 2 act as if prices are given. What does this mean? It means, for 1, that he ignores 2, and behaves as if the only thing governing his behavior is the pair (or vector) of prices (p_1, p_2). How does (p_1, p_2) govern his behavior? Well, suppose he has zero apples, worth 10¢ each, and ten grapefruits, worth 25¢ each. In all probability he will want to eat some apples as well as some grapefruits, so he will have to sell some of his grapefruits, to buy the apples he wants. If he decides he wants to consume A apples and G grapefruits, the value of the bundle (A, G) must be less than or equal to the value of the bundle he starts with, namely $(0,10)$, otherwise, he can't afford (A,G). This means that (A,G) must satisfy

$$10¢ \cdot A + 25¢ \cdot G \le 10¢ \cdot 0 + 25¢ \cdot 10 = 250¢$$

In general, in a price-governed exchange world, person 1 chooses a bundle x_1 to maximize u_1 (x_1) subject to the constraint

$$p_1 x_{11} + p_2 x_{12} \le p_1 \omega_{11} + p_2 \omega_{12}$$

Figure 3-1 represents his problem. The dashed lines show the outside boundaries of the Edgeworth box diagram, which 1 is now ignoring, because he believes that the only thing which constrains him is the set of prices (p_1, p_2). We have drawn a line, called a *budget* or *price line,* through ω_1 to represent the set of points which satisfy

$$p_1 x_{11} + p_2 x_{12} = p_1 \omega_{11} + p_2 \omega_{12}$$

The absolute value of the slope of this line is p_1/p_2. Every bundle (x_{11}, x_{12}) which lies on or below the line satisfies

$$p_1 x_{11} + p_2 x_{12} \le p_1 \omega_{11} + p_2 \omega_{12}$$

We have shaded in the set of bundles of goods which lie in this region.

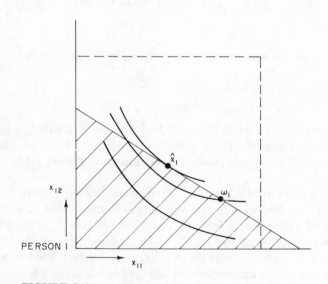

FIGURE 3-1

Given his budget line, which depends only on ω_1 and (p_1, p_2), Person 1 chooses a best bundle of goods. If he has indifference curves like the ones drawn, he will choose the bundle $\hat{x}_1$, where one of his indifference curves just touches, or is tangent to, his budget line.

If Person 1's preferences are unusual, $\hat{x}_1$ might not lie on the budget line. For example, if he is indifferent about all bundles, he might choose a bundle below the line. In what follows, however, we typically assume that people generally prefer larger quantities of goods to smaller, and this assumption will guarantee that the chosen bundle is on the budget line. Also observe that $\hat{x}_1$ might fall outside of the Edgeworth box, outside of the dashed line.

Now we put person 2 explicitly back into the picture. Let us assume for simplicity that the total quantity of each good is 1 unit, so the Edgeworth box diagram must be 1 unit on each side.

Where is person 2's budget line? Formally it is given by

$$p_1 x_{21} + p_2 x_{22} = p_1 \omega_{21} + p_2 \omega_{22}$$

If we substitute 1's quantities for 2's in this equation, according to the rules

$$x_{1j} + x_{2j} = \omega_{1j} + \omega_{2j} = 1 \text{ for } j = 1,2$$

we get

$$p_1(1 - x_{11}) + p_2(1 - x_{12}) = p_1(1 - \omega_{11}) + p_2(1 - \omega_{12})$$

or

$$p_1 x_{11} - p_1 + p_2 x_{12} - p_2 = p_1 \omega_{11} - p_1 + p_2 \omega_{12} - p_2$$

or

$$p_1 x_{11} + p_2 x_{12} = p_1 \omega_{11} + p_2 \omega_{12}$$

which is exactly 1's budget line equation. Therefore, 2's budget line coincides with 1's inside the Edgeworth box. Outside the box the two budget lines are cut off differently, since the goods axes for the two traders are different.

Person 2 can afford any bundle on or below (with respect to his origin) his budget line; he can consume any bundle in the shaded area of Figure 3-2. The figure includes a few of 2's indifference curves. Evidently, given the prices p_1 and p_2, person 2 will choose the bundle $\hat{x}_2$.

The next step is to combine the two diagrams into one. We will now drop the extensions of the budget line outside the boundaries of the box, as they play no important role in what follows. In Figure 3-3 we show the budget

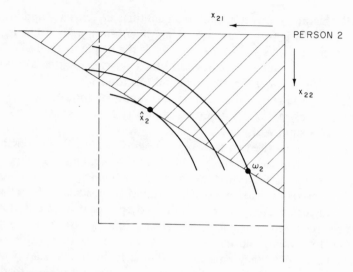

FIGURE 3-2

line through the initial allocation ω, the two crucial indifference curves of persons 1 and 2 that are tangent to the budget line, and the desired bundles of persons 1 and 2, $\hat{x}_1$ and $\hat{x}_2$. Note that we have indicated the quantities $\hat{x}_{11}$, $\hat{x}_{12}$, $\hat{x}_{21}$ and $\hat{x}_{22}$ on the sides of the box.

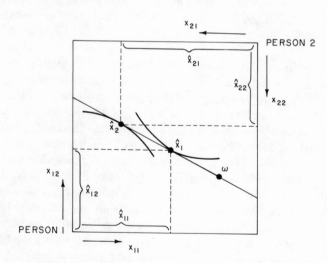

FIGURE 3-3

As the picture is drawn, the desired quantities $\hat{x}_{11}$, $\hat{x}_{12}$, $\hat{x}_{21}$ and $\hat{x}_{22}$ are inconsistent. This is so because $\hat{x}_{11} + \hat{x}_{21} > \omega_{11} + \omega_{21} = 1$, the length of the box; and $\hat{x}_{12} + \hat{x}_{22} < \omega_{12} + \omega_{22} = 1$, the height of the box. The two people want to consume more of good 1 than exists. And, this is impossible.

We call $\hat{x}_{11} + \hat{x}_{21}$ the (total) demand for good 1; $\hat{x}_{12} + \hat{x}_{22}$ the (total) demand for good 2; $\omega_{11} + \omega_{21}$ the (total) supply of good 1; and $\omega_{12} + \omega_{22}$ the (total) supply of good 2. In this example there is excess demand for good 1, and excess supply of good 2.

If the desires of the two traders are not consistent, it is impossible for them to trade from ω to $(\hat{x}_1, \hat{x}_2)$. Therefore, something must give. Either one or both will be frustrated, or the prices will change.

In the everyday world, excess demand means shortages. When there are shortages, if prices are unregulated, they go up. For if there are shortages, there are frustrated consumers who offer to pay a little more to get the quantities they want, and there are sellers who realize that they can boost prices and still sell all they want to sell. Similarly, in the everyday world, excess supply means surpluses. When there are surpluses, prices tend to go down. (This phenomenon might be masked in an economy in which there is persistent inflation which hides price declines. But even if all absolute prices are rising, the goods for which there are surpluses will fall in price relative to other goods. And, only relative prices matter in our exchange economy model, since doubling all prices has no real effect on any consumer's budget equation.) When there are surpluses, sellers have unplanned and unwanted inventories, so they have "special sales." Buyers see extra stocks of merchandise, so they try to bargain with sellers, again pushing prices down.

Let's now incorporate these natural price movements in our analysis. Good 1 is in excess demand, and good 2 is in excess supply. Therefore, p_1 will tend to rise, and p_2 will tend to drop, or, at any rate, p_1 will tend to rise relative to p_2. Therefore, p_1/p_2 will go up, and the budget line will get steeper. This shift will continue until supply equals demand for both goods, that is, until the desired bundles $\hat{x}_1$ and $\hat{x}_2$ of the two traders coincide.

An allocation $\hat{x} = (\hat{x}_1, \hat{x}_2)$, where the traders are consistently maximizing their respective utilities, subject to their budget constraints, is called a competitive equilibrium allocation. It is competitive because both traders are acting as price takers, which is presumably how people act in large competitive markets with lots of traders, and it is an equilibrium because their consumption plans are consistent; there is no excess supply or excess demand for either good; and there is no reason for prices to change further. A competitive equilibrium allocation is illustrated in Figure 3-4.

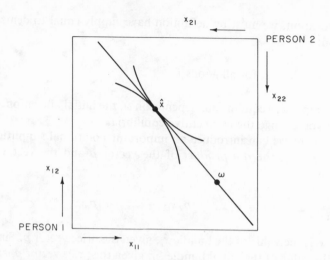

FIGURE 3-4

The figure suggests a very important result. Since the two traders' indifference curves are tangent to the same budget line at $\hat{x}$, they are also tangent to each other. Consequently, $\hat{x}$ is Pareto optimal. It is also clear that each person likes $\hat{x}$ at least as much (in fact more) than he likes ω. Consequently, $\hat{x}$ is in the core.

COMPETITIVE EQUILIBRIUM IN AN EXCHANGE ECONOMY: FORMAL PRELIMINARIES

We formally define a competitive equilibrium for an economy of selfish traders as follows. Suppose there are n people and m goods. The allocation $\hat{x}$, along with the price vector $p = (p_1, p_2, \ldots, p_n)$, form a *competitive equilibrium* if, for all i,

$\hat{x}_i$ maximizes $u_i(x_i)$ subject to the budget constraint

$$p_1 x_{i1} + p_2 x_{i2} + \ldots + p_m x_{im} \leq p_1 \omega_{i1} + p_2 \omega_{i2} + \ldots + p_m \omega_{im}$$

Let's make three remarks about the definition. First, $p_1 x_{i1} + p_2 x_{i2} + \ldots + p_m x_{im}$ is the value of the bundle x_i, while $p_1 \omega_{i1} + p_2 \omega_{i2} + \ldots + p_m \omega_{im}$ is the value of the bundle ω_i. The budget inequality then says that, when valued at the prices given by p, the value of what person i consumes must be less than or equal to the value of what he starts with. Second, since

$\hat{x}$ is an allocation, we must by definition have supply equal to demand for every good:

$$\sum_{i=1}^{n} \hat{x}_{ij} = \sum_{i=1}^{n} \omega_{ij}, \text{ for all goods } j$$

Third, a competitive equilibrium depends on ω, the initial allocation. If you change ω, you change the competitive equilibria.

At this point we can introduce an important notational simplification. We define $p \cdot x_i$, the *dot product* of the vector p and the vector x_i, as follows:

$$p \cdot x_i = \sum_{j=1}^{m} p_j x_{ij} = p_1 x_{i1} + p_2 x_{i2} + \ldots + p_m x_{im}$$

Thus $p \cdot x_i$ is the value of the bundle x_i, given the price vector p. Similarly, $p \cdot \omega_i$ is the value of the initial bundle ω_i, given the price vector p, and person i's budget constraint can be compactly rewritten

$$p \cdot x_i \leq p \cdot \omega_i$$

Now for the theorems below we need a formalization of the idea that a person prefers more goods to less. Suppose person i is selfish, so his utility depends only on his own consumption. Let x_i be any bundle of goods for him. If i would prefer to x_i any bundle y_i that includes more of every good, then i's utility function is said to be monotonic. That is, u_i is *monotonic* if $y_{ij} > x_{ij}$ for all j implies $u_i(y_i) > u_i(x_i)$.

For one of the theorems below we need two simple preliminary observations, in addition to the definitions and notations developed so far. The first observation says if i prefers some other bundle to the bundle he chooses to buy, that other bundle must be too expensive for him: it must be more valuable than the bundle he starts with. This makes splendid sense, for if the preferred bundle weren't too expensive for him, he would buy it, since his goal, after all, is to maximize his utility. The second observation says that if i likes some other bundle at least as much as the bundle he chooses to buy, that other bundle can't be less valuable than the bundle he starts with. This depends on the prior assumption of monotonicity, but it too makes fine sense. For if the other bundle were actually less valuable than the bundle he starts with, he could afford a bundle that is slightly more expensive than the other bundle, one that contains slightly more of every good. He would prefer this third bundle to the bundle he chooses to buy. So he would buy it instead, since his goal is, again, to maximize his utility.

Let's turn to the formal statements of these observations.

Observation 1. Let $(\hat{x},p)$ be a competitive equilibrium. If $u_i(y_i) > u_i(\hat{x}_i)$ for some bundle y_i, then

$$p \cdot y_i > p \cdot \omega_i$$

Proof. If this were not the case, then $\hat{x}_i$ would not be the bundle that maximizes the utility function u_i subject to i's budget constraint, which would contradict the assumption that $(\hat{x},p)$ is a competitive equilibrium. Q.E.D.

Observation 2. Let $(\hat{x},p)$ be a competitive equilibrium. Assume i has a monotonic utility function. If $u_i(y_i) \geq u_i(\hat{x}_i)$ for some bundle y_i, then

$$p \cdot y_i \geq p \cdot \omega_i$$

Proof. Suppose to the contrary that $p \cdot y_i < p \cdot \omega_i$. Define a bundle z_i by adding a small quality ϵ of every good to the bundle y_i:

$$z_{ij} = y_{ij} + \epsilon \text{ for all } j$$

Choose ϵ small enough so that

$$\begin{aligned} p \cdot z_i &= p_1 y_{i1} + p_1 \epsilon + p_2 y_{i2} + p_2 \epsilon + \ldots + p_m y_{im} + p_m \epsilon \\ &= p \cdot y_i + \epsilon(p_1 + p_2 + \ldots + p_m) \\ &\leq p \cdot \omega_i. \end{aligned}$$

This can be done since, by assumption, $p \cdot y_i < p \cdot \omega_i$. By the monotonicity assumption, person i prefers the bundle z_i to the bundle y_i. That is,

$$u_i(z_i) > u_i(y_i) \geq u_i(\hat{x}_i).$$

Therefore, $u_i(z_i) > u_i(\hat{x}_i)$, while $p \cdot z_i \leq p \cdot \omega_i$, which again contradicts the assumption that $(\hat{x},p)$ is a competitive equilibrium.

Q.E.D.

This completes our formal preliminaries to the first main result.

THE FIRST FUNDAMENTAL THEOREM OF WELFARE ECONOMICS

Since around the time of Adam Smith (*Wealth of Nations,* 1776), economists have argued that the price system has a special virtue that other allocative systems might not share. The price system induces selfish individuals, independently maximizing their private well being, to bring the economy to a socially optimal state. The invisible hand of competition transforms private greed into public welfare. Why should this be the case? In the complicated real world, people see prices and adjust their behavior accordingly, in order to maximize private welfare or private profit. High prices steer people away from wasteful uses of resources and technology, low prices attract them to effective production processes, effective technologies, and effective ways to satisfy wants. With prices giving the signals, wants are fulfilled in an economical way.

Moreover, the system works automatically. When supply is greater than demand, prices fall; when demand is greater than supply, prices rise. There is no need for an expensive or cumbersome centralized bureaucracy to tell us what to do; the hand of competition will lead in the right direction, and without force or coercion.

In the simple world of exchange, the market mechanism automatically distributes goods among people in an optimal way. The person who likes coffee will end up with a lot of coffee, while the one who likes tea will end up with a lot of tea. The person who likes bread will have bread, while the one who likes potatoes will have potatoes. Each consumer will get the bundle of goods he likes best (given his budget constraint), and all those diverse desires will be invisibly reconciled through the adjustment of prices.

Let us be more precise. First, a socially optimal state in the exchange economy model is an allocation that is in the core — one with the property that no coalition of traders, large or small, could better itself by an internal redistribution of its own resources. Second, the outcome of a competitive system or the market mechanism is simply a competitive equilibrium: An allocation $\hat{x}$ and a price vector p with the property that, given his initial holdings ω_i and the prices p, each and every trader is (selfishly) maximizing his own (selfish) utility function. So the fundamental theorem whose seed is in Adam Smith is: "A competitive equilibrium allocation is in the core."

In the last chapter, we saw that it is generally computationally impossible to determine whether or not an allocation is in the core via an examination of all possible blocking coalitions. There are just too many possible coalitions or groups of traders. But the fundamental theorem points the way to arriving at a core allocation: Use the competitive mechanism; use the free market.

Now we can analyze the theorem to see whether or not it is right. Very few meaningful propositions are always true, and the one at hand is not one of the few. In fact, we can construct a clear example, with two selfish traders and two goods, where the proposition is false.

Consider a two-person, two-good economy, in which person 1 has the following odd utility function:

$$u_1(x_1) = \begin{cases} 1 \text{ when } x_{11} + x_{12} < 1 \\ x_{11} + x_{12} \text{ when } x_{11} + x_{12} \geq 1 \end{cases}$$

Note that this utility function is not monotonic in the region where $x_{11} + x_{12} < 1$. That is, person 1 is indifferent among all bundles satisfying $x_{11} + x_{12} < 1$; if you start at one such bundle, and give him just a little more of both goods (so that $x_{11} + x_{12} < 1$ remains true), then he is no better off. He is said to have a "fat" indifference curve in this region. Let person 2's utility function be

$$u_2(x_2) = x_{21} x_{22}$$

Suppose the initial allocation is $\omega_1 = (1,0)$, $\omega_2 = (0,1)$.

Now let $p = (1,1)$, let $\hat{x}_1 = (\frac{1}{2},\frac{1}{2})$, and $\hat{x}_2 = (\frac{1}{2},\frac{1}{2})$. Obviously $\hat{x}$ is an allocation. The totals of the two goods are 1 and 1, as they must be. With the prices $p = (1,1)$, and the initial bundle $\omega_1 = (1,0)$, person 1 can afford any bundle that costs no more than $p_1\omega_{11} + p_2\omega_{12} = 1$. That is, he can afford any bundle in his fat region of indifference, as well as any bundle on the line $x_{11} + x_{12} = 1$. But all these bundles give him 1 unit of utility. Consequently, $\hat{x}_1$ maximizes person 1's utility subject to his budget constant. With the prices $p = (1,1)$ and the initial bundle $\omega_2 = (0,1)$, person 2 can afford any bundle satisfying

$$p_1 x_{21} + p_2 x_{22} \leq p_1 \omega_{21} + p_2 \omega_{22} = 1$$

He finds the best such bundle using the tangency condition:

$$\text{MRS for person 2} = \frac{p_1}{p_2}$$

or

$$\frac{x_{22}}{x_{21}} = \frac{p_1}{p_2} = 1.$$

The bundle $\hat{x}_2 = (\frac{1}{2},\frac{1}{2})$ solves person 2's problem; so $\hat{x}_2$ maximizes person 2's utility subject to his budget constraint.

In short, $\hat{x}$ is a competitive equilibrium allocation. But it is not Pareto optimal, and therefore it is not in the core. There are allocations that make person 2 better off and person 1 no worse off. For instance, let $\hat{y}_1 = (0,0)$ and $\hat{y}_2 = (1,1)$. Then $u_1(\hat{y}_1) = 1 \geq u_1(\hat{x}_1) = 1$, while $u_2(\hat{y}_2) = 1 > u_2(\hat{x}_2) = \frac{1}{4}$.

The source of the difficulty in this example is the first person's fat indifference curve. But this fat indifference curve is really quite bizarre. People with fat indifference curves in the everyday world are the ones who literally throw their money away. Lots of us claim that we know someone else who throws money away, but we all deny that we do it ourselves! (Putting money in a bank for future use is not throwing it away, nor is donating it to a worthwhile charity.) In short, fat indifference curves can be comfortably assumed away. They are in fact ruled out by the assumption of monotonic preferences.

How does Adam Smith's fundamental argument stand up when monotonicity is assumed? It turns out that in our exchange model, with selfish monotonic utility functions, the competitive mechanism automatically distributes goods among people in an optimal way. A competitive equilibrium allocation is in the core, and the market does achieve a socially desirable state of affairs.

Let's now turn to a formal statement and proof of this most basic theorem of welfare economics.

First Fundamental Theorem of Welfare Economics. If all traders have monotonic selfish utility functions, and if $(\hat{x},p)$ is a competitive equilibrium, then $\hat{x}$ is in the core (and is, therefore, Pareto optimal as well).

Proof. Suppose $(\hat{x},p)$ is a competitive equilibrium.

Suppose, contrary to the theorem, that $\hat{x}$ is not in the core.

Then some coalition can block $\hat{x}$ from ω. Let us say S can block x, and let us say it can do so with the bundles $\{s_i\}_{i \text{ in } s}$. This means that

$$\sum_{i \text{ in } S} s_{ij} = \sum_{i \text{ in } S} \omega_{ij} \text{ for all goods } j \tag{i}$$

$$u_i(s_i) \geq u_i(\hat{x}_i) \text{ for all } i \text{ in } S \tag{ii}$$

$$u_i(s_i) > u_i(\hat{x}_i) \text{ for at least one } i \text{ in } S \tag{iii}$$

Combining (ii) with Observation 2, we have

$$p \cdot s_i \geq p \cdot \omega_i \text{ for all traders } i \text{ in } S$$

Combining (iii) with Observation 1, we have

$$p \cdot s_i > p \cdot \omega_i \text{ for at least one } i \text{ in } S$$

Now let us add these inequalities over all the traders in S, to get

$$\sum_{i \text{ in } S} p \cdot s_i > \sum_{i \text{ in } S} p \cdot \omega_i$$

This inequality can be rewritten

$$\sum_{i \text{ in } S} (p_1 s_{i1} + p_2 s_{i2} + \ldots + p_m s_{im})$$

$$> \sum_{i \text{ in } S} (p_1 \omega_{i1} + p_2 \omega_{i2} + \ldots + p_m \omega_{im})$$

Rearranging, we have

$$p_1 \sum_{i \text{ in } S} s_{i1} + p_2 \sum_{i \text{ in } S} s_{i2} + \ldots + p_m \sum_{i \text{ in } S} s_{im}$$

$$> p_1 \sum_{i \text{ in } S} \omega_{i1} + p_2 \sum_{i \text{ in } S} \omega_{i2} + \ldots + p_m \sum_{i \text{ in } S} \omega_{im}$$

or

$$p_1 \left[\sum_{i \text{ in } S} s_{i1} - \sum_{i \text{ in } S} \omega_{i1} \right] + p_2 \left[\sum_{i \text{ in } S} s_{i2} - \sum_{i \text{ in } S} \omega_{i2} \right]$$

$$+ \ldots + p_m \left[\sum_{i \text{ in } S} s_{im} - \sum_{i \text{ in } S} \omega_{im} \right] > 0$$

But by (i), every term in brackets is zero. Therefore, the assumption that $\hat{x}$ is not in the core leads to a contradiction, which proves the theorem.

Q.E.D.

THE SECOND FUNDAMENTAL THEOREM OF WELFARE ECONOMICS

The first fundamental theorem says that a competitive equilibrium allocation is in the core, and is Pareto optimal. The competitive market, in other words, brings about a distribution of goods that is desirable in the sense that no group of traders could do better on its own. Moreover, it brings about this desirable distribution automatically: prices tend to rise in response to excess demand and tend to fall in response to excess supply; the prices adjust by themselves to solve the distribution problem.

However, the ideal distribution of goods brought about by the competitive mechanism depends heavily on the initial allocation. That is, the competitive allocation and the core are determined by the initial allocation ω, as well as by preferences, and if, for example, the initial allocation is very unequal, so will be the competitive allocation.

This is an important objection to complete reliance on the competitive market: it might produce great inequalities. What does this mean in a real economy? An economy with production as well as exchange has people selling (or renting) their assets to firms, as well as buying and consuming goods and services. People sell their labor, or rent their capital goods. Some people have lots of capital to rent, and some people have very valuable labor to sell. Usually we think of industrialists, doctors and lawyers in this regard, but T.V. personalities, rock music stars, and movie stars are better examples. And some people have no capital to lend or rent, and very little valuable labor to sell. Some people have few talents, few skills, and maybe not even much muscle power. There are haves, and there are have nots. And the have nots might be have nots through no fault of their own. They might be disabled, afflicted by disease, or just very unlucky. The free market mechanism will produce a distribution of goods that gives Rolls-Royces and homes in Palm Springs to the rock stars. The distribution will give Fords and suburban tract homes to most of us. But it will give worn-out shoes and crowded tenements to the have nots. And the result will very likely be Pareto optimal and in the core.

We can illustrate the inequality that might result from a competitive equilibrium allocation in an Edgeworth box diagram.

In Figure 3–5, ω is an initial allocation that strongly favors person 1, and $\hat{x}$ is the competitive equilibrium based on it. A Pareto optimal allocation like y might seem preferable to $\hat{x}$ on equity grounds. So the question arises: Can the competitive mechanism with some modifications be used to move the economy to an alternative Pareto optimal allocation like y, even given the initial distribution ω?

Do we really need to ask this question? Examination of Figure 3–5 seems to indicate an obvious solution to the inequality problem. Simply make person 1 give to person 2 $\omega_{11} - y_{11}$ units of good 1, and $\omega_{12} - y_{12}$ units of good 2. End of discussion. (Person 1 doesn't want to do this, of course, but reducing inequality almost always means causing someone to do something he doesn't want to do.)

This obvious solution to the inequality problem involves the direct transfer of quantities of various goods from one person to another. Why can't this solution be used in general, for cases more complicated than the one drawn in the figure? It cannot be used for the same reason that a proposed allocation cannot be checked to see whether or not it is in the core by examining all possible blocking coalitions. That is, when there are many people and many goods the direct transfer solution is computationally impossible. It is just too burdensome to work.

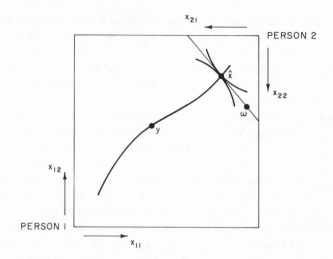

FIGURE 3-5

Consider the economy of the United States, with its more than 200 million consumers. How many different goods do we have? Obviously, the answer to this question depends on the level of aggregation we use: we might say food is a good, rather than apples, tomatoes, bread, etc. But if we talk about reasonable levels of aggregation, there are surely hundreds of things we want to identify as distinct goods. And if we walk into a large department store, we can count tens of thousands of different items; in a large supermarket there are probably tens of thousands of different food, grocery, and household goods available. So on a finely disaggregated level, there are hundreds of thousands of different goods being produced and consumed in the United States. Now imagine the problem of directly transferring either hundreds, or hundreds of thousands, of goods among hundreds of millions of people. Could a central authority, say a branch of the U.S. Government, effect such a transfer in a reasonable way?

To answer that question we can look at a recent effort by the U.S. Government to partially direct the reallocation of one good: gasoline. The United States Department of Energy employs some 20 thousand people (of whom, in truth, only a fraction work on the chore of gas allocation). It attempted, in the spring and summer of 1979, to direct the distribution of gasoline in the United States, on a regional basis. That is, it attempted to dictate how much each state should get, and how the gas should be distributed between urban and rural areas within each state. It did not attempt to decide how much each driver should get. Now the Energy Department allocated gasoline by, in effect, short circuiting the market mechanism. Gasoline sellers were not allowed to adjust their prices freely, and they were not allowed to decide by themselves where to sell what they want to sell. Their actions were governed by Department regulations, which were literally thousands of pages in length.

Did the Energy Department, with its thousands of employees and thousands of pages of regulations, succeed in distributing gasoline to U.S. consumers in a reasonable way? The answer to the question is a rather clear No. With the suppression of the price mechanisms a new rationing device appeared: the gas station line. Consumers spent, in the aggregate, millions of manhours waiting in lines. They burned, in the aggregate, millions of gallons of gasoline simply looking for open gas stations or waiting on lines. They ran into each other's cars while jockeying for positions on lines. They actually shot and killed each other over gallons of gas. This was a distribution system that wasted time, gasoline, people's nerves, and even occasionally lives. The attempt to partially direct of the distribution of one good was a dramatic failure.

Now, imagine the complexities of having a central authority effect a transfer of hundreds or thousands of goods among 200 million people. If an initial allocation is unequal or inequitable in a large economy, like the U.S. economy, and if a more equitable allocation is sought on equity grounds, a movement from the initial allocation to the more equitable allocations might theoretically be brought about by a centralized and purely nonmarket mechanism. A central authority might theoretically inform everyone of the precise quantities of the thousands of goods to which he is entitled. But the costs, the wastes, and the information requisites of such nonmarket reallocations are enormous.

Back then, to the question: Can the automatic, decentralized, competitive market mechanism with some modifications be used to move an economy to a more equitable Pareto optimal allocation? In terms of Figure 3–5, can a modified market mechanism be used to get the economy from ω to a point like y?

The answer is generally yes, and the modified mechanism works like this. Instead of transferring quantities of hundreds on thousands of goods among millions of people, a central authority transfers cash. That is, generalized purchasing power, or money, is taken from some people, and given to others. After people's bank accounts have been lightened, or enhanced, as the case may be, they are left to their own devices, and the market proceeds to work as usual. Prices adjust to automatically equate supply and demand in each market, and a new, more equitable competitive equilibrium allocation comes about. The new allocation is Pareto optimal. But it is probably not in the core for the original, pretransfer allocation.

The cash transfer system has important advantages over the direct transfer of goods system. First, it is not computationally staggering. A single human mind can grasp the idea that everyone should have a minimum (cash) income of X dollars. A single human mind cannot devise a good distribution of tens of thousands of goods among hundreds of millions of people. Second, it preserves people's freedom of choice. Adjusting a person's bank book and then letting him do his shopping is less onerous than adjusting his consumption bundle directly. And third, adjusting bank balances will not create the disasterous and wasteful market problems that direct transfers have created in, for instance, the market for gasoline.

Now let's concentrate on the meaning of the cash-transfer system in the context of our exchange economy model. This might be confusing, since we have said there is no cash, no money, in the exchange model: goods trade for goods. That position must be modified. To picture what is going on here, imagine that everyone has an account with a central bank. The bank lists, in person i's account, all the goods he has. Initially the account lists ω_i. Now suppose there is some list of prices for the goods, or price vector p. At the bottom of person i's account book, the bank evaluates i's goods. Initially, this value is $p_1\omega_{i1} + p_2\omega_{i2} + \ldots + p_m\omega_{im}$, or $p \cdot \omega_i$. If there are no cash transfers and if i wants to trade his initial bundle ω_i for a consumption bundle x_i, i must clear it through the bank, which approves the transaction if

$$p \cdot x_i \leq p \cdot \omega_i$$

that is, if $p \cdot x_i$ is less than or equal to the value of i's account. What we have described so far is just a variation of our basic exchange model, made a little complex by the existence of the bank, whose sole function is to keep an eye on people's budget constraints.

When there are cash transfers, the bank is instructed by the authority running the system to add an amount T_i to person i's bottom line amount $p \cdot w_i$. The number T_i could be positive or negative. The righthand side of i's budget inequality becomes $p \cdot \omega_i + T_i$. And now if i wants to trade his initial bundle ω_i plus his transfer T_i for the consumption bundle x_i, he must clear it through the bank, which approves the transaction if and only if

$$p \cdot x_i \leq p \cdot \omega_i + T_i$$

What does the central authority do to effect a more equitable allocation of goods? It assigns positive T_i's to those people who are judged too poor, and negative T_i's to those who are judged too rich. In other words, it transfers bank balances from the rich to the poor. Once the balances are transferred, the individuals buy and sell as usual and the market mechanism is allowed to work by itself.

We have asserted that a modified mechanism can be devised to get the economy to an equitable allocation, like y in Figure 3–5. At this point we must indicate the formal nature of the problem, and be more precise about the assertion. Mathematically, the problem is this. Suppose we are given an initial allocation ω, and a (desired) Pareto optimal allocation y. Does there exist a vector of bank balance transfers $(T_1, T_2, \ldots, T_n)$ and a price vector $p = (p_1, \ldots, p_m)$, such that, for every person i, y_i maximizes u_i subject to $p \cdot y_i \leq p \cdot \omega_i + T_i$?

The affirmative answer depends on three assumptions about the utility functions: (1) selfishness and (2) monotonicity, both of which have already been defined, and (3) convex indifference curves. Formally, we say u_i has *convex indifference curves* if the following is true: If $u_i(x_i) \geq u_i(y_i)$ for two different bundles x_i and y_i, then $u_i(z_i) \geq u_i(x_i)$ for any bundle z_i that lies on the straight-line segment connecting x_i and y_i. The idea of convexity for indifference curves is illustrated in the figure below. Figure 3–6a shows indifference curves that are convex; while 3–6b shows indifference curves that aren't. Note that the figure illustrates the $u_i(x_i) = u_i(y_i)$ case, and that it assumes monotonicity.

The formal assertion that a modified competitive mechanism can be used to get the economy to almost any desired Pareto optimal allocation is called the Second Fundamental Theorem of Welfare Economics. The proof of this

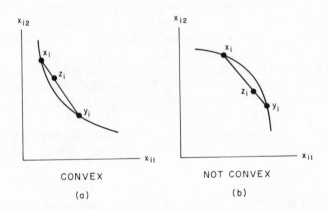

CONVEX
(a)

NOT CONVEX
(b)

FIGURE 3–6

important result is considerably more complex than the proof of the First Fundamental Theorem, so we shall not include it here.

Instead we only state the theorem for the general n-person, m-good case:

Second Fundamental Theorem of Welfare Economics. Suppose all traders have selfish, monotonic utility functions, and convex indifference curves. Let y be any Pareto optimal allocation that assigns positive quantitives of every good to every trader: $y_{ij} > 0$ for all i and j.

Then there exists a vector of bank balance transfers ($T_1, T_2, \ldots, T_n$) and a price vector $p = (p_1, \ldots, p_m)$ such that y and p are a competitive equilibrium given the transfers. That is, for all i, y_i maximizes u_i subject to $p \cdot y_i \leq p \cdot \omega_i + T_i$.

Let's make some observations about the theorem at this point.

First, the assumption that $y_{ij} > 0$ for all i and j, which seems quite restrictive, is made largely for mathematical convenience, and can be greatly weakened without affecting the conclusion of the theorem.

Second, the T_i's must sum to zero: All transfers to people must be financed by taxing other people. This is so because monotonicity ensures that people will want to spend to the limits of their budgets; therefore, for all i,

$$p \cdot y_i = p \cdot \omega_i + T_i$$

Adding over all the i and rearranging terms gives

$$\sum_{j=1}^{m} p_j \sum_{i=1}^{n} y_{ij} = \sum_{j=1}^{m} p_j \sum_{i=1}^{n} \omega_{ij} + \sum_{i=1}^{n} T_i$$

or

$$\sum_{i=1}^{n} T_i = \sum_{j=1}^{m} p_j \left[\sum_{i=1}^{n} y_{ij} - \sum_{i=1}^{n} \omega_{ij} \right] = \sum_{j=1}^{m} p_j [0] = 0$$

There is no way to induce the desired change by simply printing money and giving it to the poor. Some people must be taxed so that others can be subsidized.

Third, the theorem does not indicate how y ought to be chosen! We have argued that y is a more equitable allocation than the original ω, or the competitive allocation that would arise without transfers. But the decision to pick a particular y is made, somehow, by some people, and the process they use to make that decision is left in the dark at this point. In subsequent chapters we will discuss at some length the problem of choosing y.

Fourth and finally, the Second Fundamental Theorem says that the competitive mechanism, with modifications, is even more useful, and more robust, than the First Fundamental Theorem indicates. Even if unmodified competition brings about distributions of goods that are inequitable, the price mechanism with modifications can be used to bring about almost any equitable and optimal allocation.

AN ALGEBRAIC EXAMPLE

Consider first a consumer, person 1, with a linear utility function, $u_1 = x_{11} + 2x_{12}$, and an initial bundle $\omega_1 = (1,\frac{1}{2})$. If he is faced with prices $p = (p_1, p_2)$, he will want to buy the best bundle he can afford, that is, the best bundle x_1 satisfying

$$p_1 x_{11} + p_2 x_{12} \leq p_1 \cdot 1 + p_2 \cdot \frac{1}{2}$$

His indifference curves are straight lines, with slope, in absolute value, equal to

$$\text{MRS person } 1 = \frac{\text{MU of good } 1}{\text{MU of good } 2} = \frac{1}{2}$$

Figure 3–7a illustrates indifference curves and a budget line for person 1. The dark line is 1's budget line; the absolute value of its slope, which evidently exceeds $\frac{1}{2}$, is equal to p_1/p_2. Given this p_1/p_2, person 1 wants to consume the bundle $\hat{x}_1$. For a different p_1/p_2, he wants to consume a different bundle: As p_1/p_2 rises, the budget line pivots around ω_1 and gets steeper, and the desired bundle $\hat{x}_1$ climbs up the vertical axis. As p_1/p_2 drops, the budget line gets flatter, and the desired bundle $\hat{x}_1$ climbs down the vertical axis, until $p_1/p_2 = \frac{1}{2}$. When $p_1/p_2 = \frac{1}{2}$, the budget line coincides with 1's indifference curve through ω, and every bundle on that indifference maximizes 1's utility subject to his budget constraint. When $p_1/p_2 < \frac{1}{2}$, 1's desired bundle $\hat{x}_1$ moves to the horizontal axis, and as the budget line gets flatter, the desired bundle $\hat{x}_1$ moves out the horizontal axis. The locus of all desired bundles, for all possible prices, is the dashed line in Figure 3–7b. This is the path that $\hat{x}_1$ traces as p_1/p_2 goes from zero to infinity, and it is called person 1's *offer curve*. Figure 3–7b also includes the budget line that appears in 3–7a. Note that when we have the offer curve and the budget line we can read off the bundle $\hat{x}_1$ that 1 wants to consume. This is the point (other than ω_1) where the offer curve and the budget line intersect.

Now suppose we have another consumer, say person 2, with the utility function

$$u_2 = x_{21} x_{22}$$

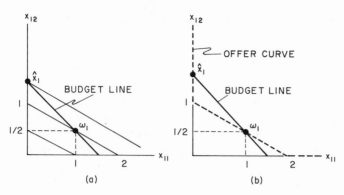

FIGURE 3-7

and the initial bundle $\omega_2 = (0, \frac{1}{2})$. If person 2 is faced with prices $p = (p_1, p_2)$, he will want to buy the best bundle he can afford, that is, the best bundle x_2 satisfying

$$p_1 x_{21} + p_2 x_{22} \leq p_1 \cdot 0 + p_2 \cdot \frac{1}{2}$$

Since his utility function is monotonic he will always want to consume at a point on, rather than below, his budget line; so the bundle he buys will satisfy

$$p_1 x_{21} + p_2 x_{22} = p_1 \cdot 0 + p_2 \cdot \frac{1}{2}$$

Person 2's indifference curves are hyperbolic, and the absolute value of the slope of an indifference curve for him is given by

$$\text{MRS person 2} = \frac{\text{MU of good 1}}{\text{MU of good 2}} = \frac{x_{22}}{x_{21}}$$

With these indifference curves, his utility maximizing bundles will always be at points of tangency of his indifference curves and budget lines. That is, for the bundles person 2 wants to consume we will have

$$\text{MRS person 2} = \frac{x_{22}}{x_{21}} = \frac{p_1}{p_2}$$

Consequently, person 2's choices are governed by two equations

$$p_1 x_{21} + p_2 x_{22} = \frac{1}{2} p_2$$

and

$$p_2 x_{22} = p_1 x_{21}$$

The solution to this pair of equations is

$$x_{21} = \frac{1}{4}\frac{p_2}{p_1} \text{ and } x_{22} = \frac{1}{4}$$

This is the algebraic form of person 2's offer curve.

Now consider an economy made up of persons 1 and 2. We have pictured it in an Edgeworth box diagram in Figure 3-8. To minimize complexity, all the figure shows is the offer curve of person 1 (taken from Figure 3-6b), the offer curve of person 2 (the dashed line where $x_{22} = \frac{1}{4}$), and the locus of Pareto optimal points where the two individuals' indifference curves are tangent. (This is determined by setting MRS for person 1 = MRS for person 2, or $x_{22}/x_{21} = \frac{1}{2}$.) The initial allocation is the point ω.

The two offer curves intersect at the point $\hat{x}$, or $\hat{x}_1 = (\frac{1}{2}, \frac{3}{4})$, $\hat{x}_2 = (\frac{1}{2}, \frac{1}{4})$. This means that for the appropriate prices person 1 wants to consume $\hat{x}_1$ and person 2 wants to consume $\hat{x}_2$. What are the prices? The budget line needed to get the two to $\hat{x}$ goes through ω and $\hat{x}$; so its slope in absolute value is $\frac{1}{2}$. Consequently, $p_1/p_2 = \frac{1}{2}$ is required, and, since one of the prices can be chosen arbitrarily, the price vector $p = (p_1, p_2) = (1, 2)$ works fine. In short, $p = (1, 2)$ and $\hat{x}_1 = (\frac{1}{2}, \frac{3}{4})$, $\hat{x}_2 = (\frac{1}{2}, \frac{1}{4})$ is a competitive equilibrium based on ω.

The First Fundamental Theorem says that $\hat{x}$ is Pareto optimal, and in the core. The figure shows it is Pareto optimal because it lies on the locus of tangencies, and it's in the core because it is Pareto optimal and it makes each individual at least as well off as ω.

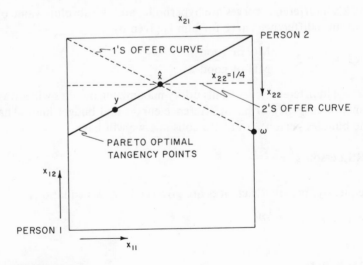

FIGURE 3-8

Now we turn to the Second Fundamental Theorem. Suppose $\hat{x}$ is judged objectionable because it gives too much to person 1. Consider the Pareto optimal allocation y given by $y_1 = (\frac{1}{4}, \frac{5}{8})$, $y_2 = (\frac{3}{4}, \frac{3}{8})$. Suppose we want to get to y from ω via a modified competitive mechanism. What bank balance transfers T_1 and T_2 are required?

The first thing to notice about this example is that person 1, whose indifference curves are straight lines with slope $\frac{1}{2}$, in absolute value, will only choose y_1 to maximize his utility if his budget line also has slope $\frac{1}{2}$ in absolute value. Consequently, the two people will end up at y only if $p_1/p_2 = \frac{1}{2}$. Again, one price can be chosen arbitrarily, so assume $p = (p_1, p_2) = (1, 2)$ is the competitive equilibrium price vector.

Next note that person 1 will choose point y_1 only if y_1 satisfies the equation

$$p \cdot y_1 = p \cdot \omega_1 + T_1$$

Similarly, y_2 must satisfy the equation

$$p \cdot y_2 = p \cdot \omega_2 + T_2$$

Substituting $(1,2)$ for p, and the given values for y_1, ω_1, y_2 and ω_2, we find that

$$T_1 = -\tfrac{1}{2} \text{ and } T_2 = +\tfrac{1}{2}$$

(Obviously, these magnitudes depended on our setting $p_1 = 1$. If we let $p_1 = 2$, then p_2, T_1 and T_2 would have to be doubled.)

The reader should check that when $p = (1,2)$, $T_1 = -\frac{1}{2}$ and $T_2 = +\frac{1}{2}$, person 1 will actually maximize his utility at y_1, and person 2 will actually maximize his utility at y_2.

EXERCISES

1. Let $u_1 = 3x_{11} + x_{12}$ and

    $$u_2 = x_{21}x_{22}.$$

    Let the initial allocation be $\omega_1 = (2,1)$, $\omega_2 = (1,2)$. Solve for the competitive equilibrium.
2. An economy is made up of two individuals and two goods. Their utility functions are:

    $$u_1 = x_{11} + x_{12}$$
    $$u_2 = 5x_{21}x_{22}.$$

Their initial endowments are:

$$\omega_1 = (100,0)$$
$$\omega_2 = (0,50).$$

Let the price of the second good, p_2, be 1.

a.   Find 1's offer curve. (Hint: Do it graphically, and pay particular attention to what happens when $p_1 = 1$.)

b.   Graph a representative indifference curve for person 2. Is it symmetric around the line $x_{21} = x_{22}$?

c.   Find a competitive equilibrium.

3.   Consider an economy with two people who have the utility functions and initial endowments given below:

$$u_1 = 2x_{11} + x_{12} \quad \omega_1 = \left(\tfrac{1}{2}, \tfrac{1}{2}\right)$$
$$u_2 = x_{21} + 2x_{22} \quad \omega_2 = \left(\tfrac{1}{2}, \tfrac{1}{2}\right).$$

a.   Solve for a competitive equilibrium.

b.   Show that MRS person 1 = MRS person 2 doesn't hold at the competitive equilibrium.

c.   Is the competitive equilibrium allocation Pareto optimal? Why?

4.   Again consider the two-person, two-goods economy given by

$$u_1 = 2x_{11} + x_{12} \quad \omega_1 = \left(\tfrac{1}{2}, \tfrac{1}{2}\right)$$
$$u_2 = x_{21} + 2x_{22} \quad \omega_2 = \left(\tfrac{1}{2}, \tfrac{1}{2}\right).$$

Suppose someone decides that $y_1 = (\tfrac{3}{4},0)$, $y_2 = (\tfrac{1}{4},1)$ is the best allocation. Show how y could be achieved via the modified competitive mechanism, with the appropriate bank balance transfers.

5.   Consider the economy given by

$$u_1 = x_{11}x_{12} \qquad \omega_1 = (1,0)$$
$$u_2 = 2x_{21} + x_{22} \qquad \omega_2 = (0,1).$$

a.   Solve for the set of Pareto optimal allocations. Where is the core?

b.   Draw an Edgeworth box diagram to represent the economy.

c.   Solve for the competitive equilibrium.

d.   Calculate bank balance transfers T_1 and T_2, and prices p_1 and p_2, such that the equilibrium of the modified competitive mechanism is $y_1 = (\tfrac{1}{4},\tfrac{1}{2})$, $y_2 = (\tfrac{3}{4},\tfrac{1}{2})$.

SELECTED REFERENCES

(Items marked with an asterisk (*) are mathematically difficult.)

*1. K. J. Arrow, "An Extension of the Basic Theorems of Classical Welfare Economics," *Second Berkeley Symposium on Mathematical Statistics and Probability* (J. Neyman, ed.), University of California Press, 1951, pp. 507–532.

In this article Arrow proves the fundamental theorems in a model with exchange and production. There are three main contributions. 1. Arrow formulates the theorems in precise mathematical terms. 2. He uses the theory of convex sets rather than the calculus arguments of earlier authors. 3. Using this powerful mathematical tool, he relaxes the unrealistic assumption made by earlier writers that all quantities of goods produced and consumed by all people are strictly greater than zero.

*2. G. Debreu, *Theory of Value,* John Wiley and Sons, Inc., New York, 1959, Chapters 5 and 6.

Chapter 5 provides an elegant proof of a theorem about the Walrasian model of an economy with exchange and production: Debreu proves that under reasonable assumptions, a competitive equilibrium in fact exists. Consequently, our theorems about the optimality of the competitive equilibrium aren't vacuous!

Chapter 6 provides rigorous proofs for general versions of the two fundamental theorems of welfare economics.

3. O. Lange, "The Foundations of Welfare Economics," *Econometrica,* V. 10, 1942, pp. 215–218.

Lange derives conditions for maximizing person *i*'s utility subject to the constraint that all other people's utilities be held constant, that is, conditions for a Pareto optimum. He uses calculus with Lagrange multipliers to do this. The equations he derives "contain *in nuce* most theorems of welfare economics, e.g., all the propositions in Pigou's *Economics of Welfare.*" However, he does not explicitly present the fundamental theorems.

4. A. P. Lerner, "The Concept of Monopoly and the Measurement of Monopoly Power," *Review of Economic Studies,* V. 1, 1934, pp. 157–175.

Although this article is principally about monopoly, it contains a clear statement of the first fundamental theorem, with an intuitive, nonrigorous argument. A competitive situation in an economy is optimal because utility maximizing individuals set marginal rates of substitution equal to price ratios, and profit-maximizing competitive firms set prices equal to marginal costs. Consequently, there is no possibility of further trade between individuals, or of further arrangements between individuals and firms, that would make some people better off and no one worse off.

5. P. K. Newman, *The Theory of Exchange,* Prentice-Hall, Inc., Englewood Cliffs, 1965, Chapters 3, 4, 5.

Newman gives a detailed exposition of exchange theory. He includes excellent notes on the literature.

6.   A. C. Pigou, *The Economics of Welfare,* MacMillan and Co., London, 1920.
     Part II, Chapters I, II, and III.
     Pigou provides the 1920 version of the first fundamental theorem. In this
     version, the "free play of self-interest" generally leads to the maximization of
     the "national dividend," which is roughly analogous to the modern concept of
     gross national product. So competition maximizes a measure of total output.
     Pigou is not particularly concerned with Pareto optimality as the outcome of
     competition, since he feels the national dividend is a reasonable measure of
     economic welfare.

7.   J. Quirk and R. Saposnik, *Introduction to General Equilibrium Theory and
     Welfare Economics,* McGraw-Hill, New York, 1968, Chapter 4, especially 4-5.
     This text includes a good exposition of the fundamental theorems, as well as
     material on the existence of competitive equilibria.

8.   J. A. Schumpeter, *History of Economic Analysis,* Edited by E. B. Schumpeter,
     Oxford University Press, 1954.
     Part II, Chapter 3 provides an uncomplimentary but useful guide to "Adam
     Smith and the *Wealth of Nations.*" According to Schumpeter, Smith was
     heavy on examples and weak on analysis. Smith's espousal of laissez faire pol-
     icies might follow from the first fundamental theorem, but Smith had no clear
     view of the theorem.
     Part IV, Chapter 7 provides a section on "The Walrasian Theory of General
     Equilibrium." This is excellent even though its completion was interrupted by
     Schumpeter's death.

9.   G. J. Stigler, *Production and Distribution Theories,* The MacMillan Company,
     New York, 1941.
     Stigler devotes Chapter IX to an explanation of the Walrasian general equi-
     librium system.

10. L. Walras, *Elements of Pure Economics* (Translated by William Jaffe), George
     Allen and Unwin, Ltd., London, 1954.
     This is a translation of *Eléments d' économie politique pure,* 1926 Edition.
     Parts II and III are particularly relevant.
     Walras must be given most of the credit for developing two important ana-
     lytical tools that we use. (1) The general equilibrium framework which puts all
     consumers, all goods, and in its general form all producers, together in one
     closed model. In the model the consumers maximize utility subject to their bud-
     get constraints, and supply equals demand for all goods. (2) The "taton-
     nement" price adjustment story, in which a set of prices is called out, desired
     supplies and demands at those prices are collected, and the prices are adjusted
     in response to excess supplies and demands. When at last there is no excess sup-
     ply or demand in any market, actual transactions are made.
     We should note, incidentally, that there is a real question about whether
     such a (hypothetical) price adjustment mechanism would be stable: Would it
     really eventually lead to a set of market-clearing prices? We have and will con-
     tinue to ignore the stability problem in this book. See Quirk and Saposnik for
     references on stability.

4 PRODUCTION AND OPTIMALITY

INTRODUCTION

In the last two chapters we focussed on models of exchange. In those models, the quantities of the various goods are fixed; nothing is produced. In this chapter, we will focus on a model of production. This model has firms, goods that are used as inputs in the production process, and goods that are produced as outputs. But it has no consumers. If the exchange model was half the story, the production model is the other half. Near the end of the chapter we will indicate how the two models might be merged.

The typical textbook treatment of production starts with production functions, the analogs of utility functions. These functions indicate precisely what levels of output a firm can achieve with given inputs. For instance, the Cobb-Douglas production function $q = L^{2/3} K^{1/3}$ says that with 27 units of labor (L) and 8 units of capital (K), it is possible to produce $(27)^{2/3} \times (8)^{1/2} = 9 \times 2 = 18$ units of output (q). The model of production developed below, however, is slightly more abstract than the typical production function approach.

We shall characterize firms not with production functions, but with production sets. To explain this, we first need to say something about what goods are inputs and what are outputs.

65

Let's assume as before that there are M goods. In the production model, some goods are used to produce other goods. These are inputs. For instance, unskilled labor, farm land, iron ore, and seed corn are used to produce, respectively, lots of things, farm products, iron, and corn. Now some of these inputs are not themselves produced. Such goods are occasionally called pure inputs. For instance, uncleared land, oil, natural gas, and minerals in the ground are not produced, at least not by people. On the other hand, some inputs are themselves produced. These are sometimes called intermediate goods. For instance, tools, machinery, trained workers, and buildings are all to various extents produced and then used to produce other goods. Finally, some of the goods in the production model are produced only for consumption. They are not used in the production of other goods. Examples of such pure outputs or final consumption goods are easy to name: ice cream, TV sets, some books, most records, clothing (except, perhaps, uniforms and work clothes), trips to Disneyworld, and so on.

The existence of intermediate goods can make the analysis of production a little complicated. For instance, a drill bit is an output for the Hughes Tool Corporation, and an input for Exxon Corporation. Gasoline is an output for Exxon Corporation, but an input on a wheat farm in Nebraska. Wheat is an output for the wheat farm, but an input for Wonder Bread Bakeries. Bread is an output for the bakery company, and probably, most often, a genuine consumption good. (Unless, of course, some is eaten by a machinist in a cafeteria of the Hughes Tool Corporation.)

Fortunately, all this complexity is nicely sorted out in our production model. Firms are characterized in our model by sets of production vectors, or input-output vectors. We shall typically index firms with the letter k. We write

$$y_k = (y_{k1}, y_{k2}, \ldots, y_{km})$$

for a production vector for the kth firm. The quantity y_{k1} is an amount of good 1; y_{k2} is an amount of good 2, . . ., y_{km} is an amount of good m. The following sign convention is crucial:

If firm k uses good j as an input, y_{kj} is negative.
If firm k produces good j as an output, y_{kj} is positive.

This simple convention is the answer to the complications of inputs, outputs, pure inputs, intermediate goods, final goods, and so on. If an entry in a production vector is positive, that good is an output for that firm; if an entry is negative, that good is an input for that firm.

The set of production vectors that are technologically feasible for firm k is called firm k's *production set*, and is written Y_k.

Let's consider an example. Suppose firm 5 can produce 1000 cars from 500 tons of steel and 2000 man-days of labor, and that cars are good 1, steel is good 2, and labor is good 3. This combination of inputs (steel and labor) and output (cars) is represented by the production vector

$$y_5 = (y_{51}, y_{52}, y_{53}) = (1000, -500, -2000)$$

The auto (output) is positive, and the steel and labor (inputs) are negative. For firm 5, the production vector $y_5 = (1000, -500, -2000)$ is technologically feasible. That is, y_5 is in Y_5. But it might be impossible for that firm to produce 1001 cars from 500 tons of steel and 2000 man-days of labor. In that case, the production vector $(1001, -500, -2000)$ is not in Y_5.

As we observed above, the sign convention sorts out inputs from outputs. But it does more: it also allows us to sensibly add up different production vectors for different firms. Suppose again that good 1 is cars, good 2 is steel, and good 3 is labor. Suppose now that we have two firms with the following production vectors:

$$y_1 = (-1, 3, -6)$$
$$y_2 = (7, -3, -14)$$

That is, firm 1 uses one car and six man-days to produce 3 tons of steel. Firm 2 uses three tons of steel and fourteen man-days to produce seven cars. Now let's add the two vectors component by component. The result we get is

$$y_1 + y_2 = (-1 + 7, 3 - 3, -6 - 14) = (6, 0, -20)$$

This says that the net output of cars between the two firms is 6, the net output of steel is 0, and the net input of labor is -20 (or the total use of labor is 20 man-days). So the vector sum, the vector derived by adding the two vectors component by component, shows net quantities.

In the analysis that follows we make several assumptions about production sets. First, we assume they are fixed; there is no technological change or progress in this simple model. Second, we assume they are independent of each other. That is, firm 1's production set Y_1 has no bearing on firm 2's production set Y_2. The firms do not interfere with or help each other technologically; there are no externalities here. One firm's choice of a production vector does not affect the technological possibilities of another firm; it does not affect the set of production vectors feasible for the other firm.

We shall also assume in our model of production that there are K firms altogether. The list of firms is fixed. (This is not as rigid an assumption as it might seem on first sight, since firms can choose to produce nothing — they need not be actively in business.) Since there are K firms, the index k for firms runs from 1 to K. A list of production vectors, with y_k in Y_k for $k = 1, 2, \ldots K$, is called a *production plan* for the economy, and is written

$$y = (y_1, y_2, \ldots, y_K)$$

A production plan for the economy shows what each and every firm is using as an input and producing as an output, and in what quantities. It details the state of every firm. And it is probably the thing in production theory that most resembles an allocation in exchange theory.

With these terms defined, we are now ready to proceed to some analysis.

OPTIMAL PRODUCTION PLANS

Figure 4-1 illustrates a production set for a firm that uses labor, good 1, to produce coal (good 2). (Obviously, most mining firms use more than labor, but for diagrams we are limited to two (or at most three) goods.)

In the diagram, the cross-hatched area is firm k's production set, Y_k. That is, every production vector in that set is technologically feasible for the firm, and none outside that set is feasible. Evidently, this firm can take labor, good 1, and transform it into coal, good 2. A typical feasible produc-

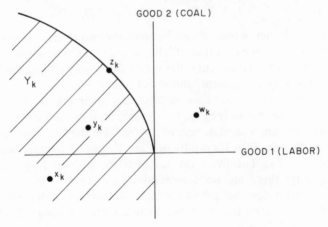

FIGURE 4-1

tion vector like y_k involves a negative quantity of labor and a positive quantity of coal. Labor is then the input, and coal is the output. But x_k is also feasible. At the point x_k, both the labor and coal coordinates are negative. This means the firm is using coal and labor and producing nothing. (It might be buying coal from a neighboring mine, and using labor to burn the coal it buys!) Clearly, x_k is a silly point; no firm would want to be there. But it is feasible. On the other, w_k is not feasible. At w_k, both the labor and the coal coordinates are positive. That is, the firm is using nothing to produce man-hours and coal. The magical formula for doing this has yet to be discovered, so w_k must lie outside of Y_k.

Now the production vector y_k makes a lot more sense than the silly production vector x_k. However, y_k itself is undesirable in the sense that other feasible production plans, such as z_k, use less labor and produce more coal. Given our sign convention, both coordinates of preferable points like z_k are greater than or equal to the corresponding coordinates of y_k, and at least one is greater:

$$y_{kj} \leq z_{kj} \text{ for all } j$$

and

$$y_{kj} < z_{kj} \text{ for at least one good } j$$

Points like z_k which are not undesirable in the above sense, are called *efficient* or *optimal production vectors* for the firm. They lie on the northeast frontier of the production set. These are the points with the property that the output of one good cannot be increased unless the output of another good is decreased, or the input of yet another good is increased.

The characterization of optimal production plans for the economy is more complicated, because what is an output for one firm might be an input for another.

Let $y = (y_1, y_2, \ldots, y_K)$ be a production plan for the economy. Since $y_{kj} > 0$ if firm k produces good j while $y_{kj} < 0$ if firm k uses good j,

$$\sum_{k=1}^{K} y_{kj}$$

is the net output in the economy of good j, if it is positive. If it is negative, it is the net input in the economy of good j. If it is zero, the total amount of good j produced by various firms equals the total used by other firms. If z is another production plan, and

$$\sum_{k=1}^{K} y_{kj} \leq \sum_{k=1}^{K} z_{kj}$$

then either:

1. Good j is a net output under both plans, and there is an equal or larger net output under z than under y.
2. Good j is a net input under both plans, and the net use of the good is equal or less under z than under y.
3. Good j is a net input under y, but a net output under z.

We shall assume that all goods, whether pure inputs, intermediate goods, or pure outputs are desirable. Therefore, it is always better to produce more (if a net output) or use less (if a net input). Therefore, if we consider only good j, we conclude that production plan z is at least as good as production plan y if

$$\sum_{k=1}^{K} y_{kj} \le \sum_{k=1}^{K} z_{kj}$$

If we think of all goods together, we must conclude that production plan z is at least as good as production plan y if

$$\sum_{k=1}^{K} y_{kj} \le \sum_{k=1}^{K} z_{kj} \text{ for all } j$$

For if the inequality holds for all goods, the net quantities of produced goods are as large under z as under y, and the net quantities of goods used are as small under z as under y.

Next, we say that a production plan z *dominates* a production plan y if

$$\sum_{k=1}^{K} y_{kj} \le \sum_{k=1}^{K} z_{kj} \text{ for all } j$$

and

$$\sum_{k=1}^{K} y_{kj} < \sum_{k=1}^{K} z_{kj} \text{ for at least one good } j$$

And finally, we say that a *production plan* for the economy is *optimal* if there exists no other production plan for the economy that dominates it. If z is optimal, there is no way to get more of an output without using more of some input or producing less of some other output. Every change from z has a real cost attached to it. There is no "free lunch."

Let's consider our two-firm, three-good example again, in which good 1 is cars, good 2 is steel, and good 3 is labor. Recall that the production plan y is given by

$$y_1 = (-1, 3, -6)$$
$$y_2 = (7, -3, -14)$$

Now let

$$z_1 = (-2,4,-6)$$
$$z_2 = (8,-3\tfrac{1}{2},-14)$$

Assume that firm 1's production set is $Y_1 = \{y_1,z_1\}$. That is, firm 1 has two and only two production vectors available to it. The first production vector is y_1. The second z_1 uses two cars and six man-days to generate 4 tons of steel. Since these are, by assumption, the only possibilities available to firm 1, they are clearly both optimal production vectors for firm 1. Assume that firm 2's production set is $Y_2 = \{y_2,z_2\}$. That is, firm 2 has two and only two production vectors available to it. We are familiar with y_2; z_2 uses three and a half tons of steel and fourteen man-days to produce eight cars. Again, both production vectors are clearly optimal for the firm.

Now consider the production plan $y = (y_1,y_2)$. Is it optimal? Although each firm's vector is optimal for it, the combination is not optimal for the economy. For the net quantities under y are

$$y_1 + y_2 = (6,0,-20)$$

The net output of cars is 6, the net output of steel is 0, and the net input of labor is 20. However, the net amounts under z are

$$z_1 + z_2 = (-2 + 8,4 - 3\tfrac{1}{2},-6 - 14) = (6,\tfrac{1}{2},-20)$$

Under plan z there is a net output of steel equal to ½ ton, while the net output of cars and the net input of labor are the same as under y. So z dominates y, and y is not an optimal production plan for the economy. The plan z is optimal, however.

COMPETITIVE EQUILIBRIUM PRODUCTION PLANS

In the section above there was no explanation of why firms might want to choose one production vector rather than another. Now we examine the behavioral assumption, the motive: We shall assume that owners or managers of firms attempt to maximize profits. We shall also assume that they act competitively, that is, they take the prices of goods as given by the market.

What is profit? The general definition is revenue less cost. Revenue for a firm is the aggregate value of the goods that the firm sells. Cost is the aggregate value of the goods that the firm buys. In terms of our model, revenue is the aggregate value of the outputs of a firm. Cost is the aggregate value of the inputs. Now if good j is an output for firm k, then $y_{kj} > 0$, $p_j y_{kj}$ represents revenue, and the contribution to profit from the firm's sale of good j is

$$p_j y_{kj}$$

On the other hand, if good j is an input for firm k, then $y_{kj} < 0$, $p_j y_{kj}$ represents cost, but the contribution to profit from the firm's use of good j is again

$$p_j y_{kj}$$

Note that $p_j y_{kj}$ is a negative number, since y_{kj} is negative.

Now consider the sum of terms

$$p_1 y_{k1} + p_2 y_{k2} + \ldots + p_m y_{km} = \sum_{j=1}^{m} p_j y_{kj} = p \cdot y_k$$

Some of these terms are positive and some of the terms are negative. The positive numbers are the contributions to revenue, and the negative numbers are the contributions to cost. Consequently,

$$p \cdot y_k$$

is equal to profit, or revenue less cost, for firm k, when it produces y_k.

We assume in what follows that firm k chooses y_k to maximize $p \cdot y_k$.

To illustrate profit maximization, we consider the firm represented in Figure 4-1. That firm uses labor, good 1, to produce coal, good 2. It maximizes

$$p \cdot y_k = p_1 y_{k1} + p_2 y_{k2}$$

Now $p_1 y_{k1}$ is a negative number, representing expenditures on labor. On the other hand, $p_2 y_{k2}$ is a positive number, representing receipts from coal sales. If we set

$$p_1 y_{k1} + p_2 y_{k2} = c$$

we get the equation for the locus of production vectors for which profit equals the constant c. In this two-good case, that locus of points is a straight line, with slope $-p_1/p_2$. Such straight lines, which are geometrically analogous to budget lines in exchange theory, are called *isoprofit lines*. Figure 4-2 shows the production set Y_k and isoprofit lines for firm k.

In the figure, ℓ_1, ℓ_2 and ℓ_3 are three different isoprofit lines. It should be clear that lines farther to the right represent higher profit levels (or higher c's in the equation $p_1 y_{k1} + p_2 y_{k2} = c$), at least when prices are positive. Consequently, ℓ_3 represents the highest profit level, of the three isoprofit lines drawn. The firm's assumed behavior is to choose the production vector which puts it on the highest possible isoprofit line. In Figure 4-2, this means the firm will choose the production vector z_k.

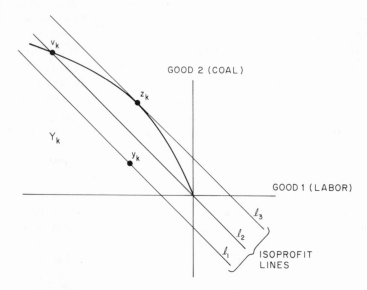

GOOD 2 (COAL)

GOOD 1 (LABOR)

ISOPROFIT LINES

FIGURE 4-2

Note that profits at z_k are higher than at the optimal production vector v_k, or at the nonoptimal production vector y_k. Also note that the profit-maximizing point z_k must be an optimal production vector for firm k. So profit maximization causes the firm to choose a vector optimal for it. But we've seen above that two production vectors optimal for each of the two firms might not be optimal for the economy. Optimality for a production plan for the economy requires more than just optimality for each production vector of each firm. It requires coordination among the firms.

In the model of an exchange economy, a competitive equilibrium is a state in which all individuals are maximizing their utilities subject to their budget constraints. In the production model, we define a competitive equilibrium as follows.

Let p be a given vector of prices of the m goods. Suppose that, for $k = 1, 2, \ldots, K$, the production vector y_k maximizes the kth firm's profit. That is, $p \cdot y_k$ is at a maximum for production vectors in Y_k. Let y be the production plan $(y_1, y_2, \ldots, y_k)$. Then y and p constitute a *competitive equilibrium* for the production economy. The essence of a competitive equilibrium is that there is one price vector p, and every firm is maximizing its profits given p.

Parallels with the exchange model are clear. In both the exchange model and the production model there is one price vector that everyone takes as given. In the exchange model, firms maximize utility. In the production model, firms maximize profit. However, utility maximization is done subject to budget constraint. Profit maximization is done subject a to the constraint that y_k be feasible, that is, in Y_k. In fact, there is no budget constraint for a firm. Also, in the exchange model, the total quantities of all the goods are fixed. In the production model, the total quantities are not fixed; only the Y_k's are fixed.

In a competitive equilibrium, each firm maximizes its profit subject to the given price vector p. We've already observed in Figure 4-2 that this implies that each firm will choose a production vector optimal for it. The question we must now ask is whether the one price vector, taken as given by all the firms, will serve to coordinate the firms' production decisions. Will y be an optimal production plan for the economy? Or, like the (y_1, y_2) in the two-firm, three-good example above, will it be dominated by some other production plan?

THE FIRST FUNDAMENTAL THEOREM OF WELFARE ECONOMICS, PRODUCTION VERSION

We are now ready to state and prove the production version of the First Fundamental Theorem. This extremely important result says that a competitive equilibrium production plan must be optimal. The competitive equilibrium price vector brings about perfect coordination of the firms' activities. In other words, in a competitive equilibrium there is no slack. It is impossible to increase the net output of one good without reducing the net output of another or increasing the net input of a third. Even though each firm is acting independently of the others, there is no possibility of unambiguous benefit through further coordination or through central planning.

The remarkable nature of this result must be emphasized. In the United States there are thousands of firms operating in fifty states. If they are profit-maximizing competitive firms and they see the same vector of prices, their decisions are optimal for the economy. Most will never communicate with each other. The firms in Rhode Island will, by and large, be unaware of the existence of the firms in Idaho. Yet, if a central authority had information about every firm on its computer, it could not unambiguously improve upon the competitive equilibrium. The best computer coupled with the largest staff of planners could not find slack in the system. Even though the competitive mechanism is decentralized and apparently chaotic, it generates an optimal production plan for the economy.

Here is the formal statement and proof of the theorem.

First Fundamental Theorem of Welfare Economics, Production Version. Suppose all prices are positive, and (y,p) is a competitive equilibrium. Then y is an optimal production plan for the economy.

Proof. Suppose instead that y is not an optimal production plan. We will show this leads to a contradiction.

If y is not a production optimum, there is a production plan for the economy $z = (z_1, z_2, \ldots, z_K)$ that dominates it. This means that

$$z_k \text{ is in } Y_k \text{ for } k = 1, 2, \ldots, K \tag{i}$$

$$\sum_{k=1}^{K} z_{kj} \geq \sum_{k=1}^{K} y_{kj}, \text{ for all goods } j \tag{ii}$$

$$\sum_{k=1}^{K} z_{kj} > \sum_{k=1}^{K} y_{kj} \text{ for at least one } j \tag{iii}$$

If we multiply each of the inequalities in (ii) and (iii) by the corresponding positive price p_j, we get

$$p_j \sum_{k=1}^{K} z_{kj} \geq p_j \sum_{k=1}^{K} y_{kj} \text{ for all } j$$

with the strict inequality holding for at least one. Adding over all j then gives

$$\sum_{j=1}^{m} p_j \sum_{k=1}^{K} z_{kj} > \sum_{j=1}^{m} p_j \sum_{k=1}^{K} y_{kj}$$

or

$$\sum_{k=1}^{K} \sum_{j=1}^{m} p_j z_{kj} > \sum_{k=1}^{K} \sum_{j=1}^{m} p_j y_{kj}$$

or

$$p \cdot z_1 + p \cdot z_2 + \ldots + p \cdot z_K >$$
$$p \cdot y_1 + p \cdot y_2 + \ldots + p \cdot y_K$$

Consequently, for at least one firm, say the kth,

$$p \cdot z_k > p \cdot y_k$$

But since z_k is feasible by (i), this means firm k is not maximizing its profits at y_k, a contradiction.

Q.E.D.

The First Fundamental Theorem obviously supports a laissez faire economic policy, since it implies that without interference, profit maximizing by competitive firms will bring about an optimal production plan. It seems to suggest that policy makers should leave competitive economic systems alone. They work. As the Sage said, if it works, don't fix it.

However, there are generally many optimal production plans. Some might involve large net outputs of housing, hospitals, food, and education. Some might involve large net outputs of automobiles, amusement parks, cigarettes, and liquor. To say that a production plan is optimal might not be enough. Most of us feel that there are good optimal production plans and there are not-so-good optimal production plans. Consequently, the First Fundamental Theorem leaves questions unanswered. Perhaps laissez faire isn't the best approach after all. It is a fine thing that the competitive mechanisms will bring the economy to a production optimum. But what if we want a different production optimum? These doubts about the first theorem bring us to the second.

THE SECOND FUNDAMENTAL THEOREM OF WELFARE ECONOMICS, PRODUCTION VERSION

In any economy it is wasteful for the productive sector to operate in a non-optimal way. There is no point in accepting one production plan for the economy when there is an alternative plan for which outputs are greater and/or inputs are less. Whether all decisions are made by individuals owners and managers of firms, operating in a climate of laissez faire, or whether crucial decisions are made by a Central Planning Board attempting to attain socially desirable production goals, optimality for production is necessary for sensible decisions. The most preferred production plan must be an optimal one.

At this point we need some more notation. Let y be a production plan for the economy. In order to represent the net inputs and outputs given y, we use the following definitions:

$$y_1^* = y_{11} + y_{21} + \ldots + y_{K1}$$
$$y_2^* = y_{12} + y_{22} + \ldots + y_{K2}$$
$$\vdots$$
$$y_m^* = y_{1m} + y_{2m} + \ldots + y_{Km}$$

That is, y_1^* is the net amount of good 1 produced (if it is positive) or used (if it is negative) under the production plan y. It is the bottom line quantity for good 1. Similarly, y_2^* is the net amount of good 2 produced (if it is positive) or used (if it is negative) under the production plan y. It is the bottom line quantity for good 2. And so on, through good m. In mathematical language, we are defining $y^* = (y_1^*, y_2^*, \ldots, y_m^*)$ to be the vector sum of y_1, $y_2, \ldots, y_K$:

$$y^* = y_1 + y_2 + \ldots + y_K$$

Now suppose that the competitive equilibrium production plan in a laissez faire economy, an economy with no political direction, is x. Then the corresponding list of net amounts is x^*. Suppose that x^* is heavy on luxury cars, liquor, and so on, and light on housing, food, etc. Let us assume that the nation's political leaders reject x^*, and the associated x. Suppose they decide that some other list of net amounts y^* is superior; let y be the associated production plan for the economy.

We are assuming here that y^* is possible, in the sense that there does exist an associated production plan y for the economy, with y_k in Y_k for every k. Sometimes some leaders decide on nonfeasible quantities of goods, in which case there is just no way that their plans can be realized. We'll stay away from the Rolls-Royce-in-every-garage, pie-in-the-sky production plans in this analysis. We are also assuming that y is optimal; it is silly to accept a non-optimal goal.

One way to achieve y^* would be to have the economy's Central Planning Board to send directives to each and every firm telling that firm exactly how much of each input it should use, and exactly how much of each output it should produce. The Board could, in other words, tell every firm what y_k to produce. Let's call this system *centralized socialism*.

Is centralized socialism practical? There are two reasons why it is not. First, it requires that the Central Planning Board send out enormous quantities of information. All the amounts of all goods used and produced by all firms are decided upon, and emanate from one Board. The information processing and transmitting requirements are prohibitive. Second, it destroys the incentives of the owners and managers of the firms. The people on the spot, directing day-to-day operations, are passive; they receive instructions and simply implement them. Consequently, they have no reasons to search for superior production processes, they have no incentives to increase outputs or reduce inputs. If the Central Planning Board mistakenly sends firm k a production vector that is not optimal for that firm, the manager has no motive to find a production vector that dominates it. Often the on-the-spot manager has information about his firm that the Central Planner doesn't, but under centralized socialism he has no incentive to use superior information or to reveal it to the Central Planner.

These practical difficulties of centralized socialism bring us back to the question. Suppose the vector of net amounts x^* associated with laissez faire is objectionable, and another list of net amounts y^*, associated with an optimal production plan y, is desired by the planners in an economy. Is there some way to achieve y^*? The Second Fundamental Theorem of Welfare Economics says that there is a way. The alternative to centralized socialism is to have the Central Planning Board issue a list of prices p, and instruct the managers of firms (or state enterprises) to maximize revenues less costs, or profits, given the prices p. We shall call this system *decentralized socialism*. Decentralized socialism re-injects the profit motive into the planned economy. It harnesses competitive forces to attain a desired list of net quantities y^*. It avoids massive intervention in the minute decisions of every firm.

Formally, the theorem says that given any optimal y, there exists some price vector p so that y and p constitute a competitive equilibrium.

In practice, the Planning Board has a y^* in mind. The theorem says that if the associated y is optimal (which makes sense), the Board can achieve it via a decentralized system, if it can find the right price vector p. The way p might actually be found probably involves trial and error; over a period of months or years the board might gradually adjust p until the desired y^* finally appears. Once the right p is hit upon, small adjustments can be made to bring about further small desired changes in y^*.

In order to provide a formal statement of the theorem, we need to define two technical terms. First, a production set Y_k is said to be *convex* if the following is true: For any two points x_k and y_k in Y_k, the straight line segment connecting those two points is entirely contained in Y_k. The reader can refer to Figure 4-1 to see a convex production set. (The reader can also refer to the definition of a convex indifference curve and Figure 3-6, which illustrates that definition. In Figure 3-6a, the set of bundles on or above the indifference curve is a convex set, while in Figure 3-6b the set of bundles on or above the indifference curve is not convex.) Second, a production set Y_k is said to be *closed* if it includes its boundaries. The Y_k in Figure 3-6 is closed, since the northeast boundary (including z_k) is part of Y_k, as is the east boundary, the lower half of the vertical axis.

Now we turn to the formal statement of the theorem. The proof is in the Appendix to this chapter.

Second Fundamental Theorem of Welfare Economics, Production Version. Suppose all production sets are convex and closed. Let y^* be any vector of net quantities whose associated production plan y is optimal.

Then there exists a price vector p, not equal to the zero vector, such that y^* could be achieved using p through decentralized socialism. That is, there exists a p such that (y, p) is a competitive equilibrium.

EXTENDING THE PRODUCTION MODEL, AND
COMBINING PRODUCTION AND EXCHANGE

The discussion above leaves certain important issues unclear. Let y be a production plan, and y^* the corresponding list of net quantities. Then $y^* = (y_1^*, y_2^*, \ldots, y_m^*)$ includes some positive numbers (for goods that are net outputs in the economy) and some negative numbers (for goods that are net inputs). Where then do the net inputs come from? Where do the net outputs go? The model is incomplete.

One way to make it more complete is to assume that there are certain fixed amounts of net inputs available to the economy, and that these amounts are owned by the Central Planning Board. This clearly makes for a fuller model in the socialist spirit, but it should be observed that this fuller model remains unfinished: the question of where the net outputs go remains unanswered. Let $s^* = (s_1^*, s_2^*, \ldots, s_m^*)$ be a vector of quantities of goods owned by the Board. All the s_j^*'s are non-negative; some might be zero. The positive quantities can be interpreted as amounts of available natural resources, like mineral ores, and farmland, or as capital equipment, and so on. One good might be interpreted as labor, if the Board owns labor in some meaningful sense. Now there is a new feasibility condition that any production plan must fulfill. In addition to the requirement that y_k be in Y_k for every k, it is necessary that the net inputs of any production plan be covered by the amounts available. That is, for any y we must have

$$s_j^* + y_j^* \geq 0 \text{ for all } j$$

The immediate effect of this condition is to constrain the set of feasible net or aggregate production vectors; it makes the aggregate production set smaller. It also changes the set of optimal production plans, since to be optimal a production plan must first be feasible. The second effect of the condition is to modify the notion of a competitive equilibrium. Up till now, a competitive equilibrium production plan has simply been one with the property that y_k maximizes firm k's profits, for all k. But the constraint that $s_j^* + y_j^* \geq 0$ for all j introduces a supply and demand condition for net input goods. If for some price vector p the aggregate net demand for good j exceeds the supply s_j^*; that is, if $y_j^* < 0$ and $s_j^* + y_j^* < 0$, then equilibrium is physically impossible. Consequently, $s_j^* + y_j^* \geq 0$ for all j is a necessary condition for a competitive equilibrium. We are led, then, to the following revision of the definition of a competitive equilibrium: y and p constitute a competitive equilibrium if (1) for all k, y_k maximizes firm k's profits over the production set Y_k, and (2) for all goods j, $s_j^* + y_j^* \geq 0$.

With these modified definitions of optimal production plans and competitive equilibrium, the two fundamental theorems go through essentially unchanged.

We should observe at this point that this model might be desocialized in spirit by assuming that s^* is privately owned, rather than owned by a Central Planning Board.

Private ownership of resources, however, brings us to a yet more complex, and fuller, model. For if resources are owned by individuals, those individuals presumably take the payments they receive for what they sell (or rent) to firms, and spend those payments on the net outputs of firms. To reflect this complexity, the models of exchange and of production must be merged. We shall indicate in general terms what such a merged production/exchange private-ownership model looks like.

Let us now assume that goods used as net inputs, and the firms themselves, are owned by private individuals. Person i's initial bundle is, as before, ω_i. We assume, as before, that $i = 1, 2, \ldots, n$. Now the initial quantities of goods in the economy are given by the following equation:

$$s_1^* = \omega_{11} + \omega_{21} + \ldots + \omega_{n1}$$
$$s_2^* = \omega_{12} + \omega_{22} + \ldots + \omega_{n2}$$
$$\vdots$$
$$s_m^* = \omega_{1m} + \omega_{2m} + \ldots + \omega_{nm}$$

In easy vector shorthand, we have

$$s^* = \omega_1 + \omega_2 + \ldots + \omega_n = \sum_{i=1}^{n} \omega_i$$

But person i owns more than ω_i at the start, he also owns shares of firms. A share of a firm gives him a right to a fraction of the profit of that firm. Let θ_{ik} be person i's fractional ownership of firm k. Since the sum of all fractional shares must be equal 1, we have

$$\sum_{i=1}^{n} \theta_{ik} = 1, \text{ for } k = 1, 2, \ldots, K$$

Now if firm k makes a profit of $p \cdot y_k$, person i receives $\theta_{ik}(p \cdot y_k)$. Since person i owns a fraction of every firm (some of these fractions obviously might be zero), his total income from profits of firms is

$$\sum_{k=1}^{K} \theta_{ik}(p \cdot y_k)$$

This profit income must appear on the income side of i's budget constraint. Therefore, in the production exchange private-ownership model, person i's budget constraint is

$$p \cdot x_i \leq p \cdot \omega_i + \sum_{k=1}^{K} \theta_{ik}(p \cdot y_k)$$

As before, x_i is a consumption bundle for i. It is assumed, of course, that i tries to maximize his utility subject to his budget constraint, so:

I. Each person i chooses x_i to maximize $u_i(x_i)$, subject to

$$p \cdot x_i \leq p \cdot \omega_i + \sum_{k=1}^{K} \theta_{ik}(p \cdot y_k)$$

Firms, of course, attempt to maximize profits. So we have:

II. Each firm k chooses y_k in Y_k to maximize $p \cdot y_k$

Finally, goods must add up. Total demands by individuals for the m goods are given by:

$x_{11} + x_{21} + \ldots + x_{n1}$, for good 1
$x_{12} + x_{22} + \ldots + x_{n2}$, for good 2
.
.
.
$x_{1m} + x_{2m} + \ldots + x_{nm}$, for good m

In vector notation, this list of total demands is

$$x_1 + x_2 + \ldots + x_n, \text{ or } \sum_{i=1}^{n} x_i$$

Total initial quantities are given by

$$s^* = \sum_{i=1}^{n} \omega_i$$

Net amounts produced (or used, if the quantities are negative) by the firms are given by the vector equation

$$y^* = y_1 + y_2 + \ldots + y_K = \sum_{k=1}^{K} y_k$$

The supply equals demand condition can then be written in compact vector form as follows:

III. $$\sum_{i=1}^{n} x_i = \sum_{i=1}^{n} \omega_i + \sum_{k=1}^{K} y_k$$

Note that the sign convention on the y_{kj}'s ensures that the righthand side of III makes sense: if the firms are, in aggregate, producers of good j, then the jth component of

$$\sum_{k=1}^{K} y_k \text{ is positive;}$$

if the firms are, in aggregate, users of good j, then the jth component of

$$\sum_{k=1}^{K} y_k \text{ is negative.}$$

In this production/exchange private-ownership model, a *competitive equilibrium* is (I) a price vector p, (II) a vector of consumption bundles $x = (x_1, x_2, \ldots, x_n)$, one for each person, and (III) a production plan for the economy $y = (y_1, y_2, \ldots, y_K)$, that satisfy I, II, and III above.

Let's now call a consumption-production plan given by a vector of consumption bundles $x = (x_1, x_2, \ldots, x_n)$ and a production plan for the economy $y = (y_1, y_2, \ldots, y_K)$ feasible if: $x_{ij} \geq 0$ for all i and j, y_k is in Y_k for all k, and III is satisfied. A feasible consumption-production plan x, y is *dominated* if there is another feasible consumption-production plan x', y' with the property that all individuals like x' as well as x, and some individuals like x' better than x. Note that dominance is once again defined in terms of individuals' utility levels, as it was in the model of exchange, rather than in terms of output quantities. Finally, we call feasible consumption-production plan x, y *Pareto optimal* if it is undominated by any feasible plan.

With this rather general model, and with these definitions, the two fundamental theorems can be rigorously formulated and proved. In essence, they are similar to the partial versions given above. The First Fundamental Theorem says that a competitive equilibrium in the production/exchange economy is Pareto optimal. And the Second Fundamental Theorem says that virtually any Pareto optimal consumption-production plan can be reached via a modified competitive mechanism. With the appropriate cash transfers, and/or stock ownership transfers, virtually any Pareto optimal arrangement can be achieved.

AN ALGEBRAIC EXAMPLE IN A SIMPLE PRODUCTION MODEL

We return in this section to a simple production model and provide an algebraic example. Suppose there are two firms, and assume there are just two goods. We assume that firm 1 can use good 1 to produce good 2 according to a square root production function: its (maximum) output of good 2 is equal to the square root of the input of good 1. Formally the production function is

$$y_{12} = \sqrt{-y_{11}}$$

We need the minus sign before the y_{11} because good 1 is used by firm 1 as an input, so y_{11} is a negative number. To define firm 1's production set Y_1, we allow for the fact that firm 1 can waste some of the input, so the output is at most equal to the square root of the input. Y_1 is then the set of points satisfying

$$y_{12} \leq \sqrt{-y_{11}}$$

The set Y_1 is sketched in Figure 4-3a.

It turns out that the absolute value of the slope of the northeast boundary of Y_1 is given by the formula

$$\frac{1}{2} \frac{1}{\sqrt{-y_{11}}}$$

When firm 1 maximizes its profits, it finds the point where its production set touches the highest isoprofit line ℓ_2. At this point, the boundary of Y_1 is tangent to the isoprofit line ℓ_2; that is, the slope of the boundary equals the slope of the isoprofit line, or

$$\frac{1}{2} \frac{1}{\sqrt{-y_{11}}} = \frac{p_1}{p_2}$$

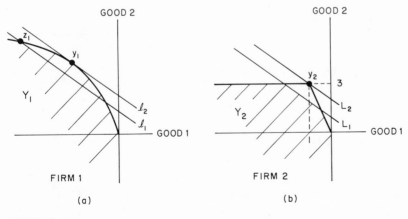

FIRM 1

(a)

FIRM 2

(b)

FIGURE 4-3

For convenience, we take p_2 to be 1, and solve for $-y_{11}$.

$$-y_{11} = \frac{1}{4 p_1^2}$$

Let's assume that the production set Y_2 has the angular shape sketched in Figure 4–3b (which may not be drawn to the same scale as Figure 4–2a.) Formally, Y_2 is the set of points satisfying

$$y_{22} \leq \begin{cases} -3y_{11} \text{ for } -1 \leq y_{11} \leq 0 \\ \\ 3 \text{ for } y_{11} < -1 \end{cases}$$

Firm 2 maximizes its profits by finding the point where its production set touches the highest isoprofit line L_2. At this point, however, the slope of the isoprofit line is not equal to the slope of the boundary of Y_2, since there is a kink in that boundary at y_2 and its slope is undefined.

The isoprofit lines ℓ_1, ℓ_2 and L_1, L_2 have been drawn with the same slope since we assume both firms face the same price vector p. The pair $y = (y_1, y_2)$ and p constitute a competitive equilibrium in this economy. By the First Fundamental Theorem, y is an optimal production plan.

By the Second Fundamental Theorem, any optimal production plan can be achieved as a competitive equilibrium. That is, for any optimal production plan y there is a price vector p such that y and p are a competitive equilibrium. For instance, the production plan (z_1, y_2) happens to be optimal. The theorem says the two firms can be induced to operate at (z_1, y_2), given the right prices. What prices? At z_1, the absolute value of the slope of the boundary of Y_1 is

$$\frac{1}{2} \frac{1}{\sqrt{-z_{11}}}$$

If p_1/p_2 is chosen equal to this, one of firm 1's isoprofit lines will just touch Y_1 at z_1. So firm 1 will want to produce at z_1. Firm 2, with new flatter isoprofit lines, will still want to produce at y_2. Thus

$$(p_1, p_2) = (\tfrac{1}{2} \frac{1}{\sqrt{-z_{11}}}, 1)$$

and (z_1, y_2) constitute a competitive equilibrium, and the Central Planning Board can move the economy to (z_1, y_2) by announcing the new prices.

1. There are three firms and three commodities. Good 1 is a composite consumption good, good 2 is capital, and good 3 is labor. Firm 2 can produce the consumption good from capital and labor according to the (Cobb-Douglas) rule:

    $$y_{11} \leq (-y_{12})^{\frac{1}{3}}(-y_{13})^{\frac{2}{3}}$$

    Firm 2 can produce the consumption good from capital and labor according to the rule:

    $$y_{21} \leq -\frac{y_{22}}{3} - \frac{2y_{23}}{3}$$

    Firm 3 can produce capital from labor according to the rule:

    $$y_{32} \leq (-y_{33})^{\frac{1}{2}}$$

    a. Find a production vector for each firm (other than (0,0,0)), which is feasible for that firm, and which lies on the northeast boundary of the production set for that firm.
    b. Given the production vectors of part (a), what are the net inputs and outputs of the three goods, for the entire economy? Can you adjust your plan so the net output (or input) of capital is zero?
    c. Show that the production plan for the economy which you have chosen is not optimal. (Hint: This can be done by trial and error: you might start by having firm 1 use 1 unit less of capital and firm 2 use 1 unit more; if this doesn't work, continue with similar small switches. The odds are very small that the y_1, y_2, and y_3 you picked in part (a) constitute an optimal production plan for the economy.)
2. In the economy of problem 1, suppose the prices of the three goods are (3,1,2). Find profit-maximizing production vectors for the three firms.

    (Note: This problem requires some familiarity with the theory of the firm and profit maximization. Those familiar with these topics can solve the problem if they recall that for a Cobb-Douglas production function $q = K^{\frac{1}{3}}L^{\frac{2}{3}}$, the marginal rate of substitution of capital for labor is $2K/L$.)

APPENDIX

In order to prove the Second Fundamental Theorem, we need to use a mathematical result known as Minkowski's Theorem. Let $S_1, S_2, \ldots, S_K$ be sets of m dimensional vectors. The sum S of the sets S_1 through S_K is defined as follows: An m dimensional vector x is in the sum, or

$$x \text{ is in } S = S_1 + S_2 + \ldots + S_K$$

If and only if

$$x = x_1 + x_2 + \ldots + x_K$$

and x_1 is in S_1, x_2 is in S_2, $\ldots$, x_K is in S_K
The version of Minkowski's Theorem that we need goes as follows:

Minkowski's Theorem. Let $S_1, S_2, \ldots, S_K$ be closed convex sets of m dimensional vectors. Suppose $S = S_1 + S_2 + \ldots + S_K$, and assume that the vector s^* is on the boundary of S. Let $s^* = s_1 + s_2 + \ldots + s_K$, with s_1 in S_1, s_2 in S_2, and so on.
　　Then there exists an m dimensional vector p, not equal to the zero vector, such that, for $k = 1, 2, \ldots, K$,

$$p \cdot x_k \leq p \cdot s_k \text{ whenever } x_k \text{ is in } S_k.$$

Proof of the Second Fundamental Theorem, Production Version. Define the aggregate production set Y as follows:

$$Y = Y_1 + Y_2 + \ldots + Y_K$$

The Central Planning Board wants to achieve y^*, a vector in Y, through decentralized socialism. Let $y = (y_1, y_2, \ldots, y_K)$ be the associated production plan. Then

$$y^* = y_1 + y_2 + \ldots + y_K$$

Also, y_1 is in Y_1, y_2 is in Y_2, and so on, and, by assumption, y is an optimal production plan.

　　To apply Minkowski's Theorem, we need to establish that y^* is on the boundary of Y. If to the contrary y^* is not on the boundary of Y, there is a point z^* in Y such that $z_j^* \geq y_j^*$ for $j = 1, 2, \ldots, m$, and $z_j^* > y_j^*$ for at least one j. But if z^* is in Y, there is a production plan $z = (z_1, z_2, \ldots, z_K)$, with z_1 in Y_1, z_2 in Y_2, $\ldots$, z_K in Y_K, for which

$$z_j^* = \sum_{k=1}^{K} z_{k_j} \text{ for all } j.$$

Now we have

$$\sum_{k=1}^{K} z_{kj} \geq \sum_{k=1}^{K} y_{kj} \text{ for all } j,$$

with the strict inequality holding for at least one j. This means the production plan z dominates the production plan y, a contradiction. Consequently, y^* must be on the boundary of Y.

By Minkowski's Theorem, there exists a nonzero price vector p such that, for all k,

$$p \cdot x_i \leq p \cdot y_k \text{ for all } x_k \text{ in } Y_k$$

This means y_k maximizes profits for the kth firm. Therefore (y,p) is a competitive equilibrium.   Q.E.D.

SELECTED REFERENCES

(Items marked with an asterisk (*) are mathematically difficult.)

*1. G. Debreu, *Theory of Value,* John Wiley and Sons, Inc., New York, 1959, Chapters 3, 6.

   Chapter 3 is an axiomatic treatment of production. It covers, among other things, assumption on production sets, and profit maximization. The material is at a mathematically advanced level. Chapter 6 deals with competitive equilibrium and optimality — in other words, the fundamental theorems.

2. T. C. Koopmans, "Allocation of Resources and the Price System," *Three Essays on the State of Economic Science,* McGraw-Hill, New York, 1957.

   Koopmans' essay is an excellent reference and it doesn't require great mathematical sophistication to understand. Chapter 1 is a good treatment of sets, the sign convention, "separating hyperplane theorems," and the virtues of decentralization. The references in Part 1.8 are a useful guide to the history of the subject. Chapter 2 covers the fundamental theorems. In 2.1 there is a useful brief history of the idea of Pareto optimality, with good references.

*3. K. Lancaster, *Mathematical Economics,* Macmillan, New York, 1968, Chapter R4.

   The student with a little mathematical sophistication who wants to understand Minkowski's Theorem can use this chapter of Lancaster's text, especially R4.3. Lancaster gives a simpler version of Minkowski's Theorem than the one we use, but the extension of his version to ours is not hard.

4. O. Lange and F. M. Taylor, *On the Economic Theory of Socialism,* The University of Minnesota Press, Minneapolis, 1939.

   Oscar Lange and Abba Lerner are given much of the credit for developing the theory of what we call decentralized socialism, and for developing the Second Fundamental Theorem. Lange's essay in this book is reprinted from the *Review of Economic Studies,* V. II, October, 1936 and February, 1937. It starts out by giving credit to Ludwig Von Mises, who had previously criticized the socialists for ignoring the informational problems of running an economy from a centralized bureau. Mises's position was that economic accounting was impossible under socialism, since socialism abolished the prices that are attached to capital goods. Lange argues that the Central Planning Board can and should attach accounting prices to capital goods, and that, in fact, by attaching prices to goods the Board can direct the economy to an optimum through decentralized socialism. The Planning Board "has to fix prices and see to it that all managers of plants, industries, and resources do their accounting on the basis of the prices." "Thus, the accounting prices in a socialist economy, far from being arbitrary, have quite the same objective character as the market prices in a regime of competition."

Although Lange claims that the managers of production are "no longer guided by the aim of maximizing profit," he has the Central Planning Board impose the following rules on them: (1) cost must be minimized, and (2) price must equal marginal cost. These two rules are, of course, the ones that a profit-maximizing competitive firm follows.

5. A. P. Lerner, *The Economics of Control,* The MacMillan Company, New York, 1944.

This book is a theory of what Lerner calls a "controlled" economy, which should be contrasted with a laissez faire economy. A controlled economy is what might now be called a "mixed" one — with public and private productive sectors — although Lerner rejects that term. A controlled economy is not necessarily a collectivist, or centralized socialist, economy. It is an economy in which the "state uses its control to enable that method to prevail in each particular case which best serves the public interest."

The student should pay particular attention to Chapters 5, 6 and 7, which outline a simple theory of optimality and production in the collectivist, perfectly competitive, capitalist and controlled regimes. Chapter 5 provides a few nice remarks about the practical impossibility of centralized socialism (or collectivism), and gives a rule for successful operation of decentralized socialism (the controlled economy). The rule is, of course, logically equivalent to the rule for profit maximization for a competitive firm. Chapter 6 gives the marginal conditions necessary for an optimum in production, and indicates how perfect competition satisfies those conditions. Chapter 7 argues that the assumptions of perfect competition are in fact rarely met. Too many firms have monopoly power. Consequently, laissez faire will not bring about an optimum. The solution? A controlled economy in which government enterprises compete with private firms.

*6. E. Malinvaud, *Lectures on Microeconomic Theory,* American Elsevier Publishing Co., New York, 1972, Chapters 3, 4.

This is a modern succinct treatment of production and optimality theorems, on a graduate textbook level. It does require some mathematics, although not nearly as much as Debreu. In particular, it requires familiarity with Lagrange multipliers. Chapter 4 is especially close to the approach we have taken.

5 EXTERNALITIES

INTRODUCTION

The fundamental results of the previous chapters, the results that link optimality and competition, depend on assumptions that (1) people have selfish utility functions, and (2) firms' production set are unaffected by other firms' production decisions. In many actual cases these assumptions break down. When person A's utility depends on what person B consumes, or when A's technological production possibilities depend on what firm B does, there is an external effect. The decisions of one person or firm have a tangible, nonmarket impact on a different person or firm.

For example, suppose person A knows person B, and feels that person B eats too little or too much. Then person B's eating has a direct effect on A's utility level. This we call external effect. On the other hand, if A does not know B and does not care how much B eats, B's consumption might still have some impact on A. For whenever B buys food he affects the equilibrium price of food (perhaps by a minute amount), and therefore, B's appetite indirectly influences A's utility level. However, we do not call this an external effect. In the case of consumers, an external effect is a direct effect of one person's consumption on another person's utility level, not an indirect one that operates via the price mechanism.

What is the difference? When one person's consumption affects another's welfare through the price mechanism, when B bids up the price of food for A, the system is working in the way assumed by the two fundamental theorems. If B gets more food at the expense of A because he is willing to pay more, then the price mechanism is directing the food to the person who wants it most. And the distribution of goods that results is efficient. However, if B's consumption of food affects A's utility directly, irrespective of prices, then the price mechanism gives inappropriate signals. When B consumes food, he thinks only about his utility; he looks at the prices, and then makes a decision. But this decision has a direct impact on A's utility, and the price that B pays for food does not reflect this impact on A. Consequently, the price mechanism does not tell B of the total social benefits and costs of his actions, and the resulting distribution of goods is not, in fact, efficient.

Once we know what to look for, we can discover external effects all around us. Many of us are directly affected when we learn that other people don't have enough food to eat. When we hear that a child a thousand miles away is starving, we are worse off. When we learn that people at the other end of the country are living in tar paper shacks, we are worse off. There are externalities, then, in the consumption of food, of housing, perhaps even of medical care. Many of us are worse off when we discover that others are in severe distress because of inadequate consumption of some vitally important good.

There are also myriad mundane consumption externalities. Nonsmokers are bothered by smokers. When A smokes, B's utility level drops. Nondrinkers are occasionally bothered by drinkers. When A drinks to excess, B, a member of the Women's Christian Temperance Union, feels worse off. Those who prefer classical music are bothered by those who play rock music. Many of us are bothered by loud exhaust noises of cars, trucks, and motorcycles. When A drives his car with modified (amplified) exhaust pipes through town, hundreds or thousands of B's might be made briefly worse off.

Externalities among firms are common. One standard story has two firms located on the same river. Firm A, the upstream firm, dumps its wastes in the river, while firm B, the downstream firm, uses river water for washing and otherwise processing its outputs. If firm A increases its output (and its wastes), firm B's production suffers. To produce the same output with dirtier water, firm B must use more chemical agents, more labor, and more electricity. That is, firm B's production set shrinks. If firm A pays nothing for dumping wastes in the river, it receives no information from the price system about the external costs it is imposing on firm B. The consequence is that the price mechanism no longer ensures efficiency. (Note that if firm A were downstream, this externality problem might not arise.)

A second standard story has two firms sharing the same air. Firm A is an old-fashioned electric generating facility that burns coal and uses no scrubbing or other antipollution devices. Consequently, every kilowatt hour produced results in a belch of black smoke. Firm B is a laundry located nearby. When firm A produces more electricity (and more smoke), firm B has to cope with more dirt and grime settling down on its plant, in its machines, on its tables and presses, and on the clothing being cleaned. So firm B must use more soap, more labor, more wrapping paper, and so on, to produce the same output of clean garments. In other words, when A's output rise, firm B's production set shrinks. But A does not take these costs for B into account in its decisions, so the price mechanism provides it with misleading information. It acts as if the air is free.

A very important type of externality occurs when a firm's production decisions have direct nonmarket effects on a person's utility level. For example, a firm that stripmines for coal without reclaiming the land affects the utility levels of people who see the results. A firm that produces smoke affects the utility levels of people who breathe the smoke. The residents of Chicago, Illinois are directly affected by the output decisions of steel mills in Gary, Indiana, whenever the wind is from the east. People who live near the Three Mile Island Nuclear Reactor in Pennsylvania might be affected by the production decisions of the firm that operates that plant. People who live near coal-burning electric generators are often affected by the output decisions of those firms.

Not all externalities of this firm-person type are harmful or negative. People who live downwind from a bakery might be happier when bread production is high. Firms that build attractive plants or office buildings make people who look at those buildings better off. Many of the impressive and exciting sights of a large city are the skyscrapers built by private firms, such as the Empire State Building and the Chrysler Building in New York, the Sears and John Hancock towers in Chicago. Much of New England is dotted with handsome nineteenth century mill buildings, which still provide viewing pleasure long after the firms that built them went bankrupt or moved away.

In all of these cases, whether the externalities are in consumption or in production, whether they are positive (beneficial) or negative (hurtful), the price mechanism does not provide complete enough information to the decision maker. In the case of negative externalities, the price mechanism does not tell the decision maker how much his decision really costs. In the case of positive externalities, the price mechanism does not tell the decision maker how much his decision really helps. And it follows that the link between competition and optimality is broken.

In this chapter we shall carefully analyze two examples of external effects, one in an exchange model and one in a production model. The examples will illustrate how the external effects destroy the optimality of a competitive equilibrium.

However, the existence of externalities does not mean that markets must be disbanded. Abolishing the price mechanism because air pollution is bothersome and because flower gardens are pleasurable would be throwing the baby out with the bath water.

Since the early twentieth century economists have advocated taxes and subsidies to correct important externality-induced inefficiencies. The idea is that those who harm others through their production or consumption decisions should pay a tax to reflect that harm. The size of the tax should depend on the extent of the harm: these are not lump sum taxes like the bank balance transfers of the Second Fundamental Theorem. With the tax in their figuring, the decision makers would be led, via the tax-modified price system, to the right decisions. They would take into account the real social costs of their decisions. Similarly, consumers and firms that create external benefits should be subsidized to reflect those benefits. Again, the extent of the subsidies would depend on the extent of the benefits. With the subsidies in their figuring, the decision makers would be led, again, to the right decisions.

We will show how the appropriate taxes or subsidies ought to be figured in each of our examples, and we will show how the the tax- or subsidy-modified price mechanism once again produces an optimal distribution of goods, or an optimal production plan.

EXTERNALITIES IN AN EXCHANGE ECONOMY: AN EXAMPLE

We now look at what happens when the selfishness assumption is relaxed in an exchange economy. To illustrate the problems, we construct a simple two-person two-goods example.

Let

$$u_1(x) = x_{11}x_{12} + x_{21} \qquad \omega_1 = (10,0)$$
$$u_2(x) = u_2(x_2) = x_{21}x_{22} \qquad \omega_2 = (0,10).$$

Person 1 is altruistic; he gets some pleasure out of 2's consumption of good 1. Person 2, on the other hand, is selfish.

To start the analysis, we solve for the set of Pareto optimal allocations. First, we rewrite u_1 as

$$u_1(x) = x_{11}x_{12} + x_{21} = x_{11}x_{12} + (10 - x_{11})$$

Next we calculate the marginal rate of substitution of good 2 for good 1 for person 1:

$$\text{MRS person 1} = \frac{\text{MU of good 1}}{\text{MU of good 2}} = \frac{x_{12} - 1}{x_{11}}$$

and for person 2:

$$\text{MRS person 2} = \frac{\text{MU of good 1}}{\text{MU of good 2}} = \frac{x_{22}}{x_{21}}$$

Then, to find the locus of tangency points of the two individuals' indifference curves, we set MRS for person 1 equal to MRS for person 2:

$$\frac{x_{12} - 1}{x_{11}} = \frac{x_{22}}{x_{21}} = \frac{10 - x_{12}}{10 - x_{11}}$$

Solving this equation for x_{12} in terms of x_{11} gives

$$x_{12} = 1 + \tfrac{9}{10}x_{11}$$

Figure 5-1 shows this locus of Pareto optimal tangency points and two other allocations to which we shall soon refer.

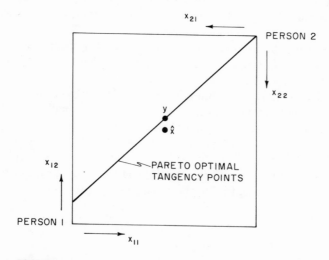

FIGURE 5-1

The next step is to calculate a competitive equilibrium. We assume that 1 and 2 act as price takers, and at this point we also suppose that 1 does not know that $x_{12} + x_{22} = 10$, and does not know that

$$u_1(x) = x_{11}x_{12} + (10 - x_{11})$$

We must make this somewhat artificial assumption in order to discuss external effects in the simple two-person case; if we do not make it, all apparently altruistic (or malevolent) utility functions could be rewritten and solved as selfish ones. If there were three or more people this artificiality would disappear.

Person 1 wants to maximize $x_{11}x_{12} + x_{21}$ subject to his budget constraint. Since he cannot choose x_{21} himself (2 has something to say about it too), we suppose he contemplates buying a quantity g of the second good, and giving it to 2. Person 2's consumption of the first good will be the quantity he purchases, which 1 cannot control, plus the gift g. Therefore, 1 wants to maximize $x_{11}x_{12}$ plus g, subject to the budget constraint

$$p_1 x_{11} + p_2 x_{12} + p_1 g \le p_1 \cdot 10 + p_2 \cdot 0 = 10p_1$$

He will clearly want to spend all his income $10\,p_1$, and we can therefore ignore the inequality.

Person 2, on the other hand, simply wants to maximize $u_2(x_2) = x_{21}x_{22}$, subject to $p_1 x_{21} + p_2 x_{22} = p_1 \cdot 0 + p_2 \cdot 10 = 10p_2$.

A competitive equilibrium in this economy is a price vector $p = (p_1, p_2)$ and consumption (+ gift) vectors $(\hat{x}_{11}, \hat{x}_{12}, g)$, $(\hat{x}_{21}, \hat{x}_{22})$, such that $(\hat{x}_{11}, \hat{x}_{12}, g)$ maximizes u_1 subject to 1's budget equation, and $(\hat{x}_{21}, \hat{x}_{22})$ maximizes u_2 subject to 2's budget equation.

To solve for the equilibrium, note that if x_{12} is greater than 1, person 1 will choose $g = 0$, that is, he will give nothing. This is so because the marginal utility of 1's private consumption of good 1 is x_{12}, whereas the marginal utility of 1's charity is 1. But it is obvious from inspection that x_{12} will be chosen greater than 1. Therefore, 1 will attempt to maximize the private part of his utility function $x_{11}x_{12}$ subject to the constraint

$$p_1 x_{11} + p_2 x_{12} = 10p_1$$

The perfect symmetry of the two individuals' maximization problems, and the symmetry of ω, lead to the conclusion that the competitive equilibrium is

$$p = (1,1)$$
$$\hat{x}_{11} = \hat{x}_{12} = \hat{x}_{21} = \hat{x}_{22} = 5$$
$$g = 0$$

The allocation $\hat{x}$ is shown in Figure 5-1. Note that $\hat{x}$ is not on the locus of tangencies in that figure; it does not satisfy the tangency condition

$$x_{12} = 1 + \tfrac{9}{10}x_{11}$$

Consequently, it is not Pareto optimal. When there are externalities present, a competitive equilibrium allocation need not be Pareto optimal, and the First Fundamental Theorem breaks down.

Recall that the exchange version of the Second Fundamental Theorem of Welfare Economics says that any Pareto optimal point can be viewed as a competitive equilibrium allocation given appropriate cash transfers. Now consider the allocation y defined by:

$$y_1 = (5, 5.5), \; y_2 = (5, 4.5)$$

Note that

$$5.5 = y_{12} = 1 + \tfrac{9}{10}y_{11} = 1 + \tfrac{9}{10} \cdot 5$$

That is, y satisfies the tangency condition; it is on the locus of tangencies in Figure 5-1. Therefore, y is Pareto optimal. Do there exist cash transfers T_1 and T_2, such that individual 1 will finish at y_1, and individual 2 will finish at y_2, when they maximize their utilities subject to their (adjusted) budget constraints

$$p_1 x_{11} + p_2 x_{12} + p_1 g \leq 10p_1 + T_1$$

and

$$p_1 x_{21} + p_2 x_{22} \leq 10p_2 + T_2?$$

It should again be clear that the gift 1 chooses will be zero, so g may be ignored. To see whether we can induce 1 and 2 to go to y via the competitive mechanism with cash transfers, we first see what is required to induce person 2 to go to y_2:

Person 2 wants to maximize $u_2(x_2) = x_{21}x_{22}$
subject to $p_1 x_{21} + p_2 x_{22} \leq 10p_2 + T_2$.

He sets his marginal rate of substitution x_{22}/x_{21} equal to the price ratio. But his MRS at y_2 is $^{4.5}\!/_5$, so we have

$$\frac{4.5}{5} = \frac{9}{10} = \frac{p_1}{p_2}$$

In order to get person 2 to the point y_2, the price ratio must be $9/10$. Let's normalize prices by setting $p_2 = 10$. Then p must equal $(9,10)$. Substituting these prices and quantities in 2's budget equation gives

$$9 \cdot 5 + 10 \cdot 4.5 = 10 \cdot 10 + T_2$$

so $T_2 = -10$. In short, person 2 will choose y_2 if $p = (9,10)$ and $T_2 = -10$.

However, if the prices are $(9,10)$ person 1 will *not* choose the point $y_1 = (5, 5.5)$. Since he will not give a gift, he will attempt to maximize the private part of his utility function, that is, $x_{11} x_{12}$. His private marginal rate of substitution at y is $5.5/5 = 11/10$, which differs from the price ratio $9/10$. He will never choose y_1 when $p = (9,10)$. Since person 2 will choose y_2 only if $p = (9,10)$ and person 1 will never choose y_1 when $p = (9,1)$, the two people cannot be induced to move to y through a cash transfer arrangement. When there are externalities present, a Pareto optimum need not be achievable via the cash transfer modified competitive mechanism, and the Second Fundamental Theorem breaks down.

PIGOUVIAN TAXES AND SUBSIDIES:
THE EXCHANGE EXAMPLE CONTINUED

Externalities weaken the link between competition and optimality. But all is not lost. There is a remedy that is consistent with a decentralized price mechanism. It is not necessary to have a central bureau (a super Environmental Protection Agency) to direct the consumption decisions of all individuals. The decentralized remedy is the introduction of per-unit (or marginal) *taxes or subsidies* on the consumption of the goods that induce the external effects. These taxes or subsidies cannot be of the lump sum cash transfer variety; we saw above that simple cash transfers won't get us to an optimal allocation. They must depend on the quantities actually consumed, for they must affect the relative prices paid by different individuals. They must be designed to encourage a person's consumption of a good if that consumption has positive external effects, and to discourage a person's consumption of a good if that consumption has negative external effects.

With this general motivation in mind, let's return to the example of the previous section. In that example, person 2's consumption of good 1 confers an external benefit on person 1. But when person 2 makes his consumption decisions in the standard competitive equilibrium model, he does not take that external benefit into account. This suggests that this consumption of good 1 ought to be subsidized.

Let s be a subsidy paid to person 2 for each unit of good 1 that he consumes. The link between competition and optimality will be rebuilt if there exist an s, a price vector p, and cash transfers T_1 and T_2, so that, when 1's budget constraint is

$$p_1 x_{11} + p_2 x_{12} \leq 10p_1 + T_1$$

and 2's budget constraint is

$$(p_1 - s)x_{21} + p_2 x_{22} \leq 10p_2 + T_2$$

the two will move to a Pareto optimal allocation through the competitive mechanism. In fact, there do exist such s, p, T_1, and T_2, and, with the appropriate choice of T_1 and T_2, one can move to whatever interior Pareto optimal allocation one desires.

For example, suppose

$$y_1 = (5, 5.5) \text{ and } y_2 = (5, 4.5)$$

is again the goal. It can be achieved this way. First consider person 1. He will again maximize the selfish part of his utility function. The marginal rate of substitution condition is

$$\frac{x_{12}}{x_{11}} = \frac{p_1}{p_2}$$

and his budget equation is

$$p_1 x_{11} + p_2 x_{12} = 10p_1 + T_1$$

If we let $T_1 = 0$, the two equations imply $x_{11} = 5$, and $x_{12} = 5p_1/p_2$. We want him to choose $y_{11} = 5$, $y_{12} = 5.5$. Therefore, if we normalize prices by setting $p_2 = 10$, we must have $p_1 = 11$.

Now turn to person 2. The marginal rate of substitution condition and the budget constraint for 2 are

$$\frac{x_{22}}{x_{21}} = \frac{p_1 - s}{p_2}$$

and

$$(p_1 - s)x_{21} + p_2 x_{22} = 10p_2 + T_2$$

But $p_1 = 11$ and $p_2 = 10$. Moreover, we want person 2 to choose the point $y_{21} = 5$, $y_{22} = 4.5$. Substituting these values in the above equations gives

$$\frac{4.5}{5} = \frac{11 - s}{10}$$

and $(11/10 - s) \cdot 5 + 1 \cdot 4.5 = 10 \cdot 1 + T_2$. Consequently, we can let $s = 2$ and $T_2 = -10$.

In short, if $T_1 = 0$, $T_2 = -10$, and if $s = 2$, the competitive mechanism, modified by T_1, T_2 and s, will take the economy to the Pareto optimal allocation y. Thus the introduction of the subsidy s re-establishes the link between competition and optimality.

These particular calculations are not especially intuitive; for policy applications we ought to have some simpler concepts to guide the choice of taxes and subsidies. To derive those concepts, we shall carry the example through a few steps further.

Recall that person 1's utility function is $u_1(x) = x_{11}x_{12} + x_{21}$. The marginal utility to person 1 of person 2's consumption of good 1 is therefore 1. The marginal utility to person 1 of his own consumption of good 1 is, in general, equal to x_{12}. At the allocation $y = ((5, 5.5), (5, 4.5))$, the marginal utility to person 1 of his own consumption of good 1 is then 5.5. Now if person 2 reduced his consumption of good 1 by a unit, person 1 would have to increase his consumption of good 1 by $\frac{1}{5.5}$ units in order to remain as well off as before. That is, there is a well-defined marginal rate of substitution of 1's own consumption of good 1 for 2's consumption of good 1, equal to person 1's marginal utility from his own consumption of good 1 divided by person 1's marginal utility from person 2's consumption of good 1. We call this particular marginal rate of substitution the *marginal external benefit* or MEB of person 2's consumption of good 1:

$$\text{MEB} = \frac{\text{MU to person 1 of person 2's consumption of good 1}}{\text{MU to person 1 of his own consumption of good 1}}.$$

This provides us with a measure of the benefit provided to 1 by 2's consumption, measured in units of good 1. At y, the MEB $= \frac{1}{5.5}$.

Now suppose we ask this question: How many dollars (or other units of currency) would person 1 have to be given to just compensate him for person 2's reducing his consumption of good 1 by 1 unit? The answer, of course, is $p_1 \cdot$ MEB, which we shall call MEB in dollars. At the point y, if $p_1 = 11$, then

$$\text{MEB in dollars} = p_1 \cdot \text{MEB} = 11 \cdot \frac{1}{5.5} = 2.$$

But we found above that the required subsidy s was 2 (that is, \$2/unit). In fact, the intuitive rule for finding the right subsidy is given by the formula

MEB in dollars $= s$.

The subsidy should just equal the value (in dollars) of the (marginal) external benefit. This makes sense: if person 2 is causing \$2 worth of external good for every extra unit of good 1 he consumes, then the appropriate way to achieve optimality is through a subsidy of \$2 per unit on each extra unit he consumes. The externality is in this way internalized; it is plugged back into the calculation of the decision maker.

What would happen if the externality were negative? Suppose, for instance, that person 1's utility function were

$$u_1(x) = x_{11}x_{12} - x_{21}$$

Then every extra unit of good 1 that person 2 consumes would make person 1 worse off, and person 1 would need to be given more of good 1 to compensate him for an increase in good 1 consumption by person 2. We would then have a *marginal external cost* associated with 2's consumption, defined as follows:

$$\text{MEC} = \frac{\text{Marginal disutility to person 1 of person 2's consumption of good 1}}{\text{MU to person 1 of his own consumption of good 1}}$$

(Or, equivalently, we could have a negative MU in the numerator and therefore a negative MEB.) We would find MEC in dollars the same way as before:

MEC in dollars $= p_1 \cdot \text{MEC}.$

And the tax required to correct the externality problem would be

MEC in dollars $= t.$

For each extra unit of good 1 that he consumes, person 2 would be required to pay a tax of t, and this tax, like the subsidy above, would internalize the externality. That is, it would be plugged into the calculations of the decision maker who is responsible for the externality.

To summarize these results: In order to re-establish the connection between competition and optimality when there are externalities present, per-
unit taxes or subsidies can be imposed on consumption, and they should be
chosen so that

MEC in dollars $= t$

or

MEB in dollars $= s$

PIGOUVIAN TAXES AND SUBSIDIES:
A PRODUCTION EXAMPLE

Now let's work through a simple production externality example. We
assume there are two firms and two goods. Both firms use good 1 to produce good 2. Firm 1 can be viewed as the "upstream" firm. Its production
set Y_1 is determined by

$$y_{12} \leq \sqrt{-y_{11}}$$

For instance, with nine units of the input good 1 ($y_{11} = -9$), it can produce up to three units of the output good 2. Firm 2 can be viewed as the
"downstream" firm. Its production set Y_2 is determined by

$$y_{22} \leq \sqrt{-y_{21}} - \tfrac{1}{2} y_{12}$$

That is, its production function is basically like firm 1's, except its output is
shifted down by an amount depending on firm 1's output. The more firm 1
produces, the larger the shift $\tfrac{1}{2} y_{12}$ and the more trouble firm 2 is in. Figure
5-2 illustrates the production sets of the two firms, as well as an (unmodified) competitive equilibrium.

In the figure the production sets Y_1 and Y_2 have the same shape, but set
Y_2 has been translated down by an amount $\tfrac{1}{2} y_{12}$.

Now suppose the prices of goods 1 and 2 are given by $p = (1,1)$. If the
isoprofit lines ℓ_1 and L_1 in the figure have slope equal to 1, in absolute
value, then the firms choose the tangency points y_1 and y_2 shown.
Formally, firm 1 wants to maximize $p \cdot y_1 = y_{12} + y_{11}$ subject to the constraint $y_{12} \leq \sqrt{-y_{11}}$. The solution to this maximization problem is

$$y_{11} = -\tfrac{1}{4}$$
$$y_{12} = \tfrac{1}{2}.$$

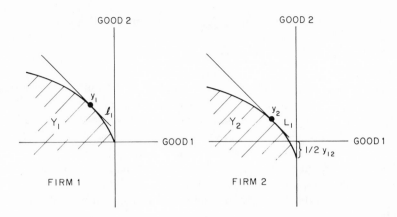

FIGURE 5-2

These are the coordinates of y_1 in Figure 5-2. With $y_1 = (-\frac{1}{4}, \frac{1}{2})$, firm 1's profit is $p \cdot y_1 = \frac{1}{4}$. Firm 2 wants to maximize $p \cdot y_2 = y_{22} + y_{21}$ subject to the constraint

$$y_{22} \leq \sqrt{-y_{21}} - \frac{1}{2}y_{12} = \sqrt{-y_{21}} - \frac{1}{4}$$

The solution to this maximization problem is

$$y_{21} = -\frac{1}{4}$$
$$y_{22} = \frac{1}{4}$$

These are the coordinates of y_2 in Figure 5-2. With this production vector, firm 1's profit is $p \cdot y_2 = 0$.

In the unmodified competitive production economy, the net output of good 2 is $\frac{1}{2} + \frac{1}{4} = \frac{3}{4}$, while the net input of good 1 is, in absolute value, $\frac{1}{4} + \frac{1}{4} = \frac{1}{2}$. Is y an optimal production plan? Or is it possible to get more good 2 produced with the same total input of good 2? Let's consider an alternative production plan in which firm 1's input of good 1 is $z_{11} = -\frac{1}{8}$, and firm 2's input of good 1 is $z_{21} = -\frac{3}{8}$. Then firm 1's output of good 2 is given by

$$z_{12} = \sqrt{-z_{11}} = \sqrt{\frac{1}{8}}$$

Firm 2's output of good 2 is given by

$$z_{22} = \sqrt{-z_{21}} - \frac{1}{2}\sqrt{z_{12}} = \sqrt{\frac{3}{8}} - \frac{1}{2}\sqrt{\frac{1}{8}}$$

The net quantity of good 2 being produced by the two firms is then

$$z_{12} + z_{22} = \sqrt{\tfrac{1}{8}} + \sqrt{\tfrac{3}{8}} - \tfrac{1}{2}\sqrt{\tfrac{1}{8}} = .79.$$

In short, the production plan z yields a higher net output of good 2 than does the production plan y, and it uses the same net input of good 1. Therefore y is not optimal. Because of the externality, the competitive equilibrium production plan is not optimal, and the production version of the First Fundamental Theorem breaks down.

It is not difficult to establish that the production version of the Second Fundamental Theorem also fails when the externality is present. The existence of externalities, then, breaks the link between competition and optimality.

What can be done? We could turn to a centralized socialist system, in which the Central Planning Board — aware of external effects just as it is aware of everything else — makes all production decisions for all firms. But this is the truly impractical solution. There is a decentralized solution exactly analogous to the tax-subsidy solution for consumption externalities. We turn to that tax system now.

If firm 1 increases its output of good 1 by 1 unit the northern frontier of firm 2's production frontier is shifted down by ½ unit. The slope of that frontier won't change anywhere, and, providing relative prices are constant and firm 2 doesn't decide to go out of business altogether, firm 2 will still maximize its profits with the same input level. But its output will change. That is, in Figure 5–2 the point y_2 will shift down, but not sideways. Consequently, the effect on firm 2 of a unit increase in y_{12} is simply to reduce firm 2's output of good 2 by ½ unit, and therefore, to reduce firm 2's profit by $p_2 \cdot$ ½ dollars. In our example, $p_2 = 1$, so the effect on firm 2 is to reduce its profit by $½.

In the discussion of consumption externalities, we saw that a positive externality should be subsidized an amount equal to the marginal external benefit in dollars; and that a negative externality should be taxed an amount equal to the marginal external cost in dollars. In our production externality example, the marginal external cost to firm 2 of firm 1's production of good 2 is equal to ½ dollars. The way to correct the externality is once again to internalize it, that is, to force firm 1 to pay this marginal cost. Let us therefore impose a tax on firm 1 of

$$t = \tfrac{1}{2}$$

That is, for every unit of good 2 that firm 1 produces, it must pay ½ dollar to a central authority. The central authority might redistribute the tax proceeds through lump sum grants, or use it in some other way. What happens when the tax is imposed?

Now firm 1 wants to maximize $p \cdot y_1 - ty_{12}$, subject to the constraint that y_1 be in Y_1. That is, it wants to maximize $y_{11} + y_{12} - \frac{1}{2} y_{12}$ or $y_{11} + \frac{1}{2} y_{12}$, subject to $y_{12} \le \sqrt{-y_{11}}$. The solution to this maximization problem is

$$y_{11} = -\frac{1}{16}$$
$$y_{12} = \frac{1}{4}$$

Firm 2 wants to maximize $p \cdot y_2$ subject to the constraint that y_2 be in Y_2. That is, it wants to maximize $y_{21} + y_{22}$ subject to

$$y_{22} \le \sqrt{-y_{21}} - \frac{1}{2} y_{12} = \sqrt{-y_{21}} - \frac{1}{8}$$

The solution to this maximization problem is

$$y_{21} = -\frac{1}{4}$$
$$y_{22} = \frac{3}{8}$$

Under this new y, the total output of good 2 is $\frac{1}{4} + \frac{3}{8} = \frac{5}{8}$, while the total input of good 1 is, in absolute value, $\frac{1}{16} + \frac{1}{4} = \frac{5}{16}$.

Is this production plan optimal? It requires a few lines of elementary calculus to establish it, but the answer is Yes. There is no way to increase total output of good 2 without also increasing the total input of good 1.

The introduction of the tax t saves the First Fundamental Theorem. The modified competitive equilibrium production plan is optimal. For the Second Fundamental Theorem we have a similar result, although now our example would have to be slightly generalized. In the example above, $p = (1,1)$. For the Second Fundamental Theorem we would have to take $p = (p_1, p_2)$. The tax t would have to be set at $p_1 \cdot \frac{1}{2}$, so that $t = $ MEC in dollars is preserved. With these modifications, we would have the result: For any optimal production plan y, there is a price vector $p = (p_1, p_2)$ and a tax rate t so that the modified market mechanism brings the production economy to y.

EXERCISES

1. An economy is made up of two people. The utility functions are:

$$u_1 (x_1) = x_{11} x_{12}$$

and

$$u_2 (x) = 2x_{21} + 2x_{22} - x_{11}$$

The initial bundles are:

$$\omega_1 = (1,0)$$
$$\omega_2 = (0,1)$$

Although 2 suffers from 1's consumption of good 1, he cannot control it, nor does he realize that the total quantity of good 1 available is 1.

a. Calculate a competitive equilibrium from ω. Draw an Edgeworth box diagram to illustrate your answer.

b. Find the locus of interior Pareto optimal points.

c. Calculate prices p_1 and p_2, a per-unit subsidy s or tax t, and lump sum cash transfers T_1 and T_2 to bring the economy to the allocation $y_1 = (\frac{1}{3}, \frac{1}{2})$, $y_2 = (\frac{2}{3}, \frac{1}{2})$.

2. Consider an economy with the following characteristics:

$$u_1(x) = x_{11}x_{12} - x_{21}x_{22} \qquad \omega_1 = (1,0)$$

$$u_2(x_2) = x_{21}^{\frac{1}{3}} x_{22}^{\frac{2}{3}} \qquad \omega_2 = (0,1)$$

Person 1 hates person 2 and projects his own tastes on him. Assume that 1 does not know the total quantities of the goods available are $(1,1)$.

Discuss the optimality (or non-optimality) of a competitive equilibrium allocation. Can you calculate taxes (or subsidies) and lump sum transfers which will bring about an efficient allocation?

Hints: 1 can't steal from 2. Also, for 2, we have the following marginal utilities:

$$\text{MU of good 1} = \frac{1}{3} x_{21}^{-\frac{2}{3}} x_{22}^{\frac{2}{3}}$$

$$\text{MU of good 2} = \frac{2}{3} x_{21}^{\frac{1}{3}} x_{22}^{-\frac{1}{3}}$$

3. (This problem requires some knowledge of calculus.) Suppose there are two firms in a production economy, each using good 1 as an input to produce good 2. They are both located in the same town, and both are bad polluters, so each one's operation has a deleterious effect on the other. Firm 1's production set Y_1 is given by

$$y_{12} \leq \sqrt{-y_{11}} - \frac{3}{4} y_{22}$$

Firm 2's production set Y_2 is given by

$$y_{22} \leq \sqrt{-y_{21}} - \frac{3}{4} y_{12}$$

Suppose the market prices of goods 1 and 2 are given by $p = (1,1)$. Assume that each firm takes the other's output as given and fixed.

a. Calculate the competitive equilibrium production plan for the economy.
b. Show that the competitive equilibrium is not an optimum.

SELECTED REFERENCES

1. F. M. Bator, "The Simple Analytics of Welfare Maximization," *American Economic Review,* 1957, pp. 23–50.
    This is listed here because it's a good companion piece for the Bator article listed below. On its own, it would belong with Chapters 3 and 4. It's basically an exposition of the two fundamental theorems, done with graphs, and without rigorous proofs.
2. F. M. Bator, "The Anatony of Market Failure," *Quarterly Journal of Economics,* 1958, pp. 351–379.
    In this article Bator discusses various different types of externalities, as well as other sources of market failures, or what we would call failures of the two fundamental theorems.
3. W. J. Baumol and W. E. Oates, *The Theory of Environmental Policy,* Prentice-Hall, Inc., Englewood Cliffs, New Jersey, 1975.
    This book provides an excellent interpretative summary of externalities, Pigouvian taxes and subsidies, environmental policy, and related issues.
4. J. M. Buchanan and W. C. Stubblebine, "Externality," *Economica,* V. 29, 1962, pp. 371–384.
    This paper attempts to clarify the definition of externality. The theoretical parts require some calculus, but there are some nice examples that don't.
5. R. H. Coase, "The Problem of Social Cost," *Journal of Law and Economics,* V. 3, 1960, pp. 1–44.
    This article solves the externality problem in a fundamentally different way. Coase suggests that many externality problems can be remedied by an appropriate assignment of rights to amenities like clean air, rather than by tax-subsidy schemes. That is, if property rights are well defined and markets in those rights function smoothly, Pareto optimality will be re-established.
6. J. E. Meade, "External Economies and Diseconomies in a Competitive Situation," *The Economic Journal,* V. 62, 1952, pp. 54–67.
    Meade shows how externality taxes and subsidies might be calculated in a production model.
7. A. C. Pigou, *The Economics of Welfare,* MacMillan and Co., Ltd., London, 1920, Part II, Chapter VI.
    Part II of Pigou's classic treatise is on "The Magnitude of the National Dividend and the Distribution of Resources Among Different Uses." Chapter VI of Part II is on divergencies between private benefit and social benefit, or what we call externalities. To solve the maldistributions created by those divergencies, Pigou suggests bounties or taxes, or what we now call Pigouvian subsidies and taxes.

6 PUBLIC GOODS

INTRODUCTION

In the last chapter we analyzed some examples of external effects, and discussed the calculation of appropriate taxes and subsidies to correct externality problems. In this chapter we carry the externality phenomenon to its logical extreme. We shall examine the theory of the production and consumption of goods whose character is essentially public, rather than private.

What do we mean by a public good? Some goods have the property that when one person uses them, all people use them. That is, their use is nonexclusive; if the goods are available to one, they are available to all. There is no practical way for one person to use them alone.

Goods that aren't like this, goods that are really private, or exclusively used by one person, are easy to think of: a glass of beer, a set of false teeth, a pair of socks, a hamburger. When A is using or consuming one of these things, then, necessarily, B isn't. Goods whose use is necessarily nonexclusive are less common, but there are many important ones: Radio and television broadcasts (unless scrambled) are nonexclusive. If A can get the TV signal and B lives nearby, then B can get the TV signal also. (Note that we are talking about the signal, not the TV set, which is a private good. Also note that we are not talking about cable TV, the access to which is again a private good.) There is no practical way to deliver radio waves to A without simultaneously delivering them to B. The signals of a lighthouse are non-exclusive. If a lighthouse is warning ship A to stay away from the shoals, then it is also necessarily warning any nearby ship B to stay clear. The outside of the Washington Monument is nonexclusive. If person A can view it and enjoy it, person B can do so as well. It wouldn't be practical to screen it and charge to let people inside the screen. On the other hand, it is practically possible to exclude people from the inside of the Washington Monument. The Statue of Liberty, viewed from the outside, is a nonexclusive good. If it's available for one to see, it's available in all.

National defense is an important nonexclusive good. If the person and property of U.S. resident A are being protected from foreign armies, then the person and property of U.S. resident B are also necessarily being protected from those armies.

Another important example is scientific and technological knowledge. Some technological knowledge is patentable and its use can be restricted, but much a larger part is not. The technology of the internal combustion engine is nonexclusive. If it is available in person A's library, it is probably available in B's. Medical knowledge is largely nonexclusive. If a cure for infection, like penecillin, is known to A's doctor, then it is known to B's. When someone discovers a cure for some form of cancer, that cure will be public knowledge, and nonexclusive in its use.

In each of these cases, when the good is there for one, it is necessarily there for all. Goods with this property are called public goods.

What are the efficiency implications of public goods? Like externalities, public goods undermine optimality in a standard competitive equilibrium. What then should be done? What are the optimal quantities for public goods? How should public goods be financed? We shall explore these and similar questions in this chapter.

THE PUBLIC GOODS MODEL

In this section we shall develop a rather special, and rather different model to analyze the problems of public goods. A good is public if it is by nature available to all: if one man uses it, everyone can use it. Public goods can be viewed as goods with extreme external effects: if person i's consumption of the good is X, then X appears in each and every person's utility function. However, we won't continue the externality and Pigouvian tax/subsidy analysis of the last chapter: it is more convenient to start anew.

The model we use here has both production and consumption, because one principal question we want to answer is this: How much of the public good should be produced? And the answer to the question depends both on people's demand for it, and on the nature of the productive sector of the economy. But in order to avoid notational and analytical complexity, our model will be exceedingly simple. We assume that there are only two goods, one private, and one public. Also we assume that the productive sector of the economy can transform units of the private good into units of the public good, in the ratio of one to one. And, therefore, we assume the equilibrium prices of the two goods are 1 and 1.

Our model will also make a crucial simplifying assumption about the nature of utility functions. We assume that person i's utility is the sum of the quantity of the private good he consumes, plus a well-behaved function of the quantity of the public good produced and available to all, including i. Such a utility function is said to be "separable" between private and public consumption. Some of the analysis below hinges on this special assumption; some does not. We make the assumption for two reasons: (1) it greatly simplifies all the mathematics, and (2) the discussion of demand revealing taxes breaks down without it.

Now let's develop some of the notation. It should be observed that this notation differs slightly from what is used in the exchange and production models treated above. First, we let

x = the quantity of the public good

Note that x is a scalar, not a vector. Also, note that x can be viewed as the quantity (or size) of the public good in physical units, or in dollars, since we assume that the prices of both the public and the private good are one. Second, we let

y_i = person i's quantity of the private good

Note that y_i is a scalar. We assume that person i's utility function u_i can be written

$$u_i = v_i(x) + y_i$$

That is, i's utility is the sum of the function v_i, which depends only on x, plus i's quantity of the private good. We also assume that v_i is continuous, smooth, and concave; that is, it looks like the one in Figure 6-1.

In the figure, the function v_i is smooth and concave, that is, it bends downward. The intercept a might be positive or negative, or v_i might even be asymptotic to the (negative half of the) vertical axis. At the point P, the ratio $\Delta v_i / \Delta x$ is person i's *marginal utility* from the public good, or approximately the amount by which his utility rises if the quantity of the public

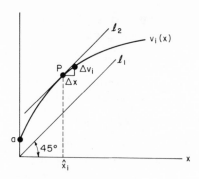

FIGURE 6-1

good is increased by 1, while his private consumption remains fixed. Note that for sufficiently small Δ's, $\Delta v_i / \Delta x$ and the slope of the v_i function at P are equal. Instead of writing MU of the public good for i, we now use this simpler notation:

$v_i'(x)$ = MU of the public good for i, when the quantity of the public good is x

We also assume that each person starts with an initial endowment of the private good. We let

ω_i = i's initial quantity of the private good

Note that ω_i is also a scalar.

In order to be *feasible*, a vector of public and private good consumption levels $(x, y_1, y_2, \ldots, y_n)$ must satisfy this condition:

$$x + \sum_{i=1}^{n} y_i = \sum_{i=1}^{n} \omega_i$$

THE SAMUELSON PUBLIC GOOD OPTIMALITY CONDITION

Let's now see how a Pareto optimal output for the public good can be found. In order to do this, we start by considering the inequality

$$v_1'(x) + v_2'(x) + \ldots + v_n'(x) > 1$$

That is, we consider an output x of the public good, such that the sum of the marginal utilities of all individuals at x exceeds 1. Let's assume for mathematical simplicity that each person's private consumption y_i exceeds his marginal utility from public consumption $v_i'(x)$. Now suppose we reduce each person's consumption of the private good by an amount $v_i'(x)$; that is, we define a new amount of private good consumption for each i:

$$\bar{y}_i = y_i - v_i'(x)$$

If we stop here, then each person's utility must drop by the amount of the private good he loses, $v_i'(x)$. But we have extracted

$$v_1'(x) + v_2'(x) + \ldots + v_n'(x) = 1 + \Delta$$

units of private good from the economy, where Δ is some number greater than zero. Now suppose we take 1 unit of private good from this total (leaving Δ) and send it to the productive sector of the economy (or the firm) to be transformed into 1 unit of public good. Then we get a new public good output of

$$\bar{x} = x + 1$$

But increasing the public good available by a unit increases each person's utility by an amount approximately equal to the marginal utility of the public good, or, for i, $v_i'(x)$. Therefore, at $(\bar{x}, \bar{y}_1, \bar{y}_2, \ldots, \bar{y}_n)$ each person is as well off as he was at $(x, y_1, y_2, \ldots, y_n)$. But Δ units of the private good are left over. This amount can be redistributed among the individual to make some (or all) better off than they used to be at $(x, y_1, y_2, \ldots, y_n)$. Consequently, if

$$v_1'(x) + v_2'(x) + \ldots + v_n'(x) > 1$$

it is possible to make some people better off and no one worse off through an appropriately financed increased in the public good x. Therefore, x is not the Pareto optimal output for the public good.

This result shows us when the output of the public good ought to increase. But as x increases, $v_i'(x)$ decreases for every i, because of the shapes of the v_i functions assumed in Figure 6-1. Unless all the private good is exhausted first, if x is continually increased, we eventually reach a point where

$$v_1'(x) + v_2'(x) + \ldots + v_n'(x) < 1$$

This inequality can be rewritten

$$v_1'(x) + v_2'(x) + \ldots + v_n'(x) + \Delta = 1$$

where Δ is again a number greater than zero. Now we can reduce the public good output by 1 unit. Suppose we let $\bar{x} = x - 1$. If we do so we reduce each person's utility by approximately $v_i'(x)$. But the unit reduction in public good output can be accompanied by a unit reduction in private good input into the productive sector. A unit of private good is saved, and available for private consumption. We can distribute it by giving each person i an amount $v_i'(x)$; that is, we can define $\bar{y}_i = y_i + v_i'(x)$, leaving the quantity Δ free for the moment. Increasing i's private consumption by $v_i'(x)$ increases his utility by $v_i'(x)$ as well. Therefore, at $(\bar{x}, \bar{y}_1, \bar{y}_2, \ldots, \bar{y}_n)$ each person is approximately as well off as he was at $(x, y_1, y_2, \ldots, y_n)$. But Δ units of the private good have been freed up. This surplus can be redistributed among the individuals to make some (or all) better off than they used to be at $(x, y_1, y_2, \ldots, y_n)$. In short, if

$$v_1'(x) + v_2'(x) + \ldots + v_n'(x) < 1$$

it is possible to make some people better off and no one worse off through a decrease in the public good x, with the savings appropriately distributed among the individuals. Therefore, x is not the Pareto optimal level of output for the public good.

We have seen that when

$$v_1'(x) + v_2'(x) + \ldots + v_n'(x) > 1$$

x is too small, and is not optimal, and that when

$$v_1'(x) + v_2'(x) + \ldots + v_n'(x) < 1$$

x is too large, and is not optimal. A necessary condition for Pareto optimality, therefore, is

$$v_1'(x) + v_2'(x) + \ldots + v_n'(x) = \sum_{i=1}^{n} v_i'(x) = 1$$

That is, the sum of the marginal utilities for the public good should equal the marginal cost of producing the public good, in terms of foregone private good. Named after Paul Samuelson, this is called the *Samuelson optimality condition for public goods*.

There is another simple way to view the Samuelson optimality condition. Consider the expression

$$v_1(x) + v_2(x) + \ldots + v_n(x) - x = \sum_{i=1}^{n} v_i(x) - x$$

This can be interpreted as the *aggregate net benefit* of the public good output level x. Now it's rather clear that if x does not maximize aggregate net benefit it cannot be Pareto optimal: If there is an alternative level of output

$\bar{x}$ that gives a higher aggregate net benefit than does x, there must be some way to shift from x to $\bar{x}$ and make everyone better off in the shift. In fact, a simple application of calculus indicates that maximizing

$$v_1(x) + v_2(x) + \ldots + v_n(x) - x$$

leads directly to the Samuelson condition.

In short, maximizing aggregate net benefit

$$\sum_{i=1}^{n} v_i(x) - x$$

is necessary for achieving the Pareto optimal output of the public good, just as the Samuelson condition

$$\sum_{i=1}^{n} v_i{}'(x) = 1$$

is necessary for achieving the Parteo optimal x. Moreover, the two conditions are also sufficient. Consequently, the Pareto optimal output of the public good is determined by the Samuelson condition, or, equivalently, the condition that aggregate net benefit be maximized.

PRIVATE FINANCING OF THE PUBLIC GOOD AND THE FREE RIDER PROBLEM

Now let's consider how the public good is financed. In this section we assume that it is privately purchased. This means individual i might pay for a certain amount of the public good, which would then be available to all. (Some examples of privately purchased public goods are privately owned parks open to the public, privately owned pieces of art on display in a public museum, and private contributions to charitable organizations.) We are assuming, then, that the unmodified (private) market mechanism is being used to supply the public good. In subsequent sections we'll analyze public (that is, government) financing of the public good.

To start the analysis, we suppose that person i takes the lead; he makes the first purchase of the public good. How much does he buy? He wants to choose an x to maximize his utility

$$u_i = v_i(x) + y$$

subject to his budget constraint

$$1 \cdot x + 1 \cdot y_i = 1 \cdot \omega_1$$

Substituting for y_i, person i wants to maximize $u_i = v_i(x) - x + \omega_i$. The graphical solution to the problem can be seen in Figure 6-1. In that figure, the lines ℓ_1 and ℓ_2 have slope 1. Maximizing $v_i(x) - x + \omega_i$ is equivalent to maximizing $v_i(x) - x$, the vertical distance between the v_i function and the line ℓ_1. This vertical distance is greatest at the point P, where v_i is tangent to the line ℓ_2. At the tangency point, the slope of the v_i function equals the slope of the line ℓ_2, or

$$v_i'(x) = 1$$

We shall let $\hat{x}_i$ be the quantity of the public good that i would choose to purchase privately. Note that the subscript i serves here only to remind us that i is making a private purchasing decision; the good is still public; and i cannot exclude others from enjoying the benefits of his purchase.

Now if person i has purchased $\hat{x}_i$ units of the public good what do the others do? Each of the others is enjoying the benefits from i's purchase without paying for those benefits. To be more precise, let's suppose first that $v_j'(\hat{x}_i) < 1$: That is, the marginal utility to person j from the public good is less than the marginal cost of the public good, given person i's (generous) decision to purchase $\hat{x}_i$ (and provide it to all). In this case, if j were to curtail his own private consumption by 1 unit, and purchase an additional unit of the public good for his (and everyone else's) extra enjoyment, he would be worse off. So he won't do it. That is, if $v_j'(\hat{x}) < 1$, person j will be content to let i buy the public good, he will not buy any himself. He will take a free ride on i's consumption of the public good. On the other hand, if $v_j'(\hat{x}) > 1$, then j would benefit if he curtailed his private consumption and purchased more units of the public good for his (and everyone else's) extra enjoyment. How much would he purchase? He would want the quantity of the public good increased until $v_j'(x) = 1$, since whenever $v_j'(x) > 1$, person j makes himself better off by reducing his consumption of the private good and increasing his (and everyone else's) consumption of the public good.

The final equilibrum in the unmodified private market for public and private goods will have these properties: For (at least) one person i, we will have $v_i'(x) = 1$. For all i, we will have $v_i'(x) \leq 1$. And the financing — the details of who pays how much — will largely be determined by who made the first purchase, who the second, and so on. But if $v_i'(x) = 1$ for some i, and if (as we are obviously assuming) $v_i(x) > 0$ for the other i's, then

$$v_1'(x) + v_2'(x) + \ldots + v_n'(x) > 1$$

That is, the sum of the marginal utilities will exceed the marginal cost of the public good, and, x will not be Pareto optimal. It will generally be possible to make some people better off and no one worse off through an appropriately financed increase in the public good. There will not be enough of the public good produced.

To get a clear intuitive idea of what's causing this insufficiency of public good production, think of the case where v_i is the same function for all i. In other words, everyone's tastes are the same. Now if a particular person, say person 1, takes the first step, and purchases $\hat{x}_1$ of the public good, what do the others do? They all take a free ride, since $\hat{x}_1 = \hat{x}_2 = \hat{x}_3 = \ldots$. Persons 2 through n are free riders on the purchase of the public good by person 1: they enjoy the benefits and pay none of the costs. It's no surprise that 1 doesn't choose the optimal quantity of the public good; he figures his own benefit against the total cost, and pays no attention to the benefits enjoyed by the free riders. And in this particular instance, there is a very large discrepancy between

$$\sum_{i=1}^{n} v_i'(x) \text{ and the marginal cost of the public good, since}$$

$$\sum_{i=1}^{n} v_i'(x) = 1 + 1 + 1 + \ldots + 1 = n >> 1$$

Consequently, there is probably a large difference between $\hat{x}_1$ and the optimal quantity of the public good.

To sum up this section, the problem with the private provision of public goods is the problem of free riders. Those who enjoy the public good without paying for it never signal their desire for it. Consequently, not enough of the public good is provided. This is why public goods ought to be, in some way, publicly financed.

THE WICKSELL-LINDAHL TAX SCHEME

We now focus on a system in which the public good is publicly financed. A central government authority called the Public Good Board decides on the output of the public good x, and collects taxes to pay for x. What would we like this system to accomplish? First, it should somehow provide for a Pareto optimal output of the public good. Any x that is not Pareto optimal is unambiguously unsatisfactory. And, second, it ought to link a person's taxes to the benefits he receives. This is partly a matter of common sense and partly a matter of justice. A person's benefits from his private consumption are clearly linked to his payments for private consumption. And that linkage works well: it produces a Pareto optimal outcome in a private-good economy. So common sense suggests the linkage might be useful in an economy with a public good. Moreover, ever since Knut Wicksell wrote about "just" taxation in 1896, economists have occasionally suggested linking taxes and benefits because it's "just" to do so. Why should a person who gets little or no utility from the public good pay the same taxes as a person who gets lots of utility from it? As Wicksell wrote, "it would seem to be a blatant injustice if someone should be forced to contribute toward the costs of some activity which does not further his interests or may even be diametrically opposed to them."

Optimality and linkage are, then, the guiding principles in the taxation system named after Wicksell and Erik Lindahl. To explain the scheme we need a little more notation. Again, this notation is specific to our discussion of public goods, and should not be confused with similar notation we have used before.

We shall let T_i stand for person i's total tax payment to the Public Good Board. With the total tax T_i, i's budget becomes

$$y_i + T_i = \omega_i$$

We are continuing to assume that the prices of the public and private goods are 1 and 1, respectively, so T_i can be viewed as a payment in dollars (or currency), or as a payment in units of the private good. We shall assume in this section that each person i has to bear a fractional share of the expenditure on the public good, and we shall let t_i stand for person i's share. Since the sum of the fractional shares of the individuals must be 1, we have

$$\sum_{i=1}^{n} t_i = 1$$

Also, if i's share is t_i and the total quantity of (or expenditure on) the public good is x, then necessarily

$$T_i = t_i x$$

Now suppose we confront individual i with this question: "If your share $t_i = \frac{1}{4}$, what quantity of the public good do you want produced?" Individual i thinks to himself: "I shall pay $T_i = \frac{1}{4} \cdot x$, so the x I want is the one that maximizes $u_i = v_i(x) + y_i$ subject to $y_i + T_i = \omega_i$, or $y_i +$ ¼ $x = \omega_i$. In short, I want the one that maximizes $v_i(x) -$ ¼ x." The graphical solution to this problem can be found by redrawing Figure 6-1 in such a way that the lines ℓ_1 and ℓ_2 have slope = ¼, rather than slope = 1. If we confront individual i with this question: "If your share $t_i = $ ½, what quantity of the public good do you want produced?" He will go through the same calculations, except with ½ where ¼ used to be. And he will obviously come up with a different answer. In Figure 6-2 we have drawn a v_i function and lines ℓ_1 and ℓ_2 for the general case: ℓ_1 and ℓ_2 have slope = t_i. The symbol $\hat{x}_i(t_i)$ represents the quantity of the public good i wants produced, given that his share of the cost is t_i.

For the general case, i wants to maximize $u_i = v_i(x) + y_i$ subject to $y_i + T_i = \omega_i$ or $y_i + t_i \cdot x = \omega_i$. In short, he wants to maximize $v_i(x) - t_i \cdot x + \omega_i$, or, equivalently, $v_i(x) - t_i \cdot x$. This quantity is greatest when the vertical distance between the v_i function and the line ℓ_i is greatest, which occurs at the point P where ℓ_2, a line parallel to ℓ_1, is tangent to v_i. At that tangency point, the slope of ℓ_2 equals the slope of v_i. But the slope of ℓ_2 is t_i, and the slope of v_i is i's marginal utility from the public good, or $v_i'(x)$. Therefore, the point P, and i's desired quantity of the public good $\hat{x}_i(t_i)$, are determined by the equation

$$v_i'(x) = t_i$$

A careful examination of Figure 6-2 should convince the reader of this general result: The higher is person i's share t_i, the lower is the quantity of the public good $\hat{x}_i(t_i)$ he wants produced. This makes intuitive sense; it's

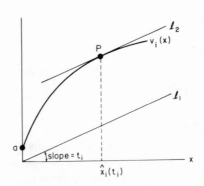

FIGURE 6-2

analogous to the Law of Demand for private goods: the higher the price of a private good, the less the individual wants to purchase, all else equal.

It is crucial to note that if the actual output of the public good happens to coincide with i's desired output of the public good, of if $x = \hat{x}_i(t_i)$, then i's marginal utility from the public good $v_i'(x)$ equals his tax share t_i. That is, his tax share is linked to his marginal benefit.

But how can the actual output be made to agree with i's desired output? After all, each of the n people has his own $\hat{x}_i(t_i)$ function, his own schedule of desired outputs contingent on t_i, and given any list of fractional shares $(t_1, t_2, \ldots, t_n)$, each person will have his own particular desired output of the public good. How can the Public Good Board find a way to insure that each and every person's tax share is linked to his marginal benefit? The Wicksell-Lindahl tax scheme answers this question.

The trick of this tax scheme is to adjust the tax shares until every person agrees on the desired output of the public good. For instance, suppose there are just two people, and, when $t_1 = t_2 = \frac{1}{2}$, person 1's desired public good output is $\hat{x}_1(\frac{1}{2}) = 10$, while person 2's desired public good output is $\hat{x}_2(\frac{1}{2}) = 20$. Given the shares $(\frac{1}{2}, \frac{1}{2})$, they disagree about the best level of output. No matter what level of output is actually chosen, for at least one of the two, his tax share will diverge from his marginal benefit. The solution? Gradually decrease t_1, and increase t_2. As t_1 decreases, 1 wants more and more of the public good produced. As t_2 increases, 2 wants less and less of the public good produced. Eventually, a point is reached when each thinks the same quantity of the public good should be produced. Say that point is reached when $t_1 = \frac{1}{3}$ and $t_2 = \frac{2}{3}$, and say $\hat{x}_1(\frac{1}{3}) = 14 = \hat{x}_2(\frac{2}{3})$. Then, the Public Good Board assigns person 1 a tax share $t_1 = \frac{1}{3}$, and person 2 a tax share $t_2 = \frac{2}{3}$, and it has 14 units of the public good produced. Under these circumstances, each person's tax share is linked to the marginal utility he gets from the public good.

Formally, a *Lindahl equilibrium* is defined to be a vector of tax shares $(t_1, t_2, \ldots, t_n)$ and a level of output $\hat{x}$ for the public good, such that, for all i, when i's tax share is t_i his desired level of public good output equals $\hat{x}$. That is, for all i, $\hat{x}$ maximizes $u_i = v_i(x) + y_i$ subject to the budget constraint $y_i + t_i x = \omega_i$.

It is clear from its definition that a Lindahl equilibrium, or the Wicksell-Lindahl tax scheme, equates tax shares and marginal benefits for every person. That is, what people pay is connected to what they get. It should be emphasized that the connection is with marginal utility rather than total utility, but at least the linkage is there. What about optimality? Does a Lindahl equilibrium level of public good output $\hat{x}$ have to be optimal? The answer is Yes.

Recall that i's desired quantity of the public good $\hat{x}_i(t_i)$ is determined by the equation

$$v_i'(x) = t_i$$

Therefore, since a Lindahl equilibrium $\hat{x}$ equals $\hat{x}_i(t_i)$ for every i, we must have

$$v_i'(\hat{x}) = t_i \text{ for all } i$$

Summing over all the i's gives

$$v_1'(\hat{x}) + v_2'(\hat{x}) + \ldots + v_n'(\hat{x}) = t_1 + t_2 + \ldots + t_n = 1$$

Consequently, the Samuelson condition is satisfied by $\hat{x}$, and $\hat{x}$ is the optimal quantity of the public good.

The Wicksell-Lindahl scheme then accomplishes the two things we set out for it: optimality and linkage. But it does have a drawback. When the Public Good Board calculates the Lindahl equilibrium, when it calculates the appropriate vector of tax shares $(t_1, t_2, \ldots, t_n)$ and the output for the public good $\hat{x}$, it relies on information it receives from the individuals. It needs each individual's $\hat{x}_i(t_i)$ schedule, which we might call i's demand schedule for the public good. Or, equivalently, it needs each individual's marginal utility function v_i', or his total utility function v_i. The three functions are really interchangeable, but the Public Good Board must ask for one of them. Now put yourself in the place of a bright individual who has just been asked to provide one of these schedules, one of these functions. Suppose you know how the Public Good Board operates; you know that you will end up with a tax share t_i equal to your marginal utility $v_i'(\hat{x})$. What will you report to the Board?

If you are at all devious, you will lie about your utility, or marginal utility, or demand function. You'll say the public good is useless to you; or you'll say that your marginal utility from the public good is zero for all relevant levels of output. You won't reveal your true demand. You'll misrepresent your preferences and take a free ride. The incentives here are not compatible with truthful answers.

And, of course, if everyone is lying like mad about his demand on marginal utility function, the Public Good Board is not likely to reach an equilibrium that links tax shares to real marginal utilities, or that is Pareto optimal given the real utility functions.

Let us note that there is also an incentive-compatibility or a demand-revealing problem in a model with only private goods. But it's much less severe. It might well be to a person's advantage to understate his demand for a private good in order to put downward pressure on the price of that good. But if he does so he'll probably end up with significantly less of the good. And if n is large, if there are many people, his misrepresentation will have very little effect on the price. So if he says "I don't want the good, it's of no use to me" he will in fact end up with a lot less of it than he would have otherwise, and he'll pay almost as much per unit as he would have otherwise. Contrast this situation to the public good model we've just analyzed. Suppose there are lots of people, and a particular person says to the Public Good Board "I don't want the good, it's of no use to me." His falsehood will induce the Board to produce a slightly smaller $\hat{x}$; but only slightly smaller, when n is large. And under the Wicksell-Lindahl tax scheme, his tax share will drop dramatically. So the person who is willing to conceal his demand for the public good will end up with almost as much of it as he would have otherwise, and he'll pay a lot less per unit than he would have otherwise!

The critical problem with the Wicksell-Lindahl tax scheme is this problem of demand-revelation. People will not want to reveal their true feelings to the Public Good Board. This is why we must look elsewhere for an ideal public finance scheme.

FIXED TAX SHARES AND MAJORITY VOTING

Before continuing the search for a theoretically ideal tax scheme, let's digress slightly, and carefully examine a realistic method for financing the public good and determining the quantity that ought to be produced. In this scheme the tax shares $t_1, t_2, \ldots, t_n$ are fixed. And the amount to produce, the quantity x, is determined by majority voting.

As an example of a fixed tax shares scheme, we might have $t_i = 1/n$, for all i. That is, each person might pay an equal share of the cost of producing x. This is obviously a commonly used scheme. As another example, the t_i's might be proportional to the ω_i's. That is, we might have

$$t_i = \frac{\omega_i}{\sum_{i=1}^{n} \omega_i} \text{ for all } i$$

The person who starts out the richest pays the highest tax; the poorest pays the lowest. Note that in both of these examples the t_i's sum to unity.

Now let's analyze what individual i wants under this system of finance. When informed that his share is t_i, i thinks of how to maximize $u_i = v_i(x) + y_i$ subject to $y_i + t_i x = \omega_i$. That is, he wants to maximize $v_i(x) - t_i x$. We've already seen in the analysis of the Wicksell-Lindahl tax scheme that person i would most prefer the level of public expenditure $\hat{x}_i(t_i)$ shown in Figure 6–2. However, if given a choice between any two public good levels x_1 and x_2, and asked to vote between those two, he would very probably vote for the one for which $v_i(x) - t_i x$ is greater.

How is an equilibrium found? Each person i has his favorite level of output $\hat{x}_i(t_i)$. For some i, this is small, for some i, it is large. For instance, if persons 1 and 2 have the same v_i function, but t_1 is big, while t_2 is small, then 1 will have a small $\hat{x}_1(t_1)$, and 2 will have a large $\hat{x}_2(t_2)$. The one who pays a bigger share will want a smaller project. Now for the sake of mathematical simplicity, let's assume here that all the $\hat{x}_i(t_i)$'s are distinct, that the people are numbered in such a way that

$$\hat{x}_1(t_1) < \hat{x}_2(t_2) < \ldots < \hat{x}_n(t_n)$$

and that the number of people n is odd. Let person M be the *median person*, the person whose $\hat{x}_M(t_M)$ is in the middle. That is, there are as many $\hat{x}_i(t_i)$'s less than $\hat{x}_M(t_M)$ as there are $\hat{x}_i(t_i)$'s greater than $x_M(t_M)$.

In the fixed tax shares, majority voting system of public finance, the Public Good Board conducts a sequence of elections, elections in which the candidates are levels of output for the public good. For simplicity, we shall assume that the list of candidates is just the set $\{\hat{x}_1(t_1), \ldots, \hat{x}_n(t_n)\}$. The Public Good Board conducts these elections until it finds a level of output $\hat{x}_i(t_i)$ which wins a majority over any other level of output $\hat{x}_j(t_j)$. The winning $\hat{x}_i(t_i)$ is the *fixed tax shares, majority voting equilibrium*.

And it turns out that the equilibrium must be $\hat{x}_M(t_M)$, that is, the desired level of output of the median voter. Let's just briefly indicate why this ought to be the case. (For a fuller treatment see Chapter 9). In what follows we will write $\hat{x}$ instead of $\hat{x}_M(t_M)$. Now consider a vote between $\hat{x}$ and some $\hat{x}_i(t_i) < \hat{x}$. Some reflection should convince you that any person $j \geq M$ will want to vote for $\hat{x}$. But since M is the median, the people numbered M or above make up a majority. So $\hat{x}$ wins a majority vote over $\hat{x}_i(t_i)$. Similarly, in a vote between $\hat{x}$ and any $\hat{x}_i(t_i) > \hat{x}$, $\hat{x}$ wins another majority, since it gets the votes of everyone numbered M or below.

What are the advantages of this system of public finance? First of all, it is relatively simple and comprehensible. It can be easily understood by the people reporting their desired quantities of the public good, and voting on hose quantities. Second, unlike the Wicksell-Lindahl scheme, the incen-ives for misrepresentation and duplicity don't stand out like a sore thumb. 3ut if subtle, these incentives might still be there. We have deliberately been /ague about the exact nature of the voting process, or what agenda the 3oard uses. It is possible that, given certain agendas, people might vote ιgainst a preferred expenditure level at one stage, in order to end up with a)etter outcome at a later stage. This possibility becomes a virtual certainty if here are two or more public good expenditure levels being chosen simul-aneously. Nonetheless, the incentives to lie are not as glaring in the fixed ax share majority voting scheme as they are in the Wicksell-Lindahl cheme.

What are the disadvantages? First of all, there is no linkage between a)erson's tax share t_i and his utility, or marginal utility from the public ;ood, except for the median person M. For M we know that t_M must equal he marginal utility from the public good at the equilibrium level of output ̂x. But for every $i \neq M$,

$$v_i'(\hat{x}) \neq t_i$$

Half of the people have tax shares less than their marginal utilities, half ιave tax shares greater.

The second and crucial disadvantage is that $\hat{x}$ is generally not Pareto)ptimal. Let's consider the Samuelson test. In the sum

$$v_1'(\hat{x}) + v_2'(\hat{x}) + \ldots + v_{M-1}'(\hat{x}) +$$
$$v_M'(\hat{x}) + v_{M+1}'(\hat{x}) + \ldots + v_n'(\hat{x})$$

ve know that the first $M - 1$ numbers are all less than the corresponding ᵢ's; we know that $v_M'(\hat{x}) = t_M$; and we know that the last $M - 1$ numbers ιre all greater than the correspondent t_i's. But we do not know, and in fact t is generally not true, that the sum of the n numbers is equal to

$$\sum_{i=1}^{n} t_i = 1.$$

That is, in general

$$v_1'(\hat{x}) + v_2'(\hat{x}) + \ldots + v_n'(\hat{x}) \neq 1$$

Therefore, in general $\hat{x}$ fails the Samuelson test; it is not Pareto optimal.

Whether $\hat{x}$ is too large, that is,

$$\sum_{i=1}^{n} v_i'(\hat{x}) < 1$$

or too small, that is,

$$\sum_{i=1}^{n} v_i'(\hat{x}) > 1$$

will depend on the circumstances. But the chances are slim that $\hat{x}$ will be just right.

THE DEMAND-REVEALING TAX SCHEME

At this point we return to our search for a theoretically ideal tax scheme. Let's examine another approach, one whose basic virtues are (1) that it leads to the optimal output for the public good, and (2) that it provides no incentives for individuals to misrepresent their demands for the public good. Because of the latter virtue (which is so dramatically missing in the Wicksell-Lindahl scheme), this public finance rule is said to solve the incentive problem or to be *incentive-compatible,* or to be *demand-revealing.* The demand revealing tax scheme was developed independently by Edward Clark and Theodore Groves in the 1970s. A similar scheme to discourage speculation in private goods markets had been developed by William Vickrey in 1961. The name "demand-revealing" was coined by T. Nicolaus Tideman and Gordon Tullock.

In the demand-revealing tax system, each individual sends a "message" to the Public Good Board, a message about his feelings for the public good. We shall assume that the message is a utility function for the public good, that is, a v_i function. This might be i's real utility-from-the-public-good function, or it might not. We shall show that i will not be able to gain by lying, so he will report his true function. But for now, when i reports a v function, it must be viewed with suspicion.

What does the Public Good Board do with the (possibly fraudulent) v functions? First, it derives from each v_i function a (possibly fraudulent) marginal utility function v_i', and, with these marginal utility functions it uses the Samuelson condition to solve for a level of expenditure on the public good. That is, it solves for an $\hat{x}$ that satisfies the equation

$$\sum_{i=1}^{n} v_i'(x) = 1$$

We saw above that this exercise is equivalent to the maximization of aggregate net benefit from the public good. Therefore, we can also say that the Board finds an $\hat{x}$ that maximizes the expression

$$\sum_{i=1}^{n} v_i(x) - x$$

Now we know that if the v_i functions are true, if individuals aren't misrepresenting their preferences, then $\hat{x}$ is a Pareto optimal level of output for the public good.

Second, the Public Good Board sets taxes. This, of course, is the delicate part, since we have seen in the case of the Wicksell-Lindahl scheme that the tax rule can tempt people to lie. In the demand-revealing scheme, the Board does not set tax shares or t_i's, it simply sets total tax payments, or T_i's. We shall assume for now that it does so according to the following rule:

$$T_i = \hat{x} - \sum_{j \neq i} v_j(\hat{x})$$

The symbol "$\sum_{j \neq i} v_j(\hat{x})$" means "sum the v_j's over all the people except i."

That is, person i's tax equals the entire cost of the public good (or its level of output) less the aggregate utility accruing to other people from the public good. For instance, suppose that $\hat{x}$ is a $1,000 bridge, and suppose there are five users who assign the following values to it:

$$v_1(\hat{x}) = 0, v_2(\hat{x}) = 500, v_3(\hat{x}) = 100, v_4(\hat{x}) = 200 \text{ and } v_5(\hat{x}) = 300.$$

Then, $T_1 = -$100$, $T_2 = 400, $T_3 = 0$, $T_4 = 100, and $T_5 = 200. Notice that T_1 is negative, which means person 1 is getting a grant rather than paying a tax. Also notice that the sum of the T_i's equals only $600, which is not enough to pay for the bridge! We'll fix up this problem of insufficient funds below.

Let's make an important observation about the rule for finding i's tax T_i: Person i's message, his reported v_i function, does not appear directly in the definition of T_i. His expressed demand for the public good does have an indirect effect on T_i, since it enters into the Board's determination of $\hat{x}$. But if i were to understate his demand, say by declaring that $v_i(x)$ were zero for all levels of x, he would still pay a tax, since T_i depends on the chosen quantity of the public good and everyone else's expressed valuation of that chosen quantity, but not i's.

Next let's see whether or not the actions of the Public Good Board provide each person with the proper incentives to honestly reveal his v_i function.

We consider a particular fixed i. Suppose persons $j = 1, 2, \ldots, i - 1$ $i + 1, \ldots, n$ have reported their v_j functions, which might be real or whimsical; i doesn't know. Person i of course wants to maximize his real utility

$$u_i = v_i(\hat{x}) + y_i$$

subject to $y_i + T_i = \omega_i$. That is, he wants to maximize $v_i(\hat{x}) - T_i + \omega_i$ or, equivalently, $v_i(\hat{x}) - T_i$. Of course, it is the Board rather than i that chooses $\hat{x}$ and T_i, which might seem to tie i's hands, but i does have the option of lying about v_i and thereby directly affecting $\hat{x}$ and indirectly affecting T_i.

Now person i, along with everyone else, knows the tax rule; he knows that the Board will always set

$$T_i = \hat{x} - \sum_{j \neq i} v_j(\hat{x})$$

Consequently, i wants to maximize the following expression for his after tax utility:

$$v_i(\hat{x}) - [\hat{x} - \sum_{j \neq i} v_j(\hat{x})].$$

At this point let's use a $\sim$ to indicate a false function, or a quantity that results when i lies, and no $\sim$ to indicate a true function, or a quantity that results when i tells the truth. If i lies, or reports $\tilde{v}_i$, the Board comes up with $\tilde{x}$, and if i tells the truth, or reports v_i, the Board comes up with $\hat{x}$. The question is, can i lie in such a way that he is (truly!) better off?

Well, person i knows that the Public Good Board always chooses $\hat{x}$ to maximize aggregate net benefit. In particular, if i tells the truth, if he reports v_i, the Board will choose $\hat{x}$ to maximize

$$\sum_{i=1}^{n} v_i(x) - x = v_i(x) + \sum_{j \neq i} v_j(x) - x = v_i(x) - [x - \sum_{j \neq i} v_j(x)]$$

That is, if i reports his true v_i, the Board will attempt to maximize precisely what i himself wants maximized: the Board's goal will coincide with i's, and i consequently has nothing to gain by lying.

More formally,

$$v_i(\hat{x}) - [\hat{x} - \sum_{j \neq i} v_j(\hat{x})] \geq v_i(x) - [x - \sum_{j \neq i} v_j(x)]$$

for all x, since the Board chooses $\hat{x}$ to maximize aggregate net benefit. In particular,

$$v_i(\hat{x}) - [\hat{x} - \sum_{j \neq i} v_j(\hat{x})] \geq v_i(\tilde{x}) - [\tilde{x} - \sum_{j \neq i} v_j(\tilde{x})]$$

for any $\tilde{x}$ that results form a false $\tilde{v}_i$. Therefore, it is never advantageous for i to misrepresent his utility from the public good. And this holds true no matter what other people ($j \neq i$) might do; whether the v_j's are true or false is irrelevant to the argument above. Consequently, telling the truth is called a *dominant strategy* for i; that is, i will maximize his utility by reporting v_i truthfully, no matter what anyone else is doing.

Since truth is a dominant strategy under the demand-revealing tax scheme, we shall assume, without doing violence to common sense, that people in fact report their true v_i's.

So far, we've shown that the demand revealing tax scheme induces people to be honest. It solves the misrepresentation problem. Also, since the Board is choosing $\hat{x}$ to maximize

$$\sum_{i=1}^{n} v_i(x) - x,$$

the demand revealing tax scheme brings about the proper Pareto optimal level of output $\hat{x}$ for the public good. These are its two important advantages.

What are its disadvantages? We must refer back at this point to our 1,000 bridge example, in which the sum of the tax payments

$$\sum_{i=1}^{5} T_i$$

was $600. Funds were insufficient to build the bridge. As we have described so far, then, the system simply might not work: tax collections might not cover the proposed expenditure $\hat{x}$.

The possibility of insufficient funds leads to a question. Is there a way to fix up the taxes so that we can always be sure that total tax receipts will cover expenditures, or

$$\sum_{i=1}^{n} T_i \geq \hat{x}$$

and so that incentives to tell the truth are preserved? The answer is Yes.

It is clear that i's incentive to tell the truth will remain if we add a term to i's tax that does not depend on v_i or $\hat{x}$. For such an addition to i's tax would remain fixed no matter what v_i he reported, and no matter what decision the Public Good Board took; i's report would have no effect on it. We shall proceed to add such a term to T_i.

Let's define

$$S_i = \underset{x}{\text{maximum}} \quad \sum_{j \neq i} [v_j(x) - \frac{x}{n}]$$

To understand the intuition here, imagine everyone is first assigned an equal $1/n^{\text{th}}$ share of the cost of x. Then person j's net benefit from x is $v_j(x) - x/n$. The sum of the net benefits of all persons except i is

$$\sum_{j \neq i} [v_j(x) - \frac{x}{n}]$$

a function of x, and S_i is the maximum value achieved by this function of x. If i were an entirely passive person, a pushover, and if he said to the Public Good Board, "Go ahead and maximize their aggregate net benefit, pay no attention to me, but do let me pay a $1/n^{\text{th}}$ share of the cost," then the Board would maximize

$$\sum_{j \neq i} [v_j(x) - \frac{x}{n}]$$

Therefore, we can interpret S_i as the maximum aggregate net benefit for all the others, when i is passive.

Now we define a new tax for i by adding S_i to i's old tax. For the rest of this section we let

$$T_i = \hat{x} - \sum_{j \neq i} v_j(\hat{x}) + S_i$$

This can be rewritten as

$$T_i = \frac{\hat{x}}{n} + S_i - \sum_{j \neq i} [v_j(\hat{x}) - \frac{\hat{x}}{n}]$$

Since S_i does not depend in any way on i's reported v_i, or on $\hat{x}$, the addition of S_i to i's tax does not affect the demand-revealing character of the tax

Telling the truth is still i's dominant strategy. Moreover, since

$$S_i = \text{maximum}_{x} \sum_{j \neq i} [v_j(x) - \frac{x}{n}] \geq \sum_{j \neq i} [v_j(\hat{x}) - \frac{\hat{x}}{n}]$$

we have

$$T_i \geq \frac{\hat{x}}{n}, \text{ and so } \sum_{i=1}^{n} T_i \geq \hat{x}.$$

Therefore, we have cured the problem of possibly insufficient tax revenues.

Also, there is now a nice intuitive interpretation of T_i. Again, we imagine that everyone is first assigned an equal $1/n^{\text{th}}$ share of the cost of x. We've noted above that S_i can be viewed as the maximum aggregate net benefit for all save i, when i is passive. What about the term

$$\sum_{j \neq i} [v_j(\hat{x}) - \frac{\hat{x}}{n}]?$$

Remember that the Board chooses $\hat{x}$ using the information about demand it receives from everybody, including i. Consequently, this term can be interpreted as the aggregate net benefit for all save i, when i is speaking up for himself. Therefore, we can interpret the new T_i as the sum of (1) i's equal share of the cost $1/n \ \hat{x}$ plus (2) the difference between the aggregate net benefit for all others when i is passive, and the aggregate net benefit for all the others when i expresses his demand. This difference itself can be viewed as the loss i imposes on the others by expressing his demand, by not being passive. So, finally, T_i is the sum of (1) i's cost share $1/n \ \hat{x}$ plus (2) the loss that i imposes on the others through his demand for the public good.

Let's note at this point that the initial assignment of equal cost shares to all, in the definition of the S_i's, could easily be relaxed. We could start out by assigning positive shares to all, shares which sum to 1. Formally, everything would go through almost as it did before.

At this point we have a tax scheme with the following properties. (1) Honesty is a dominant strategy, so everyone always tells the truth. (2) The optimal quantity $\hat{x}$ of the public good is produced. (3) The tax revenues are always sufficient to pay for $\hat{x}$.

But the analysis is not yet done. As we have defined the T_i's, we know

$$\sum_{i=1}^{n} T_i \geq \hat{x}$$

must hold. But this allows the possibility of a budget surplus for the Public Good Board. In other words, we might have

$$\sum_{i=1}^{n} T_i - \hat{x} > 0$$

What would become of this surplus?

In fact, the possibility of a surplus introduces a bizarre last twist in the analysis of the demand-revealing scheme. For suppose the Public Good Board were to return the surplus. We have been assuming throughout that individuals know exactly how the Public Good Board operates. So we must suppose that they also know the rule for returning the surplus. But if i knows that he will get back a rebate of, say, $F(i,\hat{x},v_1,v_2, \ldots, v_n)$, then we have been incorrectly calculating his tax; his tax ought to have been $T_i - F(i,\hat{x},v_1,v_2, \ldots, v_n)$, rather than T_i. And if F actually depends on $\hat{x}$ or v_1, then the incentive problem rears its head again. In short, returning the surplus (1) might make the analysis we've done so far wrong, and (2) might destroy the demand-revealing character of the properly calculated tax.

What if the surplus is not returned? What if it is, say, donated to the citizens of another country, or simply destroyed? If the surplus is not returned, we have a paradox. For now we have

$$\hat{x} + \sum_{i=1}^{n} y_i < \sum_{i=1}^{n} \omega_i$$

that is, some real goods are disappearing from the system. Some real wealth is wasted. It follows that $(\hat{x},y_1,y_2, \ldots, y_n)$ cannot be Pareto optimal, even if $\hat{x}$ satisfies the Samuelson condition, even if $\hat{x}$ is the Pareto optimal output for the public good. (Some practical authors, particularly Gordon Tullock, argue that it might be quite sensible to donate the surplus to another country, because the surplus will in fact be rather small. So the absence of Pareto optimality is not a big problem. We would be just pennies away from a Pareto optimal result here in the United States, even if the surplus were sent to New Zealand.)

The surplus problem raises a final question. Can a different, more clever definition of S_i be found, one that produces no surplus? Is it possible to find S_i functions so that, when we set

$$T_i = \hat{x} - \sum_{j \neq i} v_j(\hat{x}) + S_i$$

we have the following three virtues:

1. Truth is a dominant strategy for all i
2. $\hat{x}$ satisfies the Samuelson condition
3. $\displaystyle\sum_{i=1}^{n} T_i = \hat{x}$

Unfortunately, if we want to allow for any reasonable v_i functions, the answer to the question is No. That is, there exists no tax scheme that always satisfies conditions (1), (2), and (3). For a proof of this distressing result, the reader is referred to the Leonid Hurwicz article listed in the References section.

THE GROVES-LEDYARD TAX SCHEME

The last public finance scheme we shall consider was introduced in the late 1970s by Theodore Groves and John Ledyard. It is similar in several ways to the demand-revealing system. In the Groves-Ledyard scheme, as in the demand-revealing scheme, people send messages to the Public Good Board; the Board decides on a level of output $\hat{x}$ on the basis of those messages; and the Board sets tax payments, or T_i's, to finance $\hat{x}$. In the Groves-Ledyard scheme, as in the demand-revealing scheme, the $\hat{x}$ chosen satisfies the Samuelson condition: it is the optimal level of output for the public good. However, in contrast to the demand-revealing scheme, the Groves-Ledyard scheme produces no problematic budget surplus. This is its advantage over the demand-revealing scheme. Its disadvantages will unfold below.

Recall that in the demand-revealing scheme (and the Wicksell-Lindahl scheme as well) person i sends the Public Good Board his v_i function. In the Groves-Ledyard scheme, i's message to the Board is a desired increment in output of the public good. Thus i's message depends on the messages of all the others. For example, if the others have already expressed an aggregate desire for, say, 100 jet fighters in their nation's air force (a public good), i might say: "I want ten more," or "I want three less."

It is clear that for this scheme to work, either everyone is going to have to initially express mutually consistent desired increments, or else there is going to have to be some sort of iterative process that leads from an initial list of mutually-inconsistent desired increments to a final mutually-consistent list of desired increments. For instance, person 1 might start things going. He might propose a certain increment of the public good, contingent on everyone else's proposed increment being zero. Then person 2 might propose an increment, contingent on 1's proposal, and on all others being zero. Then 3 might propose an increment, contingent on 1's and 2's proposals. After a while, person n might propose an increment, contingent on 1's, 2's, . . ., $n-1$'s. Next, person 1 would revise his increment, since he now knows of the proposals of 2 through n. Then person 2 would revise his increment. So would persons 3, . . ., n. Then person 1 would have to revise his increment again, as would 2, 3, . . ., n, and so on and so forth, possibly ad infinitum. It is presently an open question whether or not such an iterative process would ever reach an equilibrium. (Similar processes in models of oligopolies are often unstable; they do not reach equilibria.) This is clearly one serious disadvantage of the Groves-Ledyard scheme. It might be impossible to implement because of dynamic instability problems.

Having noted this serious disadvantage, we move on. We now ignore the dynamics, and concentrate on statics. That is, we shall analyze an equilibrium, without worrying about how that equilibrium is actually reached.

We let Δ_i represent i's desired increment in the output of the public good. Δ_i, a number, is the message that i sends to the Board. Person i's message obviously depends on all the others' messages, and it depends on the rules governing the Board's behavior.

Let's turn to those rules. We assume that the Board sets the level of output of the public good according to this equation:

$$\hat{x} = \sum_{i=1}^{n} \Delta_i$$

Note that this is not what the Board does in the demand revealing scheme, but there the individuals' messages are v_i functions, and with v_i functions in hand, it makes sense to maximize aggregate net benefit. Here the messages are only increments, and the obvious thing to do with a collection of increments is to add them together, to get a public good total. We'll see below that this obvious thing to do is also the right thing to do.

We also assume that the Board sets taxes according to the following rule:

$$T_i = \frac{\hat{x}}{n} + \frac{\gamma}{2}\{\frac{n-1}{n}(\Delta_i - A_i)^2 - \sum_{j \neq i} \frac{1}{n-2}(\Delta_j - A_i)^2\}$$

where

$$A_i = \frac{1}{n-1} \sum_{j \neq i} \Delta_j = \frac{1}{n-1}(\hat{x} - \Delta_i)$$

and γ is some positive number. Let's make a few remarks about T_i. First, the $\hat{x}/n$, which represents an equal share of the cost of $\hat{x}$, could be generalized to an arbitrary fixed tax share. That is, $1/n$ could be replaced with a fixed t_i, as long as

$$\sum_{i=1}^{n} t_i = 1$$

and i's total tax would then be viewed as a fixed share of the expenditure on the public good, $t_i \hat{x}$, plus an adjustment factor. Second, the term A_i is the mean of the $n - 1$ other people's desired increments, and it therefore does not depend on Δ_i, providing Δ_j does not depend on Δ_i, for $j \neq i$. Similarly, the term

$$\sum_{j \neq i} \frac{1}{n-2} (\Delta_j - A_i)^2$$

does not depend on Δ_i, if Δ_j does not depend on Δ_i.

With the specification of the rules for finding $\hat{x}$ and T_i, we have completely described the Board's behavior. Now let's turn to i's behavior.

We assume, as usual, that i wants to maximize his after tax utility, or, equivalently, $v_i(\hat{x}) - T_i$. He chooses a Δ_i to do this. And we assume that, in finding the solution to his maximization problem, i takes Δ_j as given and fixed for all $j \neq i$.

That is, i acts as if his Δ_i has no influence on the other Δ_j's; he assumes that his message to the Board has no effect on anyone else's message to the Board. This type of assumption, called a Cournot-Nash assumption, has a long history in duopoly and oligopoly theory, dating back to M. A. Cournot in 1838, and a necessarily shorter history in game theory, dating back to J. F. Nash in 1950. We shall discuss its significance and realism a little later. For now, however, we continue with i's maximization problem.

Person i chooses Δ_i to maximize

$$v_i(\Delta_i + \sum_{j \neq i} \Delta_j) - T_i$$

or

$$v_i(\Delta_i + \sum_{j \neq i} \Delta_j) - \frac{1}{n}(\Delta_i + \sum_{j \neq i} \Delta_i) - \frac{\gamma}{2}\{\frac{n-1}{n}(\Delta_i - A_i)^2$$

$$- \sum_{j \neq i} \frac{1}{n-2} (\Delta_j - A_i)^2\}$$

Under the Cournot-Nash assumption, as far as i is concerned the only variable here is Δ_i. It follows that simple calculus can be used to derive a maximization formula. That maximization condition is:

$$v_i'(\Delta_i + \sum_{j \neq i} \Delta_j) - \frac{1}{n} - \frac{\gamma(n-1)}{n}(\Delta_i - A_i) = 0$$

or

$$v_i'(\Delta_i + \sum_{j \neq i} \Delta_j) = \frac{1}{n} + \frac{\gamma(n-1)}{n}(\Delta_i - A_i)$$

So i chooses a Δ_i to satisfy the above equation.

Now we turn to the definition of an equilibrium in the Groves-Ledyard scheme. As we indicated above, the whole business can work only if all the Δ_i messages are mutually consistent. That is, it must be the case that Δ_1 maximizes $v_1(\hat{x}) - T_1$, or satisfies 1's maximization equation, given Δ_2, $\Delta_3, \ldots, \Delta_n$. And it must be the case that Δ_2 maximizes $v_2(\hat{x}) - T_2$, or satisfies 2's maximization equation, given $\Delta_1, \Delta_3 \ldots, \Delta_n$. And so on, down through person n. That is, a *Groves-Ledyard equilibrium* is a list of increments $(\Delta_1, \Delta_2, \ldots, \Delta_n)$ and a level of output

$$\hat{x} = \sum_{i=1}^{n} \Delta_i$$

such that, for all i, Δ_i maximizes person i's after tax utility, given Δ_1, Δ_2, $\ldots, \Delta_{i-1}, \Delta_{i+1}, \ldots, \Delta_n$.

What are the properties of such an equilibrium? First, $\hat{x}$ satisfies the Samuelson condition. To see that this is the case, we sum the n maximization equations of people 1 through n.

$$\sum_{i=1}^{n} v_i'(\Delta_i + \sum_{j \neq i} \Delta_j) = \sum_{i=1}^{n} [\frac{1}{n} + \frac{\gamma(n-1)}{n}(\Delta_i - A_i)]$$

This gives

$$\sum_{i=1}^{n} v_i'(\hat{x}) = 1 + \frac{\gamma(n-1)}{n} \sum_{i=1}^{n} (\Delta_i - A_i) = 1 + 0 = 1$$

Consequently, $\hat{x}$ is the optimal output for the public good.

Second, the Groves-Ledyard tax scheme produces no embarrassing and problematic budget surplus. If $(\hat{x} - \Delta_i)/(n - 1)$ is substituted for A_i in the definition of T_i, one or two pages of unpleasant and unsubtle algebra will produce the following result:

$$T_i = \frac{\hat{x}}{n} + \frac{\gamma}{2n(n-2)}[n^2\Delta_i^2 - n \sum_{j=1}^{n} \Delta_j^2 + 2\hat{x}^2 - 2n\hat{x}\Delta_i]$$

If we then sum all the T_i's we get:

$$\sum_{i=1}^{n} T_i = \sum_{i=1}^{n} \frac{\hat{x}}{n} + \frac{\gamma}{2n(n-2)} [0] = \hat{x}$$

The Groves-Ledyard scheme collects just enough taxes to finance the public expenditure, no more and no less. This is its principle advantage over the demand revealing scheme.

Now let's return to the equilibrium concept used in this scheme, and its connection to the Cournot-Nash assumption. In the Groves-Ledyard equilibrium, each person is maximizing his own utility, contingent on what the other people are doing. We assumed above that when i maximizes $v_i(\hat{x}) - T_i$ he takes the Δ_j's as fixed. What if there is one person who doesn't do this, one person who is more sophisticated than the rest?

To be more specific, let's see what happens if person 1 knows that persons 2 through n choose their Δ_j's in the Cournot-Nash way. That is, person 1 knows that person i, for $i \neq 1$, chooses Δ_i to maximize $v_i(\hat{x}) - T_i$ taking the other Δ_j's as fixed. Then person 1 knows how Δ_1 affects person i's decision, for $i \neq 1$; person 1 knows how $\Delta_2, \Delta_3, \ldots, \Delta_n$ depend on Δ_1. If he chooses to exploit this knowledge, person 1's maximization problem changes its character, and in particular, 1's utility maximizing Δ_1 *no longer* satisfies the equation

$$v_1'(\Delta_1 + \sum_{j \neq 1} \Delta_j) = \frac{1}{n} + \frac{\gamma(n-1)}{n}(\Delta_1 - A_1)$$

A new and different equilibrium arises.

This new and different equilibrium results from a kind of "strategic" behavior on 1's part. Person 1 is not lying about Δ_1, but he is playing the game cleverly, while 2 through n are still playing it naively. What are the properties of the new equilibrium? It is still the case that

$$\sum_{i=1}^{n} T_i = \hat{x};$$

there is still no embarassing budget surplus. However, since 1's old maximization equation no longer obtains, it is no longer necessarily true that

$$\sum_{i=1}^{n} v_i'(\hat{x}) = 1$$

That is, the Samuelson condition will generally no longer hold, and $\hat{x}$ will no longer be an optimal output for the public good.

This then is another serious disadvantage of the Groves-Ledyard scheme. If one person behaves strategically, in the sense that he exploits his knowledge of how his Δ_i affects the other Δ_j's, then optimality will generally fail. Things are even worse if several people behave or attempt to behave strategically. For if person 1 tries to exploit his knowledge of how Δ_1 will affect Δ_2, and simultaneously person 2 tries to exploit his knowledge of how Δ_2 will affect Δ_1, the model breaks down. What persons 1 and 2 try to do becomes hopelessly confused. Even if they (and we) discern sensible rules to follow in setting Δ_1 and Δ_2, there may be no equilibrium of any sort. Even if there is some kind of equilibrium, there is no reason to believe it will involve an optimal $\hat{x}$. In short, if several people behave strategically, if several people attempt to exploit their knowledge of how their own Δ_i's affect other people's Δ_j's, that is, if there are several people who don't behave the way the Cournot-Nash assumption says they behave, then the Groves-Ledyard scheme is thrown into disarray.

To sum up, the Groves-Ledyard scheme will produce an optimal $\hat{x}$ and no surplus, providing all goes well, and, in particular, providing everyone acts as if his own desired increment Δ_i has no impact on other people's desired increments. But, like the Wicksell-Lindahl, the demand-revealing, and the fixed tax shares majority voting schemes, this scheme has some serious flaws.

SELECTED REFERENCES

(Items marked with an asterisk (*) are mathematically difficult.)

1. E. H. Clarke, "Multipart Pricing of Public Goods," *Public Choice*, V. 11, 1971, pp. 17–33.

    This paper is one of the seminal papers on the demand-revealing tax scheme. Clark develops a "two-part tariff" to finance the provision of a public good; it is made up of a "fixed charge" (or an assigned cost share times the cost of the public good) plus a "variable charge" that depends on the difference between the individual's desired output and the actual output of the good. The scheme has three virtues: each individual is induced to reveal his correct demand schedule, an optimal output of the public good is chosen, and tax revenues equal or exceed the cost of the public good.

    The analysis is mostly graphical and verbal, with little mathematics.

*2. J. Green and J-J. Laffont, "Characterization of Satisfactory Mechanisms for the Revelation of Preferences for Public Goods," *Econometrica*, V. 45, 1977, pp. 427–438.

    Green and Laffont extend the analysis of Groves and Loeb, that is, the analysis of demand-revealing mechanisms. Those mechanisms have the virtues that (1) truth is a dominant strategy for every individual and (2) that Pareto optimal levels of output of the public goods are always chosen. Green and Laffont show that any mechanism with these two properties must be a generalized Groves and Loeb mechanism.

3. T. Groves, "Information, Incentives, and the Internalization of Production Externalities," reprinted in S. A. Y. Lin, ed., *Theory and Measurement of Economic Externalities,* Academic Press, New York, 1976, pp. 65–86.

   This paper has a model of production externalities which are remedied by a demand-revealing tax scheme. Each of *n* firms creates external effects for the others, and each firm sends a message to a coordinating center that indicates how its profits depend on all the externalities. The center wants to coordinate the activities of the firms to maximize total profits (the analog of the Samuelson condition for a public good), and it taxes and transfers money among the firms to elicit truthful messages.

*4. T. Groves and J. Ledyard, "Optimal Allocation of Public Goods: A Solution to the 'Free Rider' Problem," *Econometrica,* V. 45, 1977, pp. 783–809.

   This is a rigorous and difficult paper that uses a general equilibrium model, with many private goods, many public goods, private firms, private markets, and a government. Section 3 of the paper analyzes the demand-revealing process in the formal general equilibrium model, and a version of the First Fundamental Theorem of Welfare Economics. Section 4 of the paper develops the model of what Groves and Ledyard call an "Optimal, Unbiased Government," or what is now called the Groves-Ledyard system. In it each individual's message to the government is interpreted as the increment of each public good the individual would like added to (or subtracted from) the total. Groves and Ledyard rigorously prove the two fundamental theorems for the optimal, unbiased government. The first establishes that a Groves-Ledyard equilibrium is Pareto optimal (and, in particular, optimal outputs of public goods are achieved and there is no government budget surplus).

   In Section 5, the paper provides a survey of some of the important theoretical literature on the free rider problem.

5. T. Groves and J. Ledyard, "Some Limitations of Demand Revealing Processes," *Public Choice,* V. XXIX-2, 1977, pp. 107–124.

   This clear and well-written article lists five drawbacks of demand-revealing tax schemes: (1) the problem of the budget surplus, (2) the possibility that an individual's tax might exceed his initial endowment and therefore bankrupt him, (3) the problem of dynamic instability of the scheme if utility functions are not separable, (4) the problem of strategic, nontruthful, behavior if utility functions are not separable, and (5) the problem of strategic behavior by coalitions. At the very end of the paper Groves and Ledyard sketch their own mechanism.

6. T. Groves and M. Loeb, "Incentives and Public Inputs," *Journal of Public Economics,* V. 4, 1975, pp. 211–226.

   This clearly written article analyzes a model of a group of firms that use a public good input. Groves and Loeb provide a demand-revealing scheme in which a Center coordinates the activities of the firms. The scheme (1) always induces firms to reveal their true demands for the input, and (2) leads to a joint profit maximum for the firms.

*7. L. Hurwicz, "On the Existence of Allocation Systems Whose Manipulative Nash Equilibria are Pareto-Optimal," unpubished paper, 1975.

This paper provides the theorem (Part A, Theorem 4) that says there is no mechanism for which (1) truth is always a dominant strategy for everyone and (2) the outcome is always Pareto optimal (and in particular there is no "budget surplus"). (See Reference 4 above, p. 795.)

8. E. Lindahl, "Just Taxation — A Positive Solution," ("Die Gerechtigkeit der Besteuerung," Lund, 1919), translated and reprinted in R. A. Musgrave and A. J. Peacock, eds., *Classics in the Theory of Public Finance,* MacMillan and Co., New York, 1958.

This extremely important article is about the distribution of the total cost of the collective goods between two categories of taxpayers, and about the appropriate extent of collective activity. The tax scheme Lindahl develops is one in which each type of taxpayer is assigned a certain fraction of the total cost, and given their assigned fractions, the two types of taxpayers agree on the appropriate extent of collective activity. It follows that the tax shares are linked to the taxpayers' valuations of the public services.

9. R. A. Musgrave and A. T. Peacock, *Classics in the Theory of Public Finance,* MacMillan and Co., New York, 1958.

In addition to providing translations of Lindahl and Wicksell, this volume has interesting classic essays in taxation and public goods by E. Barone, F. Y. Edgeworth, E. Sax, A. Wagner and other European authors. The introductory chapter by Musgrave and Peacock connects the principal contributions to the theory of public finance, starting with those of Adam Smith and ending with the ones made in the 1920's.

10. P. A. Samuelson, "The Pure Theory of Public Expenditure," *Review of Economics and Statistics,* V. 36, 1954, pp. 387–389.

This seminal paper provides a formal optimality condition for the provision of public goods — now known as the Samuelson condition. Samuelson also raises the free rider problem, which he views as insurmountable in a decentralized economic system: "*No decentralized pricing system can serve to determine optimally these levels of collective consumption.* Other kinds of "voting" or "signalling" would have to be tried. But, and this is the point sensed by Wicksell but perhaps not fully appreciated by Lindahl, now it is in the selfish interest of each person to give *false* signals, to pretend to have less interest in a given collective consumption activity than he really has, etc." (His italics.)

11. T. Nicolaus Tideman, ed., *Public Choice,* V. XXIX-2, Special Supplement to Spring, 1977.

This entire special issue of *Public Choice* is devoted to the demand-revealing and Groves-Ledyard mechanisms. Tideman's introduction is good and provides a useful bibliography. The issue includes articles by Clark, Green and Laffont, Groves and Ledyard, Loeb, Tideman, Tullock, and others.

12. W. Vickrey, "Counterspeculation, Auctions, and Competitive Sealed Tenders," *Journal of Finance,* V. 16, 1961, pp. 8–37.

Vickrey's early paper develops a mechanism to be used by a government agency that deals with monopolistic sellers and buyers. The mechanism is designed to elicit truthful information from the monopolists, and to bring about an optimal consumption and production equilibrium.

13. K. Wicksell, "A New Principle of Just Taxation," (Ein Neues Prinzip der Gerechten Besteuerung," Jena 1896), translated and reprinted in R. A. Musgrave and A. J. Peacock, eds., *Classics in the Theory of Public Finance,* MacMillan and Co., New York, 1958.

Wicksell's seminal essay argues for the principle of taxation according to benefit, to replace the principle of taxation according to ability to pay. There are two reasons to prefer taxation according to benefit: First, it allows the taxing authorities to find an appropriate extent of public expenditures. If people are taxed according to their ability to pay, the tax authorities get no information about the usefulness of public expenditures from those who are presumably "consuming" the public expenditures, namely, the taxpayers. If people are taxed according to benefit, then the tax authorities must gather some information about the usefulness of public expenditures, they must connect benefits and taxes, and this connection should lead to an appropriate level of expenditures.

Second, it is just to tax according to benefit. In fact, the greatest injustice of taxation is forcing someone to pay a tax to finance an activity which provides him no benefit, which he might actually disapprove.

Wicksell is led by this principle to the espousal of a system in which public activities, and the particular distribution of taxes used to finance them, must be approved by unanimous consent.

7 COMPENSATION CRITERIA

INTRODUCTION

We now put aside the questions of the last two chapters, about reconciling external effects and public goods with the market system, and return to the basics, the two fundamental theorems of welfare economics. The First Fundamental Theorem says, roughly, that the market mechanism leads to a Pareto optimum, barring externality or public goods complications. The Second Fundamental Theorem says, roughly, that any Pareto optimum can be reached via an appropriately modified market mechanism, e.g., in the case of an exchange economy, the right lump sum cash transfers will allow us to get to any optimum we want.

But this second theorem raises a profound question: How is the particular Pareto optimum that the theorem says we can reach to be chosen? That is, how should society choose between two Pareto optimal arrangements? Or, more generally, how should society choose between any two economic arrangements, or, in the case of an exchange economy, any two allocations?

This raises the issue touched on in Chapter 1: Are there social preferences distinct from individual preferences? We are quite comfortable with the idea that any single person has tastes, or a utility function, or a preference

138

relation R_i, any of which can indicate when x is better than y, for that person. We are comfortable with the idea that person i's preference relation R_i is complete, which means that he can always decide when x is better than y or y is better than x or they are equally good. We are comfortable with the idea that R_i is transitive. If person i likes x at least as well as y and y at least as well as z, then he likes x at least as well as z. Can the idea of a preference relation, or better, a complete preference relation, or best, a complete and transitive preference relation, be transplanted from the analysis of individual choice to the analysis of social choice? Does a group of people have a reasonable preference relation? Or is it nonsensical to attribute the characteristics of an individual to a collection of individuals?

Let's return to the Second Fundamental Theorem. It says that if the Pareto optimal allocation y is desired by society, then there are cash transfers that will, with the market mechanism, get society to y. But why y rather than x? Does society have a preference for y over x? What does this mean? The Second Fundamental Theorem of Welfare Economics raises these questions, but provides no answers. That is, the market mechanism provides no guide as to whether one Pareto optimal arrangement x is better or worse than another Pareto optimal arrangement y. In fact, it often provides no guide for the choice between x and y even if one or both is not Pareto optimal.

There are then economic questions, questions about the distribution of goods and services, that the competitive market mechanism does not answer. This chapter and the ones that follow are about attempts to answer these questions. In particular, this chapter is about economists' standard answers to the question of when one arrangement (or allocation) is better for society than another.

The question is obviously one with lots of practical ramifications. Government officials are often faced with the choice between x and y. Occasionally they consult with economists about the choice. For example, the choice might be to reduce tariffs on imported goods, or to leave them the way they are. What guidance can an economist provide? Or the choice might be to impose a special excise tax on crude oil (or a windfall-profits tax in 1979 jargon) or not to impose that tax. Can economists offer some suggestions? Or the choice might be to allow more timber harvesting on government land, or not to allow it, or to build a highway, or not to build it, and so on, almost ad infinitum. Naturally lots of these questions have a public goods character, and partial answers can be found in the previous chapter, in particular answers about the optimal extent of public expenditure and appropriate tax mechanisms. But often the questions are of the type "Is x better for society than y?" It is this particular type of question on which we focus.

NOTATIONAL PRELIMINARIES

In this chapter we shall discuss social alternatives, labelled x,y,z, etc., which might be allocations in an exchange economy, or which might be more general arrangements, like combined allocation-production plans. Or they might be simple mutually exclusive possibilities, like "build a road" or "don't build the road."

We shall lean heavily on the symbols of Chapter 1. R_i is person i's preference relation, so xR_iy means i likes x as well as i. P_i is the associated strict preference relations, and I_i is the associated indifference relation. Also, u_i is person i's utility function. We allow for external effects; so u_i is a function of x, rather than, say, x_i. Note that the symbol P will have a special meaning in this chapter, different from the meaning in Chapter 1.

THE PARETO CRITERION

Our definition of Pareto optimality for an exchange economy, and our definition of optimality in the provision of public goods, both reduce to this: If there is an alternative y that is feasible, that everyone likes as well as x and someone likes better, then x isn't optimal.

This suggests one obvious answer to the question, "When is x better for society than y?" Here is the formal definition of the Pareto criterion:

Let x and y be two alternatives. Then x is *Pareto superior* to y, which we write xPy, if

xR_iy for all individuals, and
xP_iy for at least one individual i.

So x is Pareto superior to y if all like x as well as y, and some people actually prefer x to y. We can easily illustrate the Pareto criterion in an Edgeworth box diagram.

In Figure 7-1, both people prefer allocation x to allocation y. Consequently, x is Pareto superior to y, or xPy. There is no ambiguity about x's being better for society than y. But it is not the case that xPz, and it is not the case that zPx. Should we then say that x and z are indifferent according to the Pareto criterion? Well, we don't. We just say that they are noncomparable.

What about y and z? Are they Pareto comparable? Is it the case that z is Pareto superior to y, or that y is Pareto superior to z? The answer to both questions is No. Person 1 prefers y to z, but person 2 prefers z to y. Whenever the interests of two people are opposed like this, neither yPz nor zPy can be true.

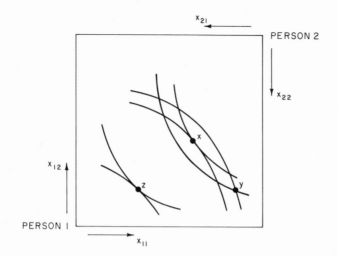

FIGURE 7-1

At this point, it is useful to be a little bit more precise about the parallel between the Pareto criterion P and an individual's preference relation R_i. The reader should first observe that P is analogous to a strict preference relation, a P_i for an individual. When we say xPy we mean x is Pareto better than y, and we don't mean that x and y might be equally good. When we need a Pareto relation analogous to a weak preference relation R_i, we define it this way.

Let x and y be two alternatives. Then x is *Pareto as-good-as y* if xR_iy for all i. From the Pareto as-good-as relation we can retrieve the Pareto superior relation P: x is Pareto superior to y, or xPy, if x is Pareto as-good-as y and y is not Pareto as-good-as x. For if x is Pareto as-good-as y, then xR_iy for all i. And if y is not Pareto as-good-as x, then for at least one i, not yR_ix, and since we assume all individuals' preference relations are complete, not yR_ix for at least one i implies xP_iy for at least one i.

The Pareto as-good-as relation is analogous to an individuals' R_i, while the Pareto superior relation is analogous to an individual's P_i. We saw in Figure 7-1 that x and z were Pareto noncomparable in the sense that neither xPz nor zPx was true. This noncomparability is still with us when we use the weaker Pareto as-good-as relation. It is not the case that x is Pareto as-good-as z, nor is it the case that z is Pareto as-good-as x. In short, the possibility of Pareto noncomparability means the Pareto as-good-as relation is not complete. And this makes it distinctly different from an individual's R_i relation.

We saw in Chapter 1 that completeness for a preference relation is crucial for the process of choice. Completeness is needed for the existence of best alternatives, for the nonemptiness of choice sets. This is true for social preference relations as well as for individual preference relations. And the lack of completeness, the pervasive problem of Pareto noncomparability, it is the fundamental drawback of the Pareto criterion.

In Figure 7-1, most of the interesting allocations are Pareto noncomparable. In practical situations, it is rarely the case that the social choice is between an alternative x and an alternative y, such that everyone likes x as well as y. The Pareto criterion can rarely be used. So economists have developed other criteria to decide when one alternative is socially preferable to another.

THE KALDOR CRITERION

To illustrate the next criterion we first construct a model that is a little more abstract than our exchange, production, and public goods models.

The usual models of an economy allow for the possibility of movement from any social state (e.g. allocation) to any other social state (e.g. allocation). Often, however, the policy maker is faced with a choice between two alternatives which are mutually exclusive—if he chooses the left fork of the road he will never be permitted the possibilities down the right fork. Some states are simply not accessible from other states.

For example, suppose the choice is to build a major road from point A to B, or not to build it. If it is built, and financed in a particular way, we have one alternative, say x. But there are many ways to finance the road, and there are many ways to transfer goods among individuals, given that the road is built. That is, given the road, or given x, there are lots of alternatives that are accessible from x, lots of distribution of goods among people contingent on the road's being built. We let $S(x)$ be the set of alternatives accessible from x. On the other hand, if the road is not built, and a particular distribution of goods holds, we have another alternative, say y. But there are many ways that the goods under y might be redistributed among individuals, or otherwise moved around; that is, given no road, there are lots of alternatives accessible from y. We let $S(y)$ be the set of alternatives accessible from y.

(As a matter of common sense it is surely the case that building the road, or x itself, is accessible from y, although y, the no-road situation, might not be accessible from x since it costs real resources to tear up a previously built road. We certainly allow that x might be $S(y)$. If the choice is to have a tariff or not to have a tariff, then it might well be the case that x is in $S(y)$ and y is in $S(x)$.)

Now we turn to the social improvement criterion devised by Nicholas Kaldor and John Hicks. Formally, we say that x is *Kaldor superior* to y, or xKy, if there exists a z in $S(x)$ such that zPy. That is, there must be a state accessible from x, which is Pareto superior to y. The existence of such a state allows for the theoretical possibility of everyone's being made better off after x is chosen, although there is no assurance that this would in fact happen.

Suppose in our road/no-road example that xKy. This means that once the road is built (path x is chosen) there exists some tax/subsidy or compensation scheme, based on x, which would produce a z that is Pareto superior to the no-road situation y. Once the road is built, in other words, the people who gained from the construction of the road could potentially transfer goods to the people who lost from the construction of the road, so that nobody ends up worse off than before the road was built.

To illustrate the Kaldor criterion graphically, it is convenient to construct what are called utility frontiers. Given an alternative z in $S(x)$, there is a utility level $u_i(z)$ for each person i, and therefore, a utility vector that depends on z, $u(z) = (u_1(z), u_2(z), \ldots, u_n(z))$. So the set of alternatives $S(x)$ generates a set of utility vectors which we shall call $U(x)$. If there are just two people, the set of utility vectors $U(x)$ can be represented by an area in a graph that shows person 1's utility u_1 on the horizontal axis and person 2's utility u_2 on the vertical axis. The northeast frontier of that area is called the *utility frontier for x*.

In Figure 7–2, $U(x)$ is the shaded area, and the utility frontier for x is labelled. The particular vector of utilities $u(x) = (u_1(x), u_2(x))$ that cor-

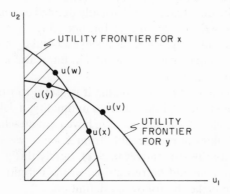

FIGURE 7–2

responds to alternative x (build the road) lies on the frontier, as does another particular vector of utilities $u(w) = (u_1(w), u_2(w))$. The alternative w is in $S(x)$, that is, it's an alternative that comes about when the road is built and a certain tax/subsidy scheme, or compensation scheme, is instituted. Clearly, person 2 likes alternative w better than alternative x, so the move from x to w involves person 1 compensating person 2 in some fashion. The utility frontier for y (don't build the road) is also labelled in the figure, and the vector of utilities $u(y) = (u_1(y), u_2(y))$ lies on the frontier for y, as does the vector of utilities for another alternative v, accessible from y.

In terms of Figure 7–2, what is Kaldor superior to what? Given alternative x (build the road), it is possible to get to alternative w. But both people prefer alternative w to alternative y; that is, $u_1(w) > u_1(y)$ and $u_2(w) > u_2(y)$. So w is Pareto superior to y. Consequently, x is Kaldor superior to y.

On the other hand, given alternative y (no road), it is possible to get to alternative v. But both people prefer alternative v to alternative x; that is, $u_1(v) > u_1(x)$ and $u_2(v) > u_2(x)$. So v is Pareto superior to x. Consequently, y is Kaldor superior to x.

In short, xKy but also yKx. That is, the criterion is inconsistent.

As it stands, Kaldor's method is an imperfect guide to social policy. In this case, at least, it says: "Build the road — but also, don't build it." This possibility of Kaldor inconsistency leads us to the next compensation criterion.

THE SCITOVSKY CRITERION

Tibor Scitovsky devised a social improvement criterion which necessarily avoids Kaldor's inconsistency. It is formally defined as follows: x is *Scitovsky superior* to y, written xSy, if xKy but not yKx.

Since it must avoid nonsensical results like "build it and don't build it," Scitovsky's criterion improves upon Kaldor's. But it also has a logical shortcoming, to which we now turn.

In order to highlight this shortcoming it is useful to first provide a new and slightly different definition of Pareto optimality, a definition that conforms with the model of this chapter. We have been attaching to each alternative x a set of states $S(x)$ accessible from x. Once we are at x, the only feasible options are the alternatives in $S(x)$. Surely this possibly restrictive feasibility condition should be recognized in the definition of optimality. Consequently, we make the following definition:

A social state x is *Pareto optimal* is there is no y in $S(x)$, that is, no y accessible from x, such that yPx.

Now let's consider what happens to the Scitovsky relation when, as in an exchange economy model, all states are accessible from each other. (When we say that all states are accessible from each other, or mutually accessible, we mean that if z is in $S(x)$ then z is also in $S(y)$, for all x, y and z.)

Proposition 1. Suppose all states are mutually accessible. Then xSy if and only if x is Pareto optimal and y is not.

Proof. Let xSy. Then xKy and not yKx. Since xKy, there exists a z accessible from x and therefore from y such that zPy. Therefore, y is not Pareto optimal. If x were not Pareto optimal, there would be a w, accessible from x and hence from y, such that wPx, which would contradict not yKx. Therefore, x is Pareto optimal.

Now suppose x is Pareto optimal and y is not. Since x is Pareto optimal, there is no z accessible from x or y with zPx. Therefore, not yKx. Since y is not, there is a w, accessible from y and hence from x, such that wPy. Therefore, xKy.

Q.E.D.

The following result is also obvious.

Proposition 2. Suppose all states are mutually accessible. Then xKy if and only if y is not Pareto optimal.

Evidently, at least in the case where all states can be reached from each other, the Scitovsky criterion does not yield any information beyond what is inherent in the notion of Pareto optimality. This is its logical shortcoming.

THE SAMUELSON CRITERION

We now turn to a compensation criterion developed by Paul Samuelson. The intuition of Samuelson's criterion is very clear, even if the formal definition isn't. We'll write down the formal definition first and then turn quickly to a diagram to see the intuition.

Formally, x is *Samuelson superior* to y, which we shall write xNy, if the following is true: For any z in $S(y)$, xKz.

To put it another way, x is Samuelson superior to y if, for any z accessible from y, there is a w accessible from x that is Pareto superior to z.

In terms of a utility frontier diagram for two individuals, for x to be Samuelson superior to y the utility frontier for x must lie to the northeast of the utility frontier for y. Figure 7-3 illustrates this criterion.

In the figure, the utility frontier for x lies outside the utility frontier for y. Consequently, for any alternative z accessible from y, there is a w accessible from x that provides at least one person with a higher utility level than z,

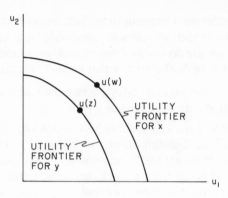

FIGURE 7-3

and neither with a lower level of utility. That is, the utility vector $u(w)$ lies to the northeast of the utility vector $u(z)$. No matter what you do, starting from y, you could do better, if you started from x.

The diagram should make it obvious that the Samuelson criterion cannot be inconsistent: it is impossible to have xNy and yNx.

However, like the Kaldor and Scitovsky criteria, the Samuelson criterion has a shortcoming when all states are mutually accessible. If all alternatives are mutually accessible, there is really only one set of feasible alternatives — the set of all alternatives — and there is only one set of possible utility vectors. Consequently, the utility frontier is unique. (It is possible to construct odd mathematical examples where there are no utility frontiers, where $U(x)$ does not have a boundary or include its boundary; however, we won't worry here about those peculiar cases.) Now if there is only one utility frontier, a brief examination of Figure 7-3 should convince the reader that xNy can never occur.

More formally, suppose the set of possible utility vectors is unique and includes its frontier. Let y be any alternative. Find a z (necessarily accessible from y) on the utility frontier — a z such that there are no feasible utility vectors to the northeast of $u(z)$. Then xNy is clearly impossible, for any x, since xKy is impossible.

In short, if all alternatives are mutually accessible, the Samuelson criterion is entirely devoid of content. No state is Samuelson superior to any other.

Before ending this discussion we ought to briefly comment on the idea that all states are mutually accessible.

In one sense, this idea is obviously wrong. Once a road has been built, real resources have gone into it, and there is no way to recapture what might have been had the road not been built. So in this sense, our criticisms of the compensation criteria of Scitovsky and Samuelson are unfair.

However, in another sense, the idea is quite plausible. For these criteria are meant to be used by decision makers before decisions are made; before the roads, for example, are built. Before the crucial decisions are made, paths are not closed, and everything is possible. Even if the policymaker is contemplating a decision with irrevocable effects, everything remains accessible as long as he is just contemplating. So in this sense, our criticisms of the Scitovsky and Samuelson compensation criteria should be taken seriously.

EXERCISES

1. The cost-benefit criterion is a widely-used tool of policymakers, and it derives from the compensation criteria of Kaldor, Scitovsky and Samuelson. To analyze it in a truly simple (and simplistic) way, suppose that there is only one good in the economy, which everyone always wants more of, and suppose an alternative $x = (x_1, x_2, \ldots, x_n)$ is just a distribution or allocation of the one good among the people in the economy. The total amount of the good is

$$\sum_{i=1}^{n} x_i$$

and we shall assume for this problem that this quantity need not be fixed. That is, if y is another alternative, it is possible to have

$$\sum_{i=1}^{n} y_i \neq \sum_{i=1}^{n} x_i$$

The sum

$$\sum_{i=1}^{n} x_i$$

can be regarded as the size of the total pie under x; while x_i is, of course, the size of person i's share of the pie under x.

In this ultra-simple model, the cost-benefit criterion says x is superior to y, which we can write xCy, if the size of the pie under x exceeds the size of the pie under y, i.e., if

$$\sum_{i=1}^{n} x_i > \sum_{i=1}^{n} y_i$$

We can interpret $S(x)$ as the set of possible distribution of a pie of size

$$\sum_{i=1}^{n} x_i$$

Show that the Kaldor criterion, the Scitovsky criterion, the Samuelson criterion, and the cost-benefit criterion are all equivalent in this one-good model. That is, show that xKy implies xSy, that xSy implies xNy, that xNy implies xCy, and that xCy implies xKy.

SELECTED REFERENCES

1. N. Kaldor, "Welfare Propositions of Economics and Interpersonal Comparisons of Utility," *Economic Journal*, V. 49, 1939, pp. 549–552.

    This is a short note about the classical argument for free trade. Kaldor observes that the repeal of the English Corn Laws could be justified on these grounds: it would be possible for the government to compensate landlords for their losses from repeal, leaving everyone better off than before. So repeal is Kaldor superior to non-repeal. In general, welfare economists should be in favor of policies that increase aggregate production, according to Kaldor.

2. P. A. Samuelson, "Evaluation of Real National Income," *The Oxford Economic Papers*, V. 2, 1950, pp. 1–29.

    This paper starts with a discussion of the question "When does an increase in real national income correspond to an increase in social welfare?" Samuelson shows that if relative prices change in a move from situation 1 to situation 2, comparing real national income at the two situations will generally give inconclusive results. This result is a fatal blow for a line of theoretical welfare economics that starts with Pigou and continues through Kaldor, Hicks, and others. (However, theoretical rigor mortis does not imply practical rigor mortis; most of today's economists, including Samuelson, are very much concerned with growth in real national income. And this concern probably makes lots of sense, in spite of negative theoretical results.)

    In the second half of the paper Samuelson analyzes production and utility frontiers (which he calls production and utility possibility functions). He applies the utility frontier analysis to the criteria of Kaldor and Scitovsky, both of which he criticizes. One of his conclusions is that "the only consistent and ethics-free definition of an increase in potential real income of a group is that based upon a uniform shift of the utility possibility function of the group."

3. A. K. Sen, *Collective Choice and Social Welfare*, Holden-Day, Inc., San Francisco, 1970, Chapters 2, 2*.

    Chapter 2 provides a short, clear, intuitive discussion of the Pareto criterion and related approaches. Chapter 2*, which is mathematical in style and notation, has a section on the Kaldor and Scitovsky criteria. Sen criticizes the Scitovsky criterion on the grounds that it might be nontransitive: it is possible to have xSy, ySz, but not xSz.

4. T. Scitovsky, "A Note on Welfare Propositions in Economics," *The Review of Economic Studies*, V. 9, 1941, pp. 77–88.

This careful article elaborates on the criterion of Kaldor (and of J. R. Hicks; see "Foundations of Welfare Economics," *Economic Journal*, V. 49, 1939). Scitovsky expresses his own criterion so clearly that it's worth quoting here:

"We propose, therefore, to make welfare propositions on the following principle. We must first see whether it is possible in the new situation so to redistribute income as to make everybody better off than he was in the initial situation; secondly, we must see whether starting from the initial situation it is not possible by a mere redistribution of income to reach a position superior to the new situation, again from everybody's point of view. If the first is possible and the second impossible, we shall say that the new situation is better than the old was. If the first is impossible but the second possible, we shall say that the new situation is worse; whereas if both are possible or both are impossible, we shall refrain from making a welfare proposition."

8 FAIRNESS AND THE RAWLS CRITERION

INTRODUCTION

The previous chapter described some of the properties and some of the shortcomings of the social improvement criteria of Pareto, Kaldor, Scitovsky and Samuelson. The question of when one alternative ought to be considered socially preferred to another remains largely unresolved. In this chapter we shall examine two new criteria for judging social states, both of which are explicitly egalitarian in their viewpoints. The first is the criterion of fairness, in the sense of non-envy. Under some distributions of goods, no person would prefer any other's bundle of goods to his own. Under other distributions, some people would prefer others' bundles to their own. We call the first kind of distribution "fair" and the second "unfair." Can this distinction be fruitfully used to indicate when one distribution is socially preferable to another? The second is the criterion of justice, developed by John Rawls. According to Rawls, alternative x is more just than alternative y if the worst-off person under x is better off than the worst-off person under y. Does this criterion provide a good basis for judging between alternatives for society?

In the section below on fairness we shall revert to the exchange theory model, and (temporarily) put aside the preference relation approach of the last chapter. This discussion will also abstract from questions of production, although production could be explicitly introduced into the fairness question. The section on the Rawls criterion, however, will mainly be in the style of the last chapter, with abstract alternatives x,y,z that might or might not be allocations of goods in an n-person, m-good exchange economy.

Now let's examine the idea of fairness in more detail, and show how fair allocations are related to competitive equilibrium allocations and Pareto optimal allocations. Then we will discuss the usefulness of the fairness criterion as a guide to which allocations are socially preferable to which.

FAIRNESS

Suppose $x = (x_1, x_2, \ldots, x_n)$ is an allocation of m goods among n people. Assume for simplicity that there are no externalities; so person i's utility depends only on his bundle of goods x_i. If $u_i(x_i) \geq u_i(x_j)$, then i likes his own bundle as well as he would like j's, and we say i does not envy j. If $u_i(x_i) \geq u_i(x_j)$ for every pair of people $\{i,j\}$, we say the allocation x is *fair*. A fair allocation x is illustrated in Figure 8–1.

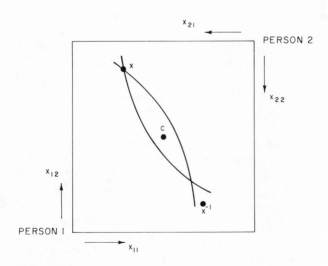

FIGURE 8–1

In this figure, the allocation $x^{-1} = (x_2, x_1)$ reverses the bundles assigned by the allocation $x = (x_1, x_2)$. That is, x^{-1} gives person 1 person 2's bundle, and it gives person 2 person 1's bundle. Geometrically x^{-1} is the mirror image of x through the center of the box. So x, c, and x^{-1} all lie on a straight line, and the distance from x to c equals the distance from x^{-1} to c.

Observe that 1's indifference curve through x passes above the allocation x^{-1}. This means that he prefers x to x^{-1}, and, consequently, $u_1(x_1) > u_1(x_2)$. Similarly, 2's indifference curve through x passes above x^{-1} ("above" in terms of 2's origin). Therefore, $u_2(x_2) > u_2(x_1)$. In short, at x neither individual would prefer the other's bundle to his own, so x is fair. Since x is obviously not Pareto optimal, the picture shows that fair allocations are not generally optimal allocations. The converse is also rather obvious: optimal allocations are not generally fair.

What then are the connections between fairness, on the one hand, and optimality on the other hand? The principal connection is indicated by the following:

Proposition 1. Suppose all people have monotonic selfish utility functions. Let the initial allocation ω be the equal allocation, that is, suppose $\omega_1 = \omega_2 = \ldots = \omega_n$. Suppose $(\hat{x}, p)$ is a competitive equilibrium.

Then $\hat{x}$ is Pareto optimal, and it is fair.

Proof. $\hat{x}$ is Pareto optimal by the First Fundamental Theorem of Welfare Economics. To see that it must be fair, recall from the definition of a competitive equilibrium that $\hat{x}_i$ must maximize $u_i(x_i)$ subject to $p \cdot x_i \leq p \cdot \omega_i$, for all i. However, the righthand side of the inequality is the same for everyone, since ω_i is the same for all i. In short, each person attempts to maximize his utility subject to the same budget constraint. Since this is true, it is impossible for i to end up with a bundle which he finds inferior to j's. Therefore, for all i and j, $u_i(\hat{x}_i) \geq u_i(\hat{x}_j)$, or the allocation $\hat{x}$ is fair.   Q.E.D.

The proposition indicates a way to achieve both Pareto optimality and fairness, at the same time. Start at the equal allocation, and allow a move to a competitive equilibrium allocation, which will be optimal and fair. And consequently, it suggests one way to choose among the Pareto optimal allocations—one way to decide when one Pareto optimal allocation is better than another. The proposition says that there exist allocations that are Pareto optimal and fair. If the choice is between an allocation that is Pareto optimal but not fair, and an allocation that is Pareto optimal and fair, choose the fair one.

Unfortunately, however, if we push the idea of fairness a little, if we pursue some of its implications, if we try to broaden Proposition 1, we start to uncover contradictions and dilemmas. Let's illustrate these difficulties with a few examples.

The first example is a three person, three good exchange economy, in which, for purposes of mathematical simplicity, each person's utility is a linear function of the amounts of the three goods he consumes. All the details are in the following table.

	Utility Function	ω_i	$u_i(\omega_i)$	x_i	$u_i(x_i)$
Person 1	$u_1(x_1) = 3x_{11} + 2x_{12} + x_{13}$	(1,1,1)	6	(3,2/3,0)	10 1/3
Person 2	$u_2(x_2) = 2x_{21} + x_{22} + 3x_{23}$	(1,1,1)	6	(0,0,2)	6
Person 3	$u_3(x_3) = x_{31} + 3x_{32} + 2x_{33}$	(1,1,1)	6	(0,7/3,1)	9

The initial allocation $\omega = (\omega_1, \omega_2, \omega_3)$ is the equal allocation, which must be fair. Although it is not a competitive equilibrium allocation based on ω, the final allocation $x = (x_1, x_2, x_3)$ is in the core. That is, no coalition or group of people can block it. The allocation x is also (necessarily) Pareto optimal. But is x fair? No it is not, since $u_2(x_1) = 6\frac{2}{3} > u_2(x_2) = 6$; that is, 2 envies 1 under x. Consequently, the example shows that even if we start at the equal allocation (the fairest of the fair), a move to the core, rather than to a competitive equilibrium, can destroy fairness.

It is true, of course, that this destruction of fairness, which subverts the spirit of Proposition 1, might be blamed on the nonprice trading in the example. Suppose we try to expand the scope of Proposition 1 by starting at a fair but not equal allocation, and then allow a move to a competitive equilibrium allocation. Is fairness preserved by such a move? The Edgeworth box diagram in Figure 8-2 shows it might not be.

In the figure, person 1's indifference curve through $\omega = (\omega_1, \omega_2)$ passes above the allocation $\omega^{-1} = (\omega_2, \omega_1)$; so he prefers his bundle under ω to person 2's. Similarly, person 2 prefers his own bundle under ω to person 1's. Consequently, ω is fair; neither one envies the other. The point $\hat{x}$ is a competitive equilibrium allocation based on ω. Person 2 prefers his own bundle at $\hat{x}$ to person 1's, since his indifference curve through $\hat{x}$ passes above $\hat{x}^{-1}$. However, person 1's indifference curve through $\hat{x}$ passes below $\hat{x}^{-1}$ and therefore 1 envies 2 at $\hat{x}$. Therefore, $\hat{x}$ is not fair. The move from ω to $\hat{x}$ destroys fairness.

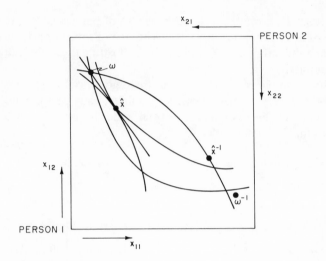

FIGURE 8-2

The first example showed that a move from the equal allocation to the core can destroy fairness. The second example showed that a move from a fair allocation to a competitive equilibrium can destroy fairness. The examples both indicate that the clever idea of Proposition 1 (starting at the equal allocation and allowing the competitive market mechanism to bring the economy to a fair and Pareto optimal allocation) can't be easily broadened. And they also show that fairness will often be destroyed by the usual economic transactions, even transactions that make everyone better off.

This last point should be emphasized. In the three-person, three-good example, the core allocation x is Pareto superior to the initial allocation ω. But ω is fair, while x is not. In the example of Figure 8-2, the competitive equilibrium allocation $\hat{x}$ is Pareto superior to the initial allocation ω. But again, ω is fair, while $\hat{x}$ is not. In both cases, the criterion of fairness is contrary to the Pareto criterion. If the choice is between ω and x in the first example, or between ω and $\hat{x}$ in the second, which is socially preferable to which? Fairness is clearly a poor guide in these cases.

In short, there is considerable tension between fairness as a social improvement criterion and the usual criteria of welfare economics. Few economists would say that fairness is, by itself, a good guide to what alternatives are better than what alternatives. Fewer still would choose fairness over the Pareto criterion when the two criteria disagree.

THE RAWLS CRITERION

No discussion of fairness would be complete without a treatment of the notion of justice developed in the 1960's by the philosopher John Rawls. In this section, we shall give a very brief (and therefore possibly unfair) characterization of Rawls' notion.

Let us imagine that a group of individuals, a society, is choosing among social alternatives, or social states. Now these alternatives, these states, are for Rawls characterized by degrees of liberty as well as by distributions of wealth or goods, but we shall focus only on the distributions of wealth or goods. Let us also suppose that the individuals who are considering the alternative states do not know what positions, what roles, they would occupy in those states. That is, person i might know that in state x there is one millionaire and one pauper, but he does not know whether he would be the millionaire or the pauper. He does not know what position he would occupy. The people in this society are making choices among the states from behind a veil of ignorance.

Now what state would they choose? To illustrate the Rawls criterion with a sensible concrete example, we assume here that there are two people and only one good (say wealth, or income). Let x be a social state in which one person's wealth is $1,000,000 and the other person's wealth is $0. Let y be a social state in which the wealth of both is $1,000. Rawls argues that the social choice between x and y, made from behind a veil of ignorance, ought to be y. Not knowing whether he would be the millionaire or the pauper under x, each person ought to prefer y, because under y each is guaranteed a tolerable level of wealth. That is, the Rawls criterion is to opt for the state that maximizes the utility of the person in the worst position, or to maximize the minimum utility. It is therefore called a *maximin criterion*.

Formally, let $x = (x_1, x_2, \ldots, x_n)$ and $y = (y_1, y_2, \ldots, y_n)$ be distributions of one good among n people.

Here $\sum\limits_{i=1}^{n} x_i$ need not equal $\sum\limits_{i=1}^{n} y_i$

We say x is *Rawls superior* to y, written xRy, if

$$\text{minimum}\{x_1, x_2, \ldots, x_n\} > \text{minimum}\{y_1, y_2, \ldots, y_n\}$$

The use of the symbol R for Rawls superiority is specific to this chapter; this R should not be confused with other social preference relations.

If it should happen that minimum $\{x_1, x_2, \ldots, x_n\}$ equals minimum $\{y_1, y_2, \ldots, y_n\}$, the logical thing to do would be to look at the second smallest of the x_j's and the second smallest of the y_j's. We won't worry too much about this nicety, however; we'll assume that the minimum of the x_j's is different from the minimum of the y_j's.

What are the properties of the Rawls criterion? First, it has clear egalitarian implications. If society is choosing among distributions of a fixed total of wealth, that is, among a set of x's for which

$$\sum_{i=1}^{n} x_i = C$$

and C is a constant, then the single distribution that is Rawls superior to all the others is the equal distribution $(C/n, C/n, \ldots, C/n)$.

Second, if choices are being made from among distributions which don't have fixed totals, the Rawls criterion can be perversely oversolicitous of the worst-off person. For instance, let

$$x = (50,100,150)$$
$$y = (90,90,90)$$
$$z = (80,250,250)$$

Then the Rawls criterion says y is better than x, which is plausible; going from x to y sacrifices some total wealth

$$\left(\sum_{i=1}^{3} x = 300 \text{ while } \sum_{i=1}^{3} y_i = 270 \right)$$

but gains lots of equality. However, the Rawls criterion also says y is better than z, and in this case it sacrifices a great deal of total wealth

$$\left(\sum_{i=1}^{3} z_i = 580 \right)$$

for the sake of some increased equality. In fact, if real people named 1, 2 and 3 were choosing between y and z from behind a veil of ignorance, and if, like most real people, they were willing to take small risks for large potential gains, they would probably choose z, in spite of Rawls' advice.

The reader should note that the criteria of Kaldor, Scitovsky and Samuelson can be easily applied in this simple one good Rawlsian example. The set of states accessible for x, that is $S(x)$, is the set of all possible distributions of the total

$$\sum_{i=1}^{n} x_i$$

$S(y)$ and $S(x)$ are defined analogously. Now according to the Kaldor, Scitovsky and Samuelson criteria, z is better than y, contrary to Rawls. That is, in a move from y to z, the gainers (persons 2 and 3) could easily compensate the loser (person 1), but not vice versa, and the utility frontier based on z lies entirely outside of the utility function for y. So the Rawls criterion is inconsistent with the usual economic compensation criteria, at least in this case.

Third, in a world in which there is more than one good, and in which individuals' tastes differ, the Rawls criterion may be impossible to apply. Suppose, for instance, that x and y are alternative distributions of m goods, where $m > 1$. Define

$$\operatorname*{minimum}_{j} u_i(x_j) = \operatorname{minimum} \{u_i(x_1), u_i(x_2), \ldots, u_i(x_n)\}$$

Now person 1 might feel that

$$\operatorname*{minimum}_{j} u_1(x_j) > \operatorname*{minimum}_{j} u_1(y_j)$$

That is, he might think that the worst that could happen to him under x, if he were assigned to any of the n positions or given any one of the n bundles, is better than the worst that could happen to him under y. However, person 2 might find that

$$\operatorname*{minimum}_{j} u_2(x_j) < \operatorname*{minimum}_{j} u_2(y_j).$$

That is, the worst under y for person 2 might be better than the worst under x. In this case, the two individuals differ about which alternative distribution has a better worst position. If there is disagreement like this behind the veil of ignorance, which distribution should be chosen? The Rawls criterion can't say.

To make this possibility clear, let's construct a simple and slightly silly example. Let x be a distribution that gives each of three people a red hat; let y be a distribution that gives each of the three a blue hat; and let z be a distribution that gives each of the three a green hat. Assume that x, y, and z are identical aside from hats. Suppose person 1 likes red better than blue and blue better than green. Suppose person 2 likes blue better than green and green better than red. Suppose person 3 likes green better than red and red better than blue. Then person 1 will rank the distributions x first, y second, and z third, even from behind a veil of ignorance. Person 2 will rank them y first, z second, and x third, from behind a veil of ignorance, while person 3 will rank them z first, x second, and y third, from behind a veil of ignorance. There is a total disagreement about which alternative is best for the worst-off person!

In sum, the Rawls criterion, like the fairness criterion, doesn't mesh well with the usual economic criteria. Just as the fairness criterion can contradict the more fundamental Pareto criterion, the Rawls criterion can contradict the criteria of Kaldor, Scitovsky and Samuelson. Moreover, the Rawls criterion is based on a maximin test that is probably contradicted by the economic behavior of most people. That is, when faced with the choice between $y = (90, 90, 90)$ and $z = (80, 250, 250)$, most of us would, from behind a veil of ignorance, place our bets on z. This in spite of Rawls' preference for y. Finally, if there are many goods and tastes differ, the Rawls criterion might simply be inapplicable.

For these reasons, the Rawls criterion, like the fairness criterion, cannot be the final answer. The question When is alternative x socially preferable to alternative y? remains open.

EXERCISES

1. a.   For the exchange economy given by

$$u_1 = x_{11}x_{12} \qquad \omega_1 = (1,0)$$
$$u_2 = 2x_{21} + x_{22} \qquad \omega_2 = (0,1)$$

   find an allocation that is both Pareto optimal and fair. (Note: This is the same economy as in Exercise 5, Chapter 3.)

   b.   For this economy, find a specific pair of points x and y such that x is fair and y is not, and y is Pareto superior to x.

2. In an m-goods exchange model, the Rawls criterion can be formulated as follows: For each possible allocation x, each person i calculates

$$\underset{j}{\text{minimum }} u_i(x_j).$$

   This is the lowest utility he can imagine under x, the level he would get if he were assigned what he views as the worst possible bundle under x. Then person i prefers allocation x to allocation y, from behind a veil of ignorance, if

$$\underset{j}{\text{minimum }} u_i(x_j) > \underset{j}{\text{minimum }} u_i(y_j)$$

   If all the individuals prefer x to y from behind a veil of ignorance, the Rawls criterion can be applied without ambiguity.

Now consider an exchange economy in which

$$u_1 = x_{11} + 2x_{12}$$

and

$$u_2 = 2x_{21} + x_{22}$$

Let $x_1 = (\frac{1}{2},\frac{1}{2})$, $x_2 = (\frac{1}{2},\frac{1}{2})$, and let $y_1 = (0,1)$, $y_2 = (1,0)$. What are person 1's behind-a-veil-of-ignorance preferences regarding allocations x and y? Person 2's? Which allocation is Rawls superior to which?

Now remove the veil of ignorance, so person 1 knows he get bundle 1, etc. Which allocation is Pareto superior to which? How does the Rawls criterion compare with the Pareto criterion?

SELECTED REFERENCES

(Items marked with asterick (*) are mathematically difficult.)

1. A. Feldman and A. Kirman, "Fairness and Envy," *American Economic Review,* V. 64, 1974, pp. 995–1005.

    This paper criticizes the notion of fairness, on the grounds that a move that makes everyone better off from a fair allocation might end up at an unfair allocation. That is, the fairness criterion might be contrary to the Pareto criterion. The paper also discusses the question of minimizing the degree of unfairness in an economy, and shows that this minimization problem can also lead to paradoxical results.

2. D. Foley, "Resource Allocation in the Public Sector," *Yale Economic Essays,* V. 7, 1967, pp. 45–98.

    Section IV of Foley's paper is on "equity," and in it he introduces the fairness as non-envy concept used here: "This [discussion about inequality] suggests a new way to define equality even when preferences are diverse: an allocation is equitable if and only if each person in the society prefers his consumption bundle to the consumption bundle of every other person in the society."

3. E. Phelps, "Recent Developments in Welfare Economics: Justice et Equité," Frontiers in Quantitative Economics, Vol. IIIB (M. Intriligator, ed.), North Holland, 1976, pp. 703–730.

    This is a sophisticated survey of many areas in economics, including justice and equity. It covers compensation criteria, Arrow's theorem, utilitarianism, and public finance models, in addition to the idea of fairness as non-envy, and the Rawlsian position.

4. E. Pazner, "Recent Thinking on Economic Justice," *Journal of Peace Science,* V. 2, 1976, pp. 143–154.

This very readable short survey of topics in the theory of fairness starts with a discussion of fair and Pareto optimal allocations in exchange economies, and in economies with production and exchange. Production makes the analysis of fairness a little bit more complicated. Some people are born with very valuable productive resources — e.g., Enrico Caruso, Babe Ruth, Reggie Jackson — and if the ownership of these resources is taxed away in the interest of fairness, productive efficiency may disappear as well. So the idea of fairness may need modification to preserve Proposition 1.

In the second half of the paper, Pazner discusses the idea of *egalitarian equivalence.* There is a very brief but useful bibliographical section at the end of the paper.

5. J. Rawls, "Constitutional Liberty and the Concept of Justice," C. J. Friedrich and J. Chapman, eds., *Justice: Nomos 8,* Atherton Press, New York, 1963.
6. J. Rawls, *A Theory of Justice,* Harvard University Press, Cambridge, 1971.
7. A. K. Sen, *Collective Choice and Social Welfare,* Holden-Day Inc., San Francisco, 1970, Chapter 9.

This is a good discussion of a number of topics related to the Rawls criterion.

8. H. R. Varian, "Equity, Envy and Efficiency," *Journal of Economic Theory* V. 9, 1974, pp. 63–91.

Varian discusses fairness in an economy with production, as well as income fairness, and coalition-fairness.

9 MAJORITY VOTING

INTRODUCTION

In Chapter 7 we saw that the social improvement criteria of Pareto, Kaldor, Scitovsky and Samuelson were all, in one way or another, unsatisfactory. In Chapter 8 we saw that the criterion of fairness is in certain ways inconsistent with other utility-based criteria, and the Rawls criterion has several objectionable properties. Therefore, we are still faced with these questions: When is alternative x socially preferable to alternative y? How can the best social alternatives be chosen from among the good ones? An ancient and obvious mechanism for answering such questions is the mechanism of voting. This chapter examines the majority voting mechanism.

We assume throughout this chapter that person i votes for x over y if he prefers x to y, and abstains if he is indifferent. This type of honest voting precludes, for example, strategically voting for one's second choice over one's first when one knows that, given expected votes by other people, the first choice cannot win. Strategic voting complications will be introduced in a succeeding chapter.

A few words are appropriate at this point about the social alternatives in this chapter and the chapters that follow. These alternatives might be allocations in an exchange economy, with or without externalities. Or they might be production plans, or production and consumption patterns in an economy with production. Or they might be levels of expenditure on a public good. Or they might be political candidates. In short, they might be just about anything that people might choose collectively. They are not, however, states viewed from behind a veil of ignorance, as in Rawls, nor are they whole sets of possibilities, as in Kaldor, Scitovsky and Samuelson. We assume here that people are quite clear about what will happen to them, as individuals, if x obtains rather than y. So it makes good sense to say something like "person i prefers x to y" or "$u_i(x) > u_i(y)$."

THE MAJORITY VOTING CRITERION

If majority rule is applied to a simple choice between two alternatives x and y, then x wins if it gets more votes than y, and they tie if they get the same number of votes. If x wins we say that x is superior to y according to the majority voting criterion, and if they tie we can say that x and y are equally good according to the majority voting criterion. We combine these two ideas with the following definition: x is as good as y according to the *majority voting criterion* if x gets at least as many votes as y. If x is as good as y according to the majority voting criterion, that is, if x beats or ties y, we write xMy. Note that the relation M, which allows social indifference, is analogous to an individual's R_i relation, rather than an individual's P_i relation.

The relation M has two cardinal virtues. First, unlike the Pareto criterion, it is always capable of judging between two alternatives. Formally, it is complete. For any two alternatives x and y, either xMy or yMx. That is for any x and y, either x beats y, or y beats x, or they tie.

Second, unlike the fairness criterion and the Rawls criterion, M is consistent with the Pareto criterion. If x is Pareto superior to y, then x must win a majority over y, which means xMy and not yMx. For if x is Pareto superior to y, some people will vote for x over y (those for whom $u_i(x) > u_i(y)$) and the rest will abstain. No one will vote for y over x.

What are M's vices? Its fundamental logical flaw, already revealed in Chapter 1, is its nontransitivity. Recall that in Chapter 1 we assumed an individual's preference relation R_i is complete and transitive. We made this assumption for two reasons: first, it is consistent with empirical research and with simple day-to-day observation; and second, if a person has complete and transitive preferences he can always make choices, according to Proposition 2 in Chapter 1. We saw in Proposition 3 in Chapter 1 that the transitivity assumption could be weakened to acyclicity without disastrous effect: if a person has complete and acyclic preferences he can always make choices. And we saw, in Proposition 5 in Chapter 1, that completeness and transitivity for a person's preferences implied the existence of a utility function for that person. In short, completeness and transitivity, or at least completeness and acyclicity, make rational choice possible for an individual. If rational choice through the use of majority rule is to be possible for society, then M had better be complete and transitive, or at least complete and acyclic. We know M is complete. Is it transitive? Or is it at least acyclic?

Unfortunately, the answer to both questions is No. This has been known at least since the time of Marie Jean Antoine Nicolas Caritat, the Marquis de Condorcet, who provide examples of voting paradoxes in his *Essai sur l'Application de l'Analyse à la Probabilité des Decisions Rendues à la Pluralité des Voix,* in 1785. The following example of a Condorcet voting paradox, which was introduced in Chapter 1, involves three people, and three alternatives $\{x,y,z\}$. Suppose the preferences of the three are as follows:

$$u_1(x) > u_1(y) > u_1(z)$$
$$u_2(y) > u_2(z) > u_2(x)$$
$$u_3(z) > u_3(x) > u_3(y)$$

In a vote between x and y, persons 1 and 3 will vote for x over y, so x beats y. In a vote between y and z, persons 1 and 2 vote for y over z, so y beats z. At this stage, we note that if M were transitive, x would have to beat z. If M were merely acyclic, z would have to not beat x. However, in a vote between x and z, person 2 and 3 vote for z. That is, z beats x, which completes the cycle. Consequently, M is neither transitive nor acyclic.

What does this imply? Since x is socially preferred to y, according to majority rule, and y is socially preferred to z, and z is socially preferred to x, there is no best alternative among the three. Each one is inferior to one of the others. Also, there is no social utility function that represents these social preferences.

Some readers might think such cycling is unlikely, bizarre, artificial, implausible, and generally of no concern to real world folks. To show that it's not, we shall make the example a little more down-to-earth. Let the set of alternatives be distributions of $100 among three people. Let x be the distribution ($50, $20, $30); that is, under x, person 1 gets $50, person 2 gets $20, and person 3 gets $30. Let y be ($30, $50, $30); that is, under y, person 1 gets $30, person 2 gets $50, and person 3 gets $70. Let z be ($20, $30, $50); that is, under z, person 1 gets $20, person 2 gets $30, and person 3 gets $50.

Then the preferences of the three individuals are

$$u_1(x) > u_1(y) > u_1(z)$$
$$u_2(y) > u_2(z) > u_2(x)$$
$$u_3(z) > u_3(x) > u_3(y)$$

These are the voting paradox preferences! But skeptics might now object that the particular distributions x, y, and z were improperly chosen. Surely there is some distribution that isn't defeated in a majority vote by some other distribution! For instance, what if we let $x' = (\$33\frac{1}{3}, \$33\frac{1}{3}, \$33\frac{1}{3})$? If we do, x' is beaten by $y' = (\$50, \$50, 0)$. And this new y' is in turn beaten by some other distribution. In fact, every distribution of \$100 among three people is defeated in a majority vote by some other distribution of the \$100 among the three. Majority voting crumbles under this very simple distributional problem.

MAJORITY VOTING AND SINGLE-PEAKEDNESS

The thrust of the section above is that majority voting might cycle, or produce illogical results. It might make social choice impossible. Yet we feel that majority voting often works; that is, we feel that there are circumstances under which majority voting yields sensible transitive results. Are there then some conditions we can find which necessarily imply that voting is transitive? The answer is Yes.

There are circumstances under which majority voting is transitive, and under which it does allow for the choice of best alternatives, and does define a social utility function. Those circumstances hinge on a certain property of the traders' tastes which we call *single-peakedness*. To explain single-peakedness, it is easiest to start with the Condorcet voting paradox example, in which tastes are not single-peaked.

Suppose that x, y, and z are lined up on an axis of alternatives, with x on the left, y on the middle, and z on the right, as in Figure 9-1a. Then when person 1's utility function u_1 is plotted above the axis of alternatives, it has a peak at x, and drops monotonically to the right of that peak, because $u_1(x) > u_1(y) > u_1(z)$. Similarly, when person 2's utility function u_2 is plotted above the axis of alternatives, it has a peak at the middle alternative y, and it drops monotonically to the left and to the right of that peak, because $u_2(y) > u_2(z) > u_2(x)$. Finally, when person 3's utility function u_3 is plotted above the axis of alternatives, it has a low peak at x, it drops at y, and it has a high peak at z, because $u_3(z) > u_3(x) > u_3(y)$. In other words, u_3 has two peaks. The important thing about Figure 9-1a is not the spacing between the alternatives, nor the absolute heights of the dots, nor

he slopes of the line segments. What is important here is that the u_3 func-
:ion has two peaks, while the u_1 and u_2 functions have only one.

Given that we have placed the alternatives in the order x, y, z, person 1's
ıtility function has one peak, person 2's utility function has one peak, and
ɔerson 3's utility function has 2 peaks. What if we were to change the order-
ng of alternatives along the horizontal axis? The reader can verify that no
natter how we permute the alternatives $\{x,y,z\}$, one trader's utility func-
ion will always show a double peak. There is no permutation of the alterna-
ives under which all traders utility functions have a single peak. We there-
ore say that these preferences do not satisfy the single-peakedness
ɔroperty, which we define formally as follows:

Suppose that there exists an ordering of the alternatives such that, given
hat ordering, the graph of each person's utility function has a peak at a
ingle point; it rises monotonically to the left of the peak, providing the
ɔeak is not at the farthest-left point, and it drops monotonically to the right
ɔf the peak, providing the peak is not at the farthest-right point. The partic-
ılar ordering of the alternatives for which this happens is called the *single-
ɔeakedness ordering*. If there does exist such a single-peakedness ordering,
he preferences R_1, R_2, . . ., R_n, or the utility functions u_1, u_2, . . ., u_n
ıre said to satisfy the *single-peakedness property*.

To make the definition clear, let's take the voting paradox preferences
ınd change u_2. Let the new u_2 function be one for which

$$u_2(y) > u_2(x) > u_2(z)$$

Now if we plot the old u_1, the new u_2, and the old u_3 functions in a picture
ike Figure 9–1a, that is, if we order the alternatives x,y,z and then plot the
ɔoints, we still get a double peak in u_3, since by assumption person 3's

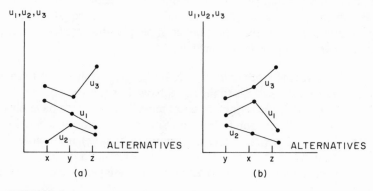

FIGURE 9–1

utility function has not changed. However, if we reorder the alternatives, if we list them y,x,z from left to right, we get the picture in Figure 9–1b. With this single-peakedness ordering, every u_1 function has one peak. Conse quently, this modified set of utility functions u_1, u_2, u_3 does satisfy the single-peakedness property.

Now consider what happens when majority voting is applied to the modi fied preferences. In a vote between x and y, person 1 and 3 vote for x, so x beats y, as before. In a vote between y and z, persons 1 and 2 vote for y, so y beats z, as before. However, in a vote between x and z, persons 1 and 2 vote for x, so x now beats z, and the voting cycle disappears!

Forcing the preferences into the single-peaked mold has abolished the voting paradox, at least in this example. In fact, the example illustrates a general result, an important theorem that provides conditions under which the majority voting relation M is complete and transitive, just like an indi vidual's preference relation. This theorem, along with the idea of single peakedness, was developed by Duncan Black in the 1940s. We now turn to a formal statement and a proof of one version of the theorem.

Black's Theorem 1.   Suppose that the number of people n is odd. If the single-peakedness property is satisfied, the majority voting relation M is transitive. That is, for any three alternatives x, y, and z, if x beats or ties y, and y beats or ties z, x must beat or tie z.

Proof.   Take three alternatives x, y, and z. To avoid trivial cases assume they are distinct. Suppose xMy and yMz. We must show xMz.

The proof will hinge on how x, y, and z appear in the single-peaked ness ordering. Since there are six possible orderings of these three alter natives, there are six cases to consider. In each case we will use one of the following two observations, which hold for any n. (1) If alternative a beats or ties alternative b, then the number of people who vote for a or abstain in the a vs. b contest, is greater than or equal to $n/2$. (2) If alternative a beats b, then the number of people who vote for a or abstain in the a vs. b contest, is greater than $n/2$.

Case 1.   The single-peakedness ordering is x,y,z. That is, x is to the left y is in the middle, and z is to the right. Now if i votes for x over y, that is if $u_i(x) > u_i(y)$, then $u_i(x) > u_i(z)$ must hold for u_i to have only one peak. (See the illustration following.) Similarly, if i abstains in the x vs. vote, that is, if $u_i(x) = u_i(y)$, then $u_i(x) > u_i(z)$ must hold. Since xMy, the number of people who vote for x or abstain in the x vs. y con test is greater than or equal to $n/2$. Since all these people must vote for over z, xMz.

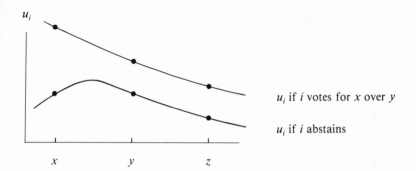

u_i if i votes for x over y

u_i if i abstains

Case 2. The single-peakedness ordering is x,z,y. Now if i votes for y over z, that is, if $u_i(y) > u_i(z)$, then $u_i(y) > u_i(x)$ must hold, for u_i to have only one peak. (See the illustration below.) Similarly, if i abstains in the y vs. z vote, that is, if $u_i(y) = u_i(z)$, then $u_i(y) > u_i(x)$ must hold. Since yMz, the number of people who vote for y or abstain in the y vs. z contest is greater than or equal to $n/2$. Since n is odd, this number is greater than $n/2$. Since all these people must vote for y over x, y must beat x. But this contradicts the assumption that xMy. Therefore, the single-peakedness ordering cannot be x,z,y.

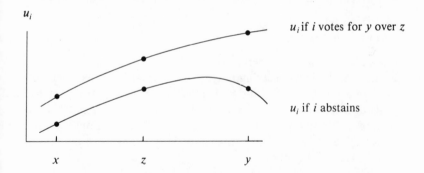

u_i if i votes for y over z

u_i if i abstains

Case 3. The single-peakedness ordering is y,x,z. We want to show that xMz. Suppose to the contrary that z beats x. Now if i votes for z over x, that is, if $u_i(z) > u_i(x)$, then $u_i(z) > u_i(y)$ must hold, for u_i to have only one peak. (See the illustration on the next page.) Similarly, if i abstains in the x vs. z vote, that is, if $u_i(x) = u_i(z)$, then $u_i(z) > u_i(y)$ must hold. Since z beats x, the number of people who vote for z or abstain in the x vs. z contest is greater than $n/2$. Since all these people must vote for z over y, z must defeat y. But this contradicts the assumption that yMz. Therefore, z cannot beat x, and so xMz.

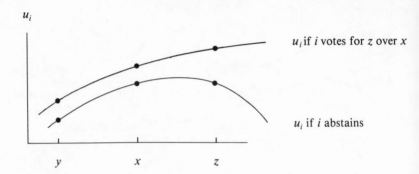

Cases 4, 5, and 6. The single-peakedness orderings are y,z,x; z,x,y; and z,y,x, respectively. These cases are mirror images of cases 2, 3 and 1 respectively, and the corresponding arguments apply.   Q.E.D

What happens to this theorem if the number of people n is even? What happens if there are say 1000 voters rather than 999? Then the theorem must be slightly modified.

To see the minor problem with single-peakedness when n is even, we consider a very simple example. Suppose there are two people and three alternatives x,y, and z. Suppose the utility functions are as follows:

$$u_1(z) > u_1(x) > u_1(y)$$
$$u_2(y) > u_2(z) > u_2(x)$$

You can check that these preferences satisfy the single-peakedness property the single-peakedness ordering is x,z,y. Now what happens when votes are taken? In a vote between x and y, there is a tie. So x and y are socially indifferent. In a vote between y and z there is another tie. So y and z are socially indifferent. But in a vote between x and z, z defeats x. Consequently, M is not transitive; it is only quasi-transitive. This brings us to our second version of Black's Theorem.

Black's Theorem 2. If the single-peakedness property is satisfied, the majority voting relation M is quasi-transitive. That is, for any three alternatives x,y, and z, if x beats y and y beats z, then x beats z.

The proof of Black's Theorem 2 is very similar to the proof of the first version, and is left as an exercise for the reader.

Now we can apply the propositions of Chapter 1 to get two corollaries.

Corollary 1. Suppose the set of alternatives is finite, and the single-peakedness property is satisfied.

Then there exists at least one alternative x that beats or ties any other alternative y. That is, xMy for all y.

We won't give a formal proof; the proof follows easily from Black's Theorem 2 above, and Propositions 1 and 3 in Chapter 1.

Corollary 2. Suppose the set of alternatives is finite, the number of people n is odd, and the single-peakedness property is satisfied.

1. Then there exists a unique alternative x that beats any other alternative y.

2. Moreover, there exists a social utility function U that exactly reflects the social preferences defined by majority voting. That is, for all alternatives x and y, xMy if and only if $U(x) \geq U(y)$.

We won't give a formal proof of this corollary either. Part 1 can be proved using Corollary 1 and assuming, contrary to what is to be proved, that there are two distinct alternatives, say x and y, each of which beats or ties all the alternatives. Using the fact that n is odd, it can be established that there is an alternative z that lies between x and y in the single-peakedness ordering, and that beats x and y. This gives a contradiction. The details are left as an exercise. Part 2 follows easily from Black's Theorem 1 above, and Proposition 5 in Chapter 1.

Let's pause to think about these results. Their basic thrust is that single-peakedness makes the majority voting relation M as sensible, as rational, as an individual's preference relation. If preferences are single-peaked, there are no paradoxes and no surprises inherent in majority voting; it is a perfectly logical way to make social choices. Majority voting becomes an acceptable vehicle for deciding when one alternative is socially preferred to another.

We have already seen, however, that the simple problem of distributing $100 among three people gives rise to voting paradoxes. How useful is single-peakedness? Is it an assumption that might actually be met? Or is it simply an empty theoretical construction? To get a feel for the answers to those questions, it's appropriate to examine a few examples.

One example has already been introduced in Chapter 6. Suppose a government is deciding on the output of a single public good. Suppose also that person i's utility function is

$$u_i = v_i(x) - y_i$$

where v_i is the type of function illustrated in Figure 6–1, x is the quantity of the public good, and y_i is i's consumption of the private good. Suppose finally that i has a fixed tax share t_i; that is, his tax bill is $t_i x$. Then i's preferences for various levels of x are given by his utility-from-the-public-good function net of taxes, or $v_i(x) - t_i x$. If this function is plotted against x, it rises monotonically to a maximum, and then declines. And this is true for every i, although different people will generally have different maxima, and functions of slightly different shapes. Therefore, preferences for the provision of one public good, financed by fixed tax shares, satisfy the single-peakedness property. Note that the single-peakedness ordering is the natural ordering — x goes from 0 at the left to $+\infty$ at the right.

Black's Theorems indicate that there will always exist a level of expenditures x that beats or ties all other proposed levels of expenditure. If levels of expenditure are subject to votes, there will be no voting cycles, no voting paradoxes. And therefore majority voting will provide a logically acceptable way to make decisions about the provision of the public good. (However, we should note the winning level of expenditure might not satisfy the Samuelson optimality condition. See Chapter 6.)

Another common single-peakedness example comes from political theory. We occasionally read about a left-right political spectrum, along which each of us has a different favorite position, and such that when we move away from our favorite position each of us is more and more unhappy:

Radical-Liberal-Moderate-Conservative-Reactionary.

The moderates love the moderate position, dislike liberal and conservative positions, and dislike radical and reactionary positions even more. The reactionaries love the reactionary position, are lukewarm about the conservative position, indifferent about the moderate position, and so on. If there is such a spectrum, then our preferences regarding political positions satisfy the single-peakedness property. Consequently, majority voting among referenda or candidates on this spectrum will be transitive, or at least quasi-transitive; there will be no voting cycles and no voting paradoxes. And there will be a position that beats or ties any other position. Clearly that winning position will be somewhere near the middle of the spectrum, and this is why, according to some political theorists, candidates in U.S. elections tend toward centrist positions. Single-peakedness has another application here.

The conclusion of this section must be that single-peakedness makes some sense, that there are interesting cases in which preferences are indeed single-peaked, and in which, by Black's Theorems, majority voting works well. But the discussion of majority voting and single-peakedness cannot stop here. In the 1960s and 1970s several economists and political scientists, particularly Charles Plott and Gerald Kramer, explored the problem of single-peakedness and voting over multidimensional sets of alternatives. They added new, disturbing results, results that we shall discuss in the next section.

MAJORITY VOTING AND SINGLE-PEAKEDNESS: THE MULTIDIMENSIONAL CASE

In Black's Theorems, the ordering of the alternatives along a single dimension plays a crucial role. A left-right political spectrum is one such unidimensional ordering. The amount spent by a town on maintaining a particular road is a unidimensional set of alternatives that is likely associated with single-peaked preferences for the town's citizens. Each person is likely to have a most preferred expenditure level, and is likely to be less and less happy with expenditure levels further and further from his most preferred level. Similarly, the amount spent by a state on public schools is a unidimensional set of alternatives likely associated with single-peaked preferences, as is the amount spent by a nation on defense. In all these single-peaked cases, Black's Theorems indicate that majority voting should give rise to sensible — i.e., transitive or quasi-transitive — results.

However, we often make choices in multidimensional sets of alternatives. For example, political candidates might have to adopt positions with regard to several unconnected issues — like gun control, abortion, unemployment, inflation, and crime — rather than to adopt one position on the left-right spectrum. A town meeting might decide simultaneously on expenditures for road maintenance and expenditures for schools — in which case the set of alternatives is most naturally two-dimensional. Or, finally, policy makers in the national government might choose among multidimensional policy alternatives in which a single alternative may be characterized by a level of unemployment, an interest rate, a rate of inflation, and an exchange rate between the yen and the dollar.

The possibility of two or more issues being decided simultaneously gives rise to new questions: Are the single-peakedness results applicable when there are multidimensional sets of alternatives? If alternatives are two-dimensional (or of higher dimensionality), and if preferences of voters are similar, in some sense, to one-dimensional single-peaked preferences, is majority voting transitive? Or do Black's Theorems collapse when the dimensionality of the set of alternatives goes from one to two or more?

The first step in answering these questions is to provide a multidimensional analog for single-peakedness. To keep the exposition simple we shall assume that social alternatives are two-dimensional vectors. Thus in this section an alternative $x = (x_1, x_2)$ specifies the levels of two variables. For example, x_1 might be the dollar amount spent on schools, a number that can range between 0 and ∞, while x_2 might be the dollar amount spent on police. Graphically, the set of alternatives is represented by the 1st quadrant of a plane, rather than by a line. Let us say that preferences are *regular* if each person has a single most preferred point on the plane, and if each person's indifference curves are roughly circular around his most preferred point. More precisely, indifference curves must be lines (they cannot be "fat"), they must have no flat segments or kinks, and they must enclose convex sets. The assumption of a most preferred point for each person is especially natural in the analysis of the provision of public services. No one wants infinite expenditures on schools or police, since those expenditures are financed through taxes.

Figure 9-2 illustrates regular preferences for three people. The set of alternatives is the set of points on the plane.

In the figure the point a represents the favorite alternative of person 1. Person 1 likes the levels of x_1 and x_2 given by the coordinates of a best. His indifference curves encircle a. This means, for example, that 1 gets the same level of utility from alternative x as he does from alternative y. Point b is the favorite of person 2, and his indifference curves are the ones encircling it; and c is the favorite of person 2, while his indifference curves are the ones encircling it.

This preference configuration provides the two-dimensional analog of single-peaked preferences: Each individual has a preference peak, and each individual's utility declines monotonically as one moves (in a straight line) from his preference peak. Moreover, if one draws a straight line (like L) anywhere through the alternative set, and looks at individuals' utility levels on that line, those utility levels are single-peaked in the Black sense. Figure 9-3 illustrates the utility levels for 1, 2 and 3 *along L*. This figure is constructed by referring to Figure 9-2 and reading off the utility levels of the three individuals along L.

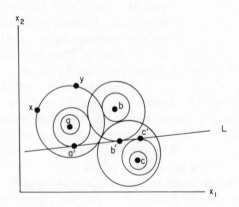

FIGURE 9-2

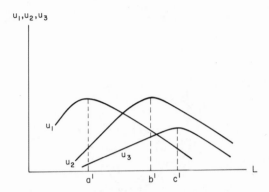

FIGURE 9-3

Note that a' is the alternative on L that person 1 likes best, and that 1's utility declines monotonically as one moves away from a' along L; similarly b' is the alternative on L that person 2 likes best, and c' is the alternative on L that 3 likes best.

Now we consider how majority voting works on a two-dimensional alternative set. The first thing to observe is that if the only alternatives considered lie on a line like L, the single-peakedness theorem holds. In this case, majority voting is transitive, or at worst, if n were even, quasi-transitive. We know by Black's Theorems that there must be an alternative that beats or ties all the rest. In the particular example of Figure 9-3, majority voting leads to the most preferred alternative of the middle, or median voter, namely person 2. That is, majority voting on L leads to b'. But constraining the voting to a line like L forces this two-dimensional problem into a one-dimensional mold. What if all alternatives are permitted on the agenda? That is, what if votes can be taken on any pair of points on the plane?

In Figure 9-4 we show three indifference curves for persons 1, 2 and 3, labeled I_1, I_2, I_3 respectively, and three alternatives x, y, and z. Note that each voter prefers any alternative on his indifference curve to any outside it, and prefers any alternative inside his indifference curve to any on it. Thus person 1 prefers x to y to z; person 2 prefers y to z to x, and person 3 prefers z to x to y.

In other words, the utility levels of the three individuals for the three alternatives are as follows:

$$u_1(x) > u_1(y) > u_1(z)$$
$$u_2(y) > u_2(z) > u_2(x)$$
$$u_3(z) > u_3(x) > u_3(y)$$

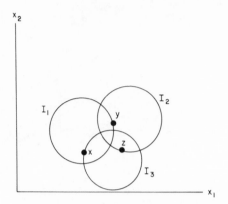

FIGURE 9-4

But these are precisely the utilities that give a voting paradox! In votes between pairs of alternatives, x beats y, y beats z, and z beats x, completing the cycle.

You can check to see that, in this three-person, two-dimensional case, every alternative, including every Pareto optimal one, is defeated by some other alternative in a majority vote. Majority voting is riddled with cycles, and leads to no socially best alternatives.

Nor is this a contrived example. In general, for a multidimensional alternative set, even if people's preferences are regular, unconstrained majority voting will be cyclic. It will almost always fail as a guide for choosing best alternatives.

There is, however, one special circumstance under which majority voting over a multidimensional set of alternatives has an equilibrium; that is, an alternative that defeats all other alternatives. Maority voting in this circumstance can indicate a socially best choice, namely the one that beats the others. (There may, however, still be cycles among inferior alternatives. This is not ruled out by Proposition 3 in Chapter 1.)

The special circumstance is illustrated in Figure 9-5.

In this figure, a is again 1's favorite, b is 2's favorite, and c is 3's favorite. What is crucial here is that person 2's favorite is on the locus of tangencies of 1's and 3's indifference curves. In this case, alternative b wins a majority over any other alternative.

The peculiarity of this case is striking, however, because the a priori likelihood that person 2's favorite is on the thin line of tangencies connecting points a and c must be zero! Moreover, this general configuration is the only regular preferences configuration that gives rise to the existence of a

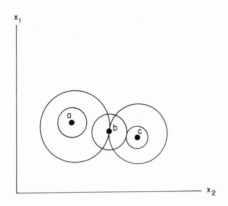

FIGURE 9-5

majority voting equilibrium, in the three person two dimensional case. A voting equilibrium exists if and only if one person's favorite alternative lies on the locus of tangencies connecting the favorites of the other two people. This is surely a rarity.

We must conclude that the connection between single-peakedness and transitivity or quasi-transitivity for majority voting depends crucially on there being a unidimensional set of alternatives. If the alternatives can be lined up, and utility functions have single peaks given that line up, majority voting is logically acceptable. If, however, the alternatives lie on a plane, and utility functions have single peaks over the plane, then majority voting will almost surely be logically unacceptable. It will almost surely be riddled with cycles. And there will almost surely be no alternative x such that xMy for all y. It will almost surely be the case that every alternative is, paradoxically, inferior to some other alternative.

EXERCISES

1. Prove Black's Theorem 2.
2. Prove Corollary 2 to Black's Theorems.
3. Suppose there are n voters, where n is an odd number, and a set of distinct alternatives $\{x_1, x_1, \ldots, x_n\}$. Suppose the voters' preferences are single-peaked, and the single-peakedness ordering is $x_1, x_2, x_3, \ldots, x_n$. Assume that x_1 is person 1's favorite alternative; x_2 is person 2's, and so on down through n. Let $m = (n + 1)/2$, so m is

the median of the n numbers, person m is the median voter, and x_m is the favorite of the median voter.

Show that x_m will win a majority over any other alternative. (Hint: Draw a picture of the utility functions over $x_1, x_2, \ldots, x_n$. Then figure out who will vote for x_m and who will vote for x_i, for an arbitrarily chosen x_i other than x_m.)

This result is essentially Black's original version of the single-peakedness theorem.

SELECTED REFERENCES

(Items marked with an asterisk (*) are mathematically difficult.)

1. D. Black, "On the Rationale of Group Decision Making," *Journal of Political Economy,* V. 56, 1948, pp. 23–34.

    In this straightforward article Black explains the idea of single-peakedness, and shows that one motion exists that wins a simple majority over every other motion.

2. D. Black, *The Theory of Committees and Elections,* Cambridge University Press, London, 1958.

    This excellent book covers lots of topics in the theory of elections. We name a few of the topics in Part I. Chapter IV discusses single-peakedness. Chapters V, VI and VII cover non-single-peaked preferences, and cycles in majority voting. Chapter X covers some election procedures other than majority voting. Part II of the book provides a history of analysis of voting, with excellent treatments of the contributions of de Borda, Condorcet, C. L. Dodgson (Lewis Carroll) as well as others. This part is essential for anyone seriously interested in the theory of elections.

3. O. Davis, M. J. Hinich, P. C. Ordeshook, "An Expository Development of a Mathematical Model of the Electoral Process," *American Political Science Review,* V. 64, 1970, pp. 426–448.

    Davis, Hinich and Ordeshook develop a model in which candidates in an election adopt positions in a multidimensional issues space. Each voter has preferences over the issues space, and a most preferred alternative; that is, a favorite position on all the issues. These preferences for individual i give rise to a *loss function* that essentially measures how much individual i dislikes candidate j. The loss is zero if candidate j's position is identical to voter i's most preferred alternative, and the loss increases as the difference between the voter's most preferred alternative and candidate j's position increases. The authors then go on to characterize some conditions under which there will exist an equilibrium position; i.e., a position that, if adopted by candidate j, will guarantee j's beating or tying any other candidate in a majority vote. It turns out that the existence of an equilibrium position is unlikely.

4. P. Fishburn, "Paradoxes of Voting," *American Political Science Review*, V. 67, 1974, pp. 537–546.

    This interesting article describes several voting paradoxes other than Condorcet's. These are paradoxes that arise for voting procedures that are different from straightforward majority rule, particularly sequential-elimination simple-majority voting, the de Borda procedure, and truncated variants of the de Borda procedure. Fishburn also presents data from computer simulations to suggest how likely (or unlikely) the paradoxes might be.

*5. G. H. Kramer, "On a Class of Equilibrium Conditions for Majority Rule," *Econometrica*, V. 41, 1973, pp. 285–297.

    Kramer examines voting over multidimensional alternatives, in a model where people have utility functions that satisfy standard properties of convexity and smoothness. He examines many "exclusionary" properties — properties which, like single-peakedness, rule out or exclude certain configurations of preferences. These properties were developed to avoid the quirks of majority rule. Kramer shows that in a standard utility-function model these exclusionary properties are extremely restrictive, "in the sense that they are incompatible with even a very modest degree of heterogeneity of tastes." Voting cycles are, therefore, the norm rather than the exception in "problems involving voting over multidimensional choice spaces."

*6. C. R. Plott, "A Notion of Equilibrium and its Possibility Under Majority Rule," *American Economic Review*, V. 57, 1967, pp. 787–806.

    In a model with a multidimensional alternative set, Plott characterizes a voting equilibrium, that is, an alternative that beats or ties any other in a majority vote. In the case where the number of people n is odd, an equilibrium point must satisfy these conditions. (1) It must be a favorite alternative for at least one person. (2) "All the individuals for which the point is not a maximum can be divided into pairs whose interests are diametrically opposed." Since it is unlikely that an arbitrary set of preferences will satisfy these conditions, it is unlikely that an equilibrium will exist.

    This article by Plott is the basis for our discussion surrounding Figure 9-5.

7. A. K. Sen, *Collective Choice and Social Welfare*, Holden-Day, Inc., San Francisco, 1970, Chapters 10, 10*.

    Chapter 10, on majority rule, provides a nice discussion of relatively recent literature on majority voting. One branch of this literature is about the likelihood of voting cycles — in an "average" "randomly selected committee," is a voting cycle a real possibility? The second branch is about extensions of the approach of Black. These extensions impose conditions (like single-peakedness) on preference relations, conditions which iron out some of the quirks in majority voting.

    Chapter 10*, which is rather mathematical, has a set of theorems on majority rule under various preference relation similarity conditions.

10 ARROW'S IMPOSSIBILITY THEOREM

INTRODUCTION

We have now looked at several ways to answer the question "When is one alternative socially preferred to another?" Each of the answers has been somehow disappointing. The Pareto criterion is incomplete; the Kaldor criterion is possibly inconsistent. The Scitovsky criterion reduces to a question of optimality vs. non-optimality. The Samuelson criterion might be completely devoid of content. The fairness and Rawls criteria might be inconsistent with the Pareto criterion. Majority voting might generate cycles, and the single-peakedness condition, which forces transitivity, is quite restrictive.

Our goal throughout has been to discover an unerring rule for generating rational social preferences, rational in the sense that an individual's preferences are rational. That is, we have been looking for a rule that generates complete and transitive social preferences, or, at least, complete and acyclic social preferences. But our series of disappointments raises some questions: Does a foolproof method exist for constructing complete and transitive social preference relations? Does a foolproof method exist for constructing complete and acyclic social preference relations? Does a foolproof method exist for finding best social alternatives? In this chapter we construct a simple model to answer the first question, and we briefly discuss the answer to the second question.

Does a foolproof method exist for constructing complete and transitive social preference relations? The answer to this question clearly depends on what we mean by foolproof. We will impose formal requirements on the method for constructing social preferences, requirements that allow a definite answer. The list of requirements, and the answer to the question, were developed by Kenneth Arrow around 1950, and the answer, to which we shall soon turn, is called Arrow's Impossibility Theorem.

THE MODEL

We now assume for the sake of simplicity that there are only two individuals, and three social alternatives x, y, and z. Also, we suppose that no individual is ever indifferent between any two alternatives. As usual, xP_iy means i prefers x to y. Individual i's preference ordering is assumed to be complete and transitive. Since there are only three alternatives and indifference is disallowed, there are only six ways individual 1 can order the alternatives. He can prefer x to y to z, or he can prefer x to z to y, or he can prefer y to x to z, and so on. The same is true of individual 2. Therefore, if any preference ordering for 1 or 2 is allowed, there are exactly $6 \times 6 = 36$ different constellations of individual preferences, or *preference profiles,* possible in this small society. Table 10–1 includes them all.

Each cell in this table shows a possible pair of rankings of the three alternatives by individuals 1 and 2. On the left side the alternatives are ordered, from top to bottom, according to person 1's preferences, and on the right side they are ordered according to 2's preferences. For example, the 1st row, 2nd column cell has 1 preferring x to y to z, and 2 preferring x to z to y.

Our concern here is whether or not there is a foolproof rule to transform any cell in Table 10–1 into a social preference relation. Such a rule is called a *collective choice rule.* A collective choice rule takes preference profiles and produces social preferences.

Let R stand for a social preference relation, so xRy means x is socially at least as good as y. P is the corresponding strict social preference relation: xPy means x is socially preferred to y; i.e., xRy and not yRx. (Don't confuse this R with the Rawls criterion, or this P with the Pareto criterion.) Finally, I is the social indifference relation: xIy means x and y are socially indifferent; i.e., xRy and yRx.

TABLE 10-1

Individuals

Choices	1	2	1	2	1	2	1	2	1	2	1	2
1st	x	x	x	x	x	y	x	y	x	z	x	z
2nd	y	y	y	z	y	x	y	z	y	x	y	y
3rd	z	z	z	y	z	z	z	x	z	y	z	x
1st	x	x	x	x	x	y	x	y	x	z	x	z
2nd	z	y	z	z	z	x	z	z	z	x	z	y
3rd	y	z	y	y	y	z	y	x	y	y	y	x
1st	y	x	y	x	y	y	y	y	y	z	y	z
2nd	x	y	x	z	x	x	x	z	x	x	x	y
3rd	z	z	z	y	z	z	z	x	z	y	z	x
1st	y	x	y	x	y	y	y	y	y	z	y	z
2nd	z	y	z	z	z	x	z	z	z	x	z	y
3rd	x	z	x	y	x	z	x	x	x	y	x	x
1st	z	x	z	x	z	y	z	y	z	z	z	z
2nd	x	y	x	z	x	x	x	z	x	x	x	y
3rd	y	z	y	y	y	z	y	x	y	y	y	x
1st	z	x	z	x	z	y	z	y	z	z	z	z
2nd	y	y	y	z	y	x	y	z	y	x	y	y
3rd	x	z	x	y	x	z	x	x	x	y	x	x

In the next section we will list five plausible requirements that will be imposed on the collective choice rule. Taken together, these five requirements define what we mean by foolproof.

REQUIREMENTS ON THE COLLECTIVE CHOICE RULE

1. Completeness and transitivity. The social preference relations generated by a collective choice rule must be complete and transitive. If some preference profile is transformed into a particular R, then for any pair of alternatives x and y, either xRy or yRx must hold, and for any triple

x,y and z,xRy and yRz must imply xRz. The requirement says that a collective choice rule must always permit comparisons between two alternatives, and that social preferences must have the nice transitivity property assumed for an individual's preferences.

We have examined collective choice rules that don't generate complete and transitive social preference relations. The Pareto criterion gives incomplete social rankings: if 1 prefers x to y and 2 prefers y to x, the two alternatives are Pareto noncomparable. Majority voting gives nontransitive social rankings. As an example in a two-person case (where the voting cycle of Condorcet cannot be generated), suppose 1 prefers x to z to y, and 2 prefers y to x to z. If a vote is taken between x and y, there is a tie (1 votes for x, and 2 votes for y). If a vote is taken between y and z, there is again a tie. According to majority voting, x and y are socially indifferent, and y and z are socially indifferent. Transitivity would require that x and z be socially indifferent. But in a vote between x and z, x gets 2 votes and z none; so x beats z, and transitivity fails.

2. Universality. A collective choice rule should work no matter what individual preferences happen to be. This means that the rule should give us a social preference ordering for every cell in Table 10-1, not just for the easy ones, like the ones where there is unanimous agreement

Universality is a significant requirement. It precludes the assumption of single-peakedness, since it says that the collective choice rule must work for all preference profiles, not just the ones where utility functions have single peaks. Why should it be imposed?

First, it is difficult to see where to draw the line between permissible and impermissible individual preferences. Which cells in Table 10-1 should be disallowed or ignored? How much diversity can be expected in society? When is there so much conflict that the very idea of social welfare becomes implausible? There are no easy answers to these questions. Second, the theorem we will prove remains valid even when the universality requirement is substantially weakened, and we will indicate how much it can be weakened in a subsequent section.

3. Pareto consistency. A collective choice rule should be consistent with the Pareto criterion. For any pair of alternatives x and y, if both individuals prefer x to y, x must be socially preferred to y.

Pareto consistency is a very mild requirement for a collective choice rule. One would not expect it to hold in societies which are ruled by external forces; in which, for example, everyone prefers lust and gambling, on the one hand, to chastity and frugality on the other; but where, according to a

Holy Book, the social state of chastity and frugality is preferable to the social state of lust and gambling. Economists naturally would recommend lust and gambling.

On a more serious note, let's recall that the fairness and Rawls criteria could produce results contrary to the Pareto criterion. In our view, this fact is an indictment of fairness and Rawls, not of Pareto. We take Pareto consistency to be fundamental.

4. Non-dictatorship. A collective choice rule must make no one a dictator. Individual i is said to be a *dictator* if his wishes prevail, no matter how j feels; that is, if $xP_i y$ implies xPy for all x and y, irrespective of P_j. Ruling out dictatorship does not mean that it is never possible to have $xP_i y$ implying xPy for all x and y. Obviously, if both people agree on the rankings of all alternatives (so that $P_1 = P_2$, as in the diagonal cells of Table 10–1), then it is perfectly reasonable to have the social preference relation agreeing with 1's (and 2's) preference relation, and in fact, the Pareto consistency requirement makes such agreement necessary. Nondictatorship simply says that 1 (or 2) must not always prevail, no matter how 2 (or 1) happens to feel.

5. Independence of irrelevant alternatives. If people's feelings change about some set of irrelevant alternatives, but do not change about the pair of alternatives x and y, then a collective choice rule must preserve the social ordering of x and y. The social preference between x and y must be independent of individual orderings on other pairs of alternatives. (We should note that this formulation of independence differs slightly from Arrow's original formulation.)

Independence is the subtlest of the five requirements, and it takes some explanation. Suppose society prefers x to y when z is a third alternative lurking in the wings. Next suppose everyone suddenly changes his mind about the desirability of z, but no one changes his mind about x vs. y. The independence requirement says that, if society is deciding on the relative merits of x and y, and only those two, it must still prefer x to y.

The standard example of an otherwise-nice collective choice rule that violates independence is *weighted voting*. This type of rule was first analyzed in 1781 by Jean-Charles de Borda, in his *Mémoire sur les Élections au Scrutin,* and it is consequently also called *de Borda voting*. It works as follows. Each person reports his preference relation, his rank ordering. A first place in a rank ordering is assigned a certain fixed weight, a second place is assigned a (smaller) fixed weight, a third place is assigned a (yet smaller) fixed weight, and so on. (In the two-person, three-alternative model of this chapter we have no ties, no cases of indifference, to worry about.) The weights that each alternative gets from each person are summed, and the social preference relation is derived from the sums of the weights.

For instance, suppose person 1 prefers z to x to y, while person 2 prefers y to x to z. Suppose a person's first choice gets a weight of five points, a second choice gets four points, and a third choice gets one point. (The weights are obviously arbitrary. It is common to use equally spaced weights, like 3, 2, and 1, but there is no logically compelling reason to do so. You may construct an example similar to this one using the common weighting scheme.) Now alternative x gets $4 + 4 = 8$ points, alternative y gets $1 + 5 = 6$ points, and alternative z gets $5 + 1 = 6$ points. Therefore, for this preference profile, x is socially preferred to y according to the weighted voting rule.

However, suppose person 1 becomes disillusioned with alternative z, and his preference ordering changes to x over y over z. If the voting is repeated, x gets $5 + 4 = 9$ points, y gets $4 + 5 = 9$ points, and z gets $1 + 1 = 2$ points. Therefore, given this new preference profile, x is socially indifferent to y. Society has become indifferent between x and y, even though neither person has changed his feelings about x and y! Consequently, weighted voting violates the independence requirement.

APPLYING THE REQUIREMENTS

At this stage we shall apply requirements 1, 2, 3 and 5 to Table 10–1. The applications should clarify the meanings of the four requirements. They will also lay the groundwork for the proof of Arrow's Impossibility Theorem.

The completeness and transitivity and the universality requirements say that, when applied to any cell of Table 10–1, a collective choice rule must generate a complete and transitive social ordering.

The Pareto consistency requirement says a collective choice rule must respect unanimous opinion: If both 1 and 2 prefer one alternative to another, then society must also prefer the one to the other. For example, given the preference profile of the first row, second column cell of Table 10–1, the Pareto requirement says x must be socially preferred to y and x must be socially preferred to z. We must have xPy and xPz. Application of Pareto consistency over the entirety of Table 10–1 gives rise to Table 10–2.

Each cell of this table is produced by applying Pareto consistency to the corresponding cell of Table 10–1, and therefore, any rule for generating social preferences must be entirely consistent with Table 10–2.

TABLE 10-2

xPy xPz yPz	xPy xPz	xPz yPz	yPz	xPy	
xPy xPz	xPy xPz zPy	xPz		xPy zPy	zPy
xPz yPz	xPz	xPz yPx yPz	yPx yPz		yPx
yPz		yPx yPz	yPx yPz zPx	zPx	yPx zPx
xPy	xPy zPy		zPx	xPy zPx zPy	zPx zPy
	zPy	yPx	yPx zPx	zPx zPy	yPx zPx zPy

Now we turn to the independent requirement. Suppose that when person 1 prefers x to y to z and person 2 prefers y to x to z (the first row, third column cell of Table 10-1) a collective choice rule declares x is socially preferred to y, or xPy. Then independence requires that xPy hold whenever xP_1y and yP_2x, not matter how 1 and 2 rank alternative z. Similarly, if yPx (or xIy) holds when person 1 prefers x to y to z and person 2 prefers y to x to z, then yPx (or xIy) must hold whenever xP_1y and yP_2x. In short, the independence requirement forces a collective choice rule to give rise to social preferences that agree over certain preference profiles.

Let's be specific about those areas of agreement. Independence requires that all the cells in Table 10-1 where xP_1y and yP_2x must yield identical social rankings of x and y. Similarly, all the cells where yP_1x and xP_2y must yield identical social rankings of x and y. There is no presumption, however, that the social ranking of x and y on the xP_1y and yP_2x cells need be the same as the social ranking of x and y on the yP_1x and xP_2y cells. Such a neutrality condition is unnecessary for the proof of the Impossibility Theorem, although it is intuitively appealing and useful in other contexts.

Independence also implies these areas of agreement. All the cells of Table 10-1 where xP_1z and zP_2x must give rise to identical social rankings of x and z; all the cells where zP_1x and xP_2z must give rise to identical social rankings of x and z; all the cells where yP_1z and zP_2y must give rise to identical social rankings of y and z; and, finally, all the cells where zP_1y and yP_2z must give rise to identical social rankings of y and z.

All of this information can be incorporated in a third table. Table 10-3a indicates where the social rankings of x and y must agree because xP_1y and yP_2x in all the X'd cells, and where the social rankings of x and y must agree because yP_1x and xP_2y in all the O'd cells. Tables 10-3b and 10-3c show the areas of agreement which arise from applications of the independence requirement to the social preferences between x and z, and y and z, respectively.

TABLE 10-3a

		X	X		X
		X	X		X
0	0			0	
0	0			0	
		X	X		X
0	0			0	

The crossed cells all produce the same x-y social rankings. The circled cells all produce the same x-y social rankings (which need not be the same as in the crossed cells).

(a)

TABLE 10–3b & c

			X	X	X
			X	X	X
			X	X	X
0	0	0			
0	0	0			
0	0	0			

The crossed cells all produce the same x-z social rankings. The circled cells all produce the same x-z social rankings (which need not be the same as in the crossed cells).

(b)

	X			X	X
0		0	0		
	X			X	X
	X			X	X
0		0	0		
0		0	0		

The crossed cells all produce the same y-z social rankings. The circled cells all produce the same y-z social ranking (which need not be the same as in the crossed cells).

(c)

With these preliminaries out of the way, we can turn to a truly remarkable theorem.

ARROW'S IMPOSSIBILITY THEOREM

At least since the time of Condorcet and de Borda in the eighteenth century, people have been concerned with the properties of rules for making social choices, election rules in practice, collective choice rules in theory. Does there exist a foolproof rule for discovering, or for defining, social preferences? Arrow showed that, if foolproof means consistent with the five requirements above, the answer is No.

We now turn to a formal statement and proof of the theorem.

Arrow's Impossibility Theorem.   Any collective choice which is consistent with the requirements of (1) completeness and transitivity, (2) universality, (3) Pareto consistency, and (4) independence of irrelevant alternatives, makes one person a dictator. Therefore, there is no rule which satisfies all five requirements.

Proof.   We start by looking at the preference profile of the first row, second column cell of Table 10-1. For these preferences Pareto consistency requires xPy and xPz (Table 10-2). There are three and only three complete and transitive social preference orderings which satisfy xPy and xPz. They are:

1. xPy, xPz and yPz
2. xPy, xPz and zPy
3. xPy, xPz and yIz

Each of these three possibilities will be considered in turn.

Case 1: yPz.   First a word about strategy. The Pareto consistency requirement tells a lot about what social preferences must be, but it leaves a lot unsaid. Table 10-2 is full of blank and partially blank spaces. We will now show how all the blanks can be filled in by repeatedly applying the independence and transitivity requirements.

If yPz holds in the first row, second column cell, then independence (Table 10-3c) requires that y be socially preferred to z whenever individual preferences about y and z are the same as they are in that cell. Therefore, yPz holds in all the cells indicated in Table 10-4a. (The cells that provide crucial steps in the proof are numbered 1 and 2.)

Now consider the first row, fifth column cell, or cell number 2 in Table 10-4a. Pareto consistency (Table 10-2) requires that xPy here, but xPy and yPz implies xPz, by transitivity. So in this cell we must also have xPz.

But if xPz holds in cell number 2, then independence (Table 10-3b) requires that x be socially preferred to z whenever individual preferences about x and z are the same as they are in that cell. Therefore, xPz holds in all the cells indicated in Table 10-4b. (The cells that provide crucial steps in the proof are numbered 2 and 3.)

Now we have xPz in cell 3. We again invoke Pareto consistency and transitivity to conclude that xPy must hold in cell 3 as well. But this

TABLE 10-4.

(a)

1. yPz			2. yPz	yPz	
yPz			yPz	yPz	
yPz			yPz	yPz	

(b)

			xPz	2. xPz	xPz
			xPz	xPz	3. xPz
			xPz	xPz	xPz

(c)

	1.		2.		
				3.	
6.					
		4.			
	5.				

allows us to use independence again, (Table 10–3a), to fill in eight more bits of information.

The filling-in process is repeated four more times. You can complete this part of the argument using the sequence of crucial cells indicated in Table 10–4c.

This filling-in process produces six diagrams like Tables 10–4a and 10–4b. Each one shows nine identical social preferences. If the information contained in all these diagrams is added to the information of

TABLE 10-5

x y z	x y z	x y z	x y z	x y z	x y z
x z y	x z y	x z y	x z y	x z y	x z y
y x z	y x z	y x z	y x z	y x z	y x z
y z x	y z x	y z x	y z x	y z x	y z x
z x y	z x y	z x y	z x y	z x y	z x y
z y x	z y x	z y x	z y x	z y x	z y x

Table 10-2, the result is the pattern of social preferences of Table 10-5.

But the social preferences shown in Table 10-5 are identical to person 1's preferences. Therefore, in Case 1, 1 is a dictator. He gets his way, no matter how 2 feels.

Case 2: zPy. If zPy holds in the 1st row, 2nd column cell, an argument analogous to the one above establishes that 2 is a dictator. The argument is left as an exercise.

Case 3: yIz. Suppose yIz holds in the first row, second column cell. Then by independence of irrelevant alternatives (Table 10-3c) yIz must also hold in the third row, second column cell, as well as the fourth row, fifth column cell. By Pareto consistency (Table 10-2), z must be socially preferred to x in the latter cell. Now by transitivity, yIz and zPx implies yPx for the fourth row, fifth column cell. By independence again (Table 10-3a), yPx in the fourth row, fifth column cell implies yPx in the third row, second column cell. Using transitivity again, yIz and yPx implies zPx in this cell. However, this contradicts Pareto consistency (Table 10-2), which says that xPz holds here. Therefore, Case 3 is impossible.

The proof of the theorem is now complete, for it has been shown that requirements 1, 2, 3, and 5 together imply that either

    i. 1 is a dictator, or

    ii. 2 is a dictator.   Q.E.D.

RELAXING THE UNIVERSALITY REQUIREMENT

We said near the beginning of this chapter that the universality requirement, which demands that a collective choice rule work for any preference profile, is overly strong. This section will indicate why. In fact, the construction of a sensible collective choice rule remains impossible even if a large number of possible preference profiles are excluded.

To show that lots of preference profiles might be dispensed with, without affecting the theorem, we will just count the cells that are crucial in our proof. In Case 1, we use the cells numbered 1–6 in Table 10-4c. In Case 2, we need another six crucial cells, but the first crucial cell is again the first row, second column cell, which we have already counted. Thus far, we have 6 + 5 or 11 cells. In Case 3, we use three crucial cells, but one is the familiar first row, second column cell, which has been counted. Therefore, the total number of crucial cells for the purposes of our proof is $11 + 2 = 13$. And the Arrow Impossibility Theorem holds even if any or all of the remaining cells are discarded. Incidentally, the crucial cells we have used are not the only ones which can establish the theorem—other sequences of steps can be used to prove it. But they are a full set, in the sense that they will do the job, and so long as they are all retained, any or all of the other cells are disposable.

In short, with a properly chosen set of thirteen preference profiles, out of the total set of thirty-six, Arrow's Theorem can be established. So universality is really a much stronger assumption than is needed to prove the theorem.

REACTIONS TO ARROW'S IMPOSSIBILITY THEOREM

Since Arrow published his seminal paper in 1950, a vast literature has grown on the Impossibility Theorem and related topics. It's interesting to think about why. The theorem provides an unambiguous answer to the question "Is there a foolproof way to derive complete and transitive social preference relations?" The answer is No. This clearly negative result casts doubts on all assertions that there is a "general will," a "social contract," a "social good," a "will of the people," a "people's government," a "people's voice," a "social benefit," and so on and so forth. That is, it casts doubts on all notions that explicitly or implicitly attribute preferences to society that are comparable to preferences for an individual. Therefore, it casts doubts on vast areas of twentieth century social thought. Of course any theorem that casts so much doubt will generate a lot of responses.

There are many possible reactions to Arrow's Theorem. The first, and perhaps most obvious reaction is this. It is quite silly in the first place to think that there might be social preferences that are analogous to individual preferences. It is nonsense to talk about social preferences since society itself is nothing more than a collection of individuals, each with his own interests. The idea that a motley collection of individuals should have social preferences that are like an individual's preferences is just an example of illegitimate reasoning by analogy. To attribute the characteristics of an individual to a society commits the logical error of personification. Arguments like these have been made by James Buchanan, Charles Plott, and others.

Now this line of reasoning could be pursued further. For instance, the idea that anyone should be interested in Pareto optimality is also silly, since each person i just wants to maximize his own utility u_i. Person i couldn't care less about optimality. Further, the idea that a government official might be interested in pursuing the public good is equally silly, first because the public good is an empty idea, and second because even if there were a public good to be pursued, public official i just wants to maximize his utility function u_i, and what's good for the public will often differ from what's good for the public official. (See Anthony Downs' *An Economic Theory of Democracy*.) Further, the idea that an economist or a political scientist might be interested in instructing the citizenry or electorate, or reforming public officials, is also silly, first because there is no public good, second because the citizens and/or the officials are only trying to maximize their own utility functions, and third becaue the economist or the political scientist is also simply interested in maximizing his u_i! And why should anyone listen to such an obviously self-serving advisor or reformer?

So this first reaction to Arrow's Theorem is logically attractive, but it can lead to varieties of nihilism that are unappealing to some people.

The second type of reaction to Arrow's Theorem accepts the legitimacy of the basic idea of social preferences, and attacks one or more of Arrow's five requirements. Let's very briefly touch on some of these lines of attack.

First, the completeness requirement might be jettisoned. For instance, some people are quite satisfied with the Pareto criterion alone, and hold that if x and y are Pareto noncomparable, only an act of God can decide between them. There is no way that a reasonable person, or government, can decide, and reasonable people or governments have no business trying to do so. One implication of this line of reasoning is that a Pareto optimal status quo, brought about, perhaps, by a competitive market mechanism, should be left untouched—government officials should not waste their time (and tax dollars) scheming about how to redistribute wealth. Nor should economists and political scientists.

Second, the transitivity requirement might be dropped, or weakened to quasi-transitivity, or acyclicity. If transitivity is dropped entirely, majority voting becomes acceptable, and its advocates simply hope embarrassing voting cycles do not arise. If cycles are potentially there, they might be suppressed by clever committee chairmen, by agenda rules, or by some other *deus ex machina*.

Or, transitivity might be weakened to quasi-transitivity. If this is done, however, a new version of Arrow's Impossibility Theorem rears its head. In this version, due to Allan Gibbard, the requirements of completeness and quasi-transitivity, universality, Pareto consistency, and independence together imply that there must exist an *oligarchy,* rather than a dictatorship. That is, there must exist a group of people G such that (1) if xP_iy for all i in G, then xPy, and (2) if xP_iy for some i in G, then xRy. Acting together members of the oligarchy can force a social preference for x over y, and acting apart, each member of the oligarchy has *veto power* over a y which he regards as inferior to x. If G has only one member, then the oligarchy is a dictatorship. If G has two members, it is a duumvirate; if it has three members, it is a triumvirate, and so on. (G might include everyone. Consider for instance, A. K. Sen's *Pareto-extension* rule, which is defined as follows. Let xRy if y is not Pareto superior to x. This rule satisfies completeness and quasi-transitivity, universality, Pareto consistency, and independence. It makes the whole group an oligarchy. And, we should note, it doesn't provide much information. It says, for example, that all Pareto optimal allocations are equally good.)

If transitivity is weakened to acyclicity, there arises yet another version of Arrow's Impossibility Theorem, a version due to Donald Brown. This result says the requirements of completeness and acyclicity, universality

Pareto consistency, and independence together imply that there must exist what Brown calls a *collegial polity,* rather than an oligarchy or a dictatorship. In a collegial polity, there may be several groups G who can force a social preference for x over y, that is, several G's such that if xP_iy for all i in G, then xPy. These groups have a nonempty intersection, and this intersection, this set of people who belong to all the powerful G-groups is called a *collegium,* which we abbreviate C. Now C need not be able to force the social preference of x over y by itself, but any group that can force that preference must include C. C is thus the elite of the powerful. As an example, suppose there are five people, and the collective choice rule defines xPy if persons 1 and 2 plus any one other person prefer x to y. Otherwise, yRx. Then the powerful G-groups are $\{1,2,3,\}$, $\{1,2,4\}$ and $\{1,2,5\}$. That is, any of these groups can force a social preference for x over y. The elite among the powerful, the collegium, is $\{1,2\}$. However, the collegium $\{1,2\}$, acting alone, cannot force a social preference for x over y.

A third reaction to Arrow's Theorem is to drop the universality requirement. This is the approach of the single-peakedness mode of analysis, and similar analyses of restrictions of allowable preference profiles. We have already seen in Chapter 9 and this chapter that this tack is disappointing.

A fourth, and for our purposes final, way is to drop the independence requirement. There are at least two reasons why one might want to move in this direction. The first is that the independence requirement is, of all the Arrow requirements, the least intuitive, the least compelling, the least understandable, and these weaknesses suggest it should be sacrificed. The second is that the independence requirement depends on there being more than one preference profile, it depends on changes in individuals' preferences. Why not constrain the entire discussion to a fixed preference profile? Why not say: "Look, we have so many people with particular preferences that are given. How might we aggregate these given preferences? What might or might not happen if preferences change is of no particular interest, because we want to aggregate the fixed preferences of our given population."

What is wrong with this position? The essential problem here is that with the independence requirement we are forced to admit only one type of collective choice rule-dictatorship, but without it we have an unlimited set of admissible collective choice rules, a real embarrassment of riches. For instance, suppose we forget about independence, suppose for simplicity that no one is ever indifferent between two alternatives, and suppose the total number of alternatives is k. Let $(a_1, a_2, a_3, \ldots, a_k)$ be any k numbers satisfying $a_1 > a_2 > a_3 > \ldots > a_k$. Consider the generalized weighted voting rule, or generalized de Borda rule, in which the weight assigned a first choice is a_1, the weight assigned a second choice is a_2, and so on. Then this collective choice rule is perfectly well behaved; it satisfies completeness

and transitivity, universality (which might be moot if we are really con
cerned with a fixed preference profile) and Pareto consistency. Indepen
dence has been jettisoned. And the rule is most certainly nondictatorial
nonoligarchic and noncollegial. But the problem here is that the outcome
the social preference relation, depends on the actual magnitudes of the
weights $(a_1, a_2, \ldots, a_k)$, and that a different set of weights will generally
give a different social preference relation. And there are infinitely many
ways to choose the weights! So the resulting social preference relation is
arbitrary, insofar as the particular weights are arbitrary.

How is a (social) choice of a set of weights going to be made? How can
we decide if one set of weights $(a_1, a_2, a_3, \ldots, a_k)$ is socially preferable to
another set of weights $(b_1, b_2, b_3, \ldots, b_k)$? The problem of social prefer
ences has not been solved in this case, it has only been thrust back onto the
choice of the weights.

EXERCISES

1. Suppose there are three people and four alternatives. Assume 1 pre
    fers w to x to y to z, 2 prefers y to z to w to x, and 3 prefers z to x to y
    to w. Find weights (a_1, a_2, a_3, a_4) so that weighted voting indicate
    the social preference is y over z over x over w. That is, y's total
    weighted vote is the highest, z's is the second highest, and so on
    Next find weights (b_1, b_2, b_3, b_4) so that weighted voting indicate
    the social preference is z over x over y over w.

2. Suppose there are four people, and no one is ever indifferent
    between two alternatives. One of the alternatives is special, and is
    labeled x_0. Consider a collective choice rule that works as follows. If
    person 1 prefers x to y, and y isn't the special alternative, then x is
    socially preferred to y. That is, $xP_1 y$ implies xPy, if $y \neq x_0$. (So per
    son 1 is a dictator except when the special alternative is at stake.) If
    persons 1 and 2, plus at least one other person, prefer x to x_0, then x
    is socially preferred to x_0. (So person 1 needs person 2 plus someone
    else to overrule the special alternative.) In all other cases, yRx.
    a. Show that this rule satisfies Pareto consistency and indepen
        dence.
    b. Show with specific examples of preferences that the rule is not
        quasi-transitive.
    c. Show that it must be acyclic.
    d. Identify the collegium.
    e. If all members of the collegium prefer x to y, does it necessaril
        follow that xPy?

3. Prove Case 2 of Arrow's Impossibility Theorem.

SELECTED REFERENCES

Articles marked with an asterisk (*) are mathematically difficult.)

1. K. J. Arrow, "A Difficulty in the Concept of Social Welfare," *The Journal of Political Economy*, V. 58, 1950, pp. 328–346.

    Arrow's 1950 paper is the source of the enormous literature on the Impossibility Theorem. (By now there are many hundreds of published papers on the topic.) After briefly surveying dictatorship, rule by convention, majority rule, and compensation criteria, Arrow turns to the question: "Can we find other methods of aggregating individual tastes which imply rational behavior on the part of the community and which will be satisfactory in other ways?" The answer is No.

2. K. J. Arrow, *Social Choice and Individual Values*, 2nd edition, John Wiley and Sons, Inc., New York, 1963.

    Arrow's excellent monograph extends and supplements his original 1950 article. The monograph is as valuable for its treatment of related topics as it is for its proof of the Impossibility Thorem. For instance, Arrow discusses compensation criteria at great length; he has a chapter on preference similarity that deals with unanimity, single-peakedness, and in the last chapter he discusses some of the issues raised in the literature on social choice since the publication of his 1950 article (and the first, 1951 edition of this monograph). The last section of the last chapter is especially interesting, since it is about whether or not rationality is a property that ought to be attributed to society.

3. D. J. Brown, "Aggregation of Preferences," *Quarterly Journal of Economics*, V. 89, 1975, pp. 456–469.

    See the references section at the end of Chapter 1.

4. J. M. Buchanan, "Individual Choice in Voting and in the Market," *Journal of Political Economy*, V. 62, 1954, pp. 334–343.

5. C. Plott, "Axiomatic Social Choice Theory: An Overview and Interpretation," *American Journal of Political Science*, V. 20, 1976, pp. 511–596.

    Plott provides an interesting and relatively nontechnical survey of Arrow's Impossibility Theorem topics in the first part of this paper. In the second, he surveys axiomatic characterizations of collective choice rules. These are statements of the form "if a rule has properties A, B and C, then it must be such-and-such."

6. A. K. Sen, *Collective Choice and Social Welfare*, Holden-Day, Inc., San Francisco, 1970, Chapters 3, 3*, 4, 4*.

    Chapter 3 is a literary treatment of Arrow's results, 3* is a mathematical treatment and a general proof. Chapters 4 and 4* are about weakening the transitivity requirement.

*6. A. K. Sen, "Social Choice Theory: A Re-examination," *Econometrica*, V. 45, 1977, pp. 53–90.

    This article surveys the technical literature on collective choice rules that generate binary social preference relations, and collective choice rules that generate choice functions. (A choice function indicates what alternatives are best from among any subset of alternatives.) Impossibility results are given for both types of rules.

11 STRATEGIC BEHAVIOR

INTRODUCTION

In the last chapter the goal was to find a foolproof collective choice rule which would transform any preference profile into a complete and transitive social preference relation. It turned out that this was impossible. Evidently we were hoping for too much. Now we shall modify that goal. We shall try to find a foolproof rule that can transform any preference profile into a single best alternative, or a single winner.

It is possible that it is less demanding for a rule to produce single winners, than to produce rankings of all the alternatives? It is possible that there exist satisfactory rules which generate single winners?

What are the differences between rules that transform preference profiles into social preference relations, or what we call collective choice rules, and rules that transform preferences profiles into single winners? We call the latter *Social Decision Functions,* or SDF's for short. According to Proposition 2 of Chapter 1, if we have a complete and transitive social preference relation we can always find best social alternatives. That is, we can always find alternatives that are socially preferred or indifferent to all the rest. But

by Proposition 3 of Chapter 1, even with a complete and acyclic social preference relation, we can always find best social alternatives. So completeness
and transitivity for the social preference relation is more than enough to
guarantee that socially best choices exist. Therefore, if we only require that
a rule generate socially best alternatives, we are asking for less than if we require that a rule generate complete and transitive social preferences. And so
the disappointment of Arrow's Impossibility Theorem might not extend to
SDF's.

This is our first reason for analyzing rules that transform preference
profiles into single winners. We might find a way to escape Arrow's di-
lemma. The second reason to analyze SDF's is more down-to-earth. Our
concern with social preference relations per se is somewhat academic. We
analyze social preferences in part because we have already analyzed individual preference relations; we are used to thinking in terms of preference relations. But there is no practical need to be able to judge between every pair of
alternatives. From a practical point of view, it is quite sufficient to say:
"Given this set of alternatives, this one is best." The practical question of
social choice is not "What is the ranking of all the alternatives?" but
"Which alternative is on top?" This is our second reason for analyzing
SDF's.

The question now is "Is there a foolproof way to find single best alternatives, is there a foolproof SDF?" Once again, the answer depends on what
we mean by foolproof.

Let's first consider the requirements that defined a foolproof collective
choice rule. (1) The completeness and transitivity requirement is not directly
applicable to SDF's, and we will drop it. (2) Universality is applicable, and
we will continue to require it. We will require that the rule always work, no
matter what individual preferences might be. (3) Pareto consistency might
easily be adapted to SDF's. For instance, one might insist that the chosen
alternative, the best alternative, always be Pareto optimal. However, we
will not insist on Pareto consistency as a requirement for foolproof SDF's;
we will drop this requirement. (4) Nondictatorship is applicable here, and
we will continue to require it. However, the definition of an SDF dictator
will differ slightly from the definition of a collective choice rule dictator. (5)
Independence of irrelevant alternatives is not directly applicable to SDF's,
and we will drop theis requirement also.

So of the Arrow requirements, we are left with universality and nondictatorship. Are there any new requirements to impose? What in fact makes a
foolproof SDF? The answer to this question is closely connected to our
analysis of public goods in Chapter 6.

Recall that the Wicksell-Lindahl tax scheme, in which a person's tax share was equal to his marginal utility from the public good, has one fatal flaw: it induces people to misrepresent their preferences, to lie to the Public Good Board. We take this flaw very seriously in this chapter, and we incorporate the idea of misrepresentation into our definition of a foolproof SDF.

If a tax scheme causes people to behave strategically, that is to lie about their marginal utilities for a public good, then we say it isn't foolproof. If a voting mechanism causes people to vote strategically, that is, to vote as if they prefer A over B over C when in fact they prefer C over B over A, then we say it isn't foolproof.

In short, the new requirement for a foolproof rule is that it provide no incentives for strategic behavior in the sense of misrepresentation of preferences. We now turn to examples of SDF's to further illustrate this requirement.

EXAMPLES OF STRATEGIC BEHAVIOR

What follows are examples of SDF's that *do* permit strategic behavior.

Example 1 is a simplified version of a problem already analyzed in Chapter 6. There is a public good, a bridge, that might or might not be built. We'll assume here that the bridge can be only one size, so the choice is to build it or not. Consequently, there are just two alternatives.

There is one good other than bridges; this is the private good, which we now simply call money. Person i's initial quantity of the private good is ω_i, and we let T_i represent the tax that i pays to finance the bridge, if the bridge is built. We assume that i's utility function is separable, and can be written this way:

$$u_i = \begin{cases} v_i + \omega_i - T_i & \text{if the bridge is built} \\ \omega_i & \text{if the bridge is not built} \end{cases}$$

The number v_i is then i's valuation of the bridge, and is analogous to the function v_i of Chapter 6. We assume that $v_i \geq 0$ for all i.

If the bridge is built, its cost is C, measured in units of the private good, or money. As usual we assume that whatever the tax system might be, each person knows how all taxes are computed.

The SDF works as follows. Each person is asked his valuation v_i. The Bridge Board goes ahead and builds the bridge if

$$\sum_{i=1}^{n} v_i \geq C$$

t does not build it if

$$\sum_{i=1}^{n} v_i < C$$

Now let's turn to the tax rules. We shall examine two possibilities. First, uppose that the tax shares are fixed and equal; or $T_i = C/n$ for all i. Sup-pose for some particular i, $v_i - C/n > 0$. Then i is better off if the bridge s built than if it is not built. When the Bridge Board asks i for his v_i, i has a lear incentive to lie, to misrepresent his preferences. In particular, i will ex-ggerate his valuation of the bridge. Similarly, if $v_i - C/n < 0$, i has a lear incentive to claim his valuation is zero. With this tax scheme, the SDF ncourages strategic behavior, and any decision the Bridge Board reaches nust be suspect.

Next suppose that i's tax is linked to his valuation, as it is in the Wicksell-Lindahl tax scheme. In particular, suppose T_i is set equal to v_i. There might e a budget surplus, which we know could destory Pareto optimality, but et's ignore that problem and concentrate on the possibility of strategic be-avior. If $T_i = v_i$, it is clear that many people, including some who value he bridge rather highly, will claim their valuations are zero! They will try to e free riders. Again, this SDF elicits false preferences, and any decision it eaches is suspect.

In short, these two very plausible tax schemes give rise to a bridge-build-ng SDF that rewards strategy. And this elicitation of false preferences, in ur view, means these tax schemes are not foolproof. (Of course there do xist demand-revealing taxes to finance this bridge, taxes which provide no ncentives for false revelation of preferences. An example is given in the xercise section below. It should be recalled, however, that the effectiveness f demand-revealing taxes depends crucially on the special assumption that dividuals i's valuation v_i is independent of ω_i and T_i.)

In the next examples we turn away from tax expenditure schemes, and ack to voting rules.

Example 2 is the weighted voting rule, or the de Borda rule, which we et in the last chapter. Here we analyze the common version of de Borda's ule. Suppose there are k alternatives. Each voter ranks the alternatives ac-ording to his order of preference. (We assume that there is no ndifference.) A voter's first choice is assigned k points, his second $k - 1$ oints, and so on down to his last choice, which is assigned one point. The otal vote for an alternative is the sum of the points assigned it by the vari-us voters, and the winner (ignoring ties) is the alternative with the highest um.

Aside from the minor complication caused by the possibility of ties, th de Borda rule takes a collection of individual preferences, and, based o thoses preferences, produces a single best alternative, or a winner.

Let see how it might work with a particular preference profile, whei there are seven voters and five alternatives. Suppose the voters have the fol lowing preferences:

Type 1	Type 2	Type 3
x	y	z
y	z	x
z	x	y
u	u	u
v	v	v
(3 people)	(2 people)	(2 people)

This table indicates that three of the people, the ones labeled "type 1," prefer x to y to z to u to v. Two of the people, the ones labeled "type 2, prefer y to z to x to u to v; and two of the people, the ones labeled "type 3," prefer z to x to y to u to v.

In this case the de Borda votes are:

$$3 \times 5 + 2 \times 3 + 2 \times 4 = 29 \text{ points for } x,$$
$$3 \times 4 + 2 \times 5 + 2 \times 3 = 28 \text{ points for } y,$$
$$3 \times 3 + 2 \times 4 + 2 \times 5 = 27 \text{ points for } z,$$
$$3 \times 2 + 2 \times 2 + 2 \times 2 = 14 \text{ points for } u, \text{ and}$$
$$3 \times 1 + 2 \times 1 + 2 \times 1 = 7 \text{ points for } v.$$

Consequently, when all individuals honestly report their preferences, a ternative x wins.

However, if one of the type 2 voters declares

y
z
u
v
x

as his preferences ordering, the de Borda votes are 28 for y, 27 for z and ? for x; so y wins.

Consequently, the de Borda rule may tempt people to vote as if the preferences are something other than what they really are. It might provie incentives for the declaration of false preferences; and therefore the dec sions it reaches are suspect. In short, it's not a foolproof SDF.(Incidentall this kind of manipulation of the de Borda rule was foreseen by de Bord imself, who is supposed to have said, "My scheme is only intended for onest men." See Duncan Black's *Theory of Committees and Elections,* Chapter XVIII-3.)

In Example 3, we return to majority voting, but majority voting modi- ed by the introduction of an agenda. We have already seen that majority oting between pairs of alternatives may produce cycles of social prefer- nce, unless individuals' preferences are single-peaked. And cycles might aake the choice of a winner impossible. However, cycles infrequently arise a the real world, partly because of single-peakedness, but also partly be- aause of the effects of committee agendas. A typical agenda rules out many airwise comparisons, and therefore makes the appearance of cycles less robable. Without cycles, majority voting does produce overall winners barring ties), and is consequently a proper SDF. To clarify these points, we arn to our concrete example.

Again, suppose there are seven voters of three types. This time, however, ssume there are three alternatives. One is the *status quo,* which we abbrevi- te SQ. The second is a *motion,* which we abbreviate M. And the third is an *nended version of the motion,* which we abbreviate AM. Assume the pref- ences are as follows:

Type 1	Type 2	Type 3
SQ	M	AM
M	AM	SQ
AM	SQ	M
(3 voters)	(2 voters)	(2 voters)

Iajority voting with no agenda produces a cycle here. The status quo de- ats the motion 5 to 2; the motion defeats the amended motion 5 to 2; but le amended motion defeats the status quo 4 to 3.

But what does a typical committee do in a case like this? Does it to hold a bte between all three pairs? In fact, it doesn't. The standard procedure is first vote on the motion (i.e., decide between M and AM), and then put e winner of that vote against the status quo. Only two votes are held, not ree. If people vote their preferences honestly, M first defeats AM, or the nendment is defeated. The final winner is SQ.

But under these circumstances, the two type 2 voters can misrepresent eir preferences, by voting as if they prefer the amended motion to the otion, and the motion to the status quo. If they do so, AM defeats M in e first round, or the amendment is adopted. Then AM defeats SQ, or the nended motion is adopted. The final winner is AM, which type 2 voters efer to SQ.

In short, the method of majority rule with the usual agenda may provide opportunities for people to profitably misrepresent their preferences. Consequently, decisions arrived at with this very widely used procedure are suspect. This SDF isn't foolproof either.

Our idea of a foolproof social decision function should be clear by now. Each of the above SDF's is unsatisfactory because it produces incentives for individuals to misrepresent their preferences, and so the decisions reached are in each case suspect. We require of a foolproof SDF that it never provide incentives for declarations of false preferences. The SDF must be immune to manipulation or cheating by dishonest individuals.

As we noted above, we also require that a foolproof SDF work for all possible preference profiles (the universality requirement), and that it be nondictatorial.

There is one last minor requirement. Suppose the set of alternatives is $\{x,y,z,u,v, \ldots \}$, and the SDF chooses y as the winner, no matter what the preferences of the individuals might be. This is clearly an unsatisfactory SDF, because it is trivial or degenerate. We shall also require nontriviality, or nondegeneracy, for our foolproof SDF.

We have seen several examples of SDF's that are not foolproof. Does there exist an SDF that meets the four requirements of universality, nontriviality, nondictatorship, and nonmanipulability?

THE GIBBARD-SATTERTHWAITE
IMPOSSIBILITY THEOREM

Does a foolproof SDF exist? The question is answered here for the simple model that was analyzed in the previous chapter. We assume that there are two people, and three alternatives, x, y, and z. We again suppose that no individual is ever indifferent between two alternatives. Each person can then have six possible rankings of the three alternatives, and there are $6 \times 6 = 36$ possible preference profiles, all of which are pictured in Table 10-1 of Chapter 10, which is reproduced in Table 11-1.

Each cell in this figure shows a preference ranking for each of the two people; so, for example, the cell in the first row, second column, indicates person 1 prefers x to y to z, and person 2 prefers x to z to y.

The universality requirement says a social decision function must work no matter what preference profile is given to it. Therefore, a social decision function for this little society is a rule which takes every cell to Table 11-1 or every preference profile, and transforms it into a winner, or a social choice. For each of the thirty-six preference profiles of Table 11-1, there are

TABLE 11-1

Individuals

Choices	1	2	1	2	1	2	1	2	1	2	1	2
1st	x	x	x	x	x	y	x	y	x	z	x	z
2nd	y	y	y	z	y	x	y	z	y	x	y	y
3rd	z	z	z	y	z	z	z	x	z	y	z	x
1st	x	x	x	x	x	y	x	y	x	z	x	z
2nd	z	y	z	z	z	x	z	z	z	x	z	y
3rd	y	z	y	y	y	z	y	x	y	y	y	x
1st	y	x	y	x	y	y	y	y	y	z	y	z
2nd	x	y	x	z	x	x	x	z	x	x	x	y
3rd	z	z	z	y	z	z	z	x	z	y	z	x
1st	y	x	y	x	y	y	y	y	y	z	y	z
2nd	z	y	z	z	z	x	z	z	z	x	z	y
3rd	x	z	x	y	x	z	x	x	x	y	x	x
1st	z	x	z	x	z	y	z	y	z	z	z	z
2nd	x	y	x	z	x	x	x	z	x	x	x	y
3rd	y	z	y	y	y	z	y	x	y	y	y	x
1st	z	x	z	x	z	y	z	y	z	z	z	z
2nd	y	y	y	z	y	x	y	z	y	x	y	y
3rd	x	z	x	y	x	z	x	x	x	y	x	x

hree possible social choices. Therefore, the number of conceivable SDF's is 3^{36}, or (approximately) 1.5×10^{17}, or a hundred and fifty thousand trillion. Our having only two people and three alternatives does not imply that only a few SDF's are available!

Any one of the many possible SDF's can be represented by another 6×6 matrix, whose entries are winners, or social choices, corresponding to the preference profiles of Table 11-1.

Table 11-2 represents one such SDF:

Each cell of Table 11-2 shows the social choice or winner, given the preference profile of the corresponding cell of Table 11-2. For example, given

TABLE 11-2

x	x	x	x	x	x
x	x	x	x	x	x
y	y	y	y	y	y
y	y	y	y	y	y
z	z	z	z	z	z
z	z	z	z	z	z

the preference profile in the first row, second column cell of Table 11-1, Ta
ble 11-2 says the winner is alternative x.

Now it should be obvious that Table 11-2 represents a very special SDF
For each choice in it is person 1's most preferred alternative. This is a *dicte
torial* SDF: the social choice is always the favorite alternative of person 1
There is, of course, one other dictatorial SDF; it would be represented b
the transpose of the Table 11-2 matrix, and it would make 2 a dictator.

But we require that a foolproof SDF must be nondictatorial. Therefore
the SDF represented in Table 11-2 is unacceptable, as is the SDF that make
2 a dictator.

We also require that a foolproof SDF be *nontrivial* or *nondegenerate*. I
terms of the simple model at hand, this means that there must be some pre
erence profile that gives rise to the choice of x, that there must be som
(other) preference profile that gives rise to the choice of y, and that ther
must be some (other) preference profile that gives rise to the choice of z. I
other words, none of the three alternatives is irrevocably excluded fro
choice. In formal terms, each of x, y and z is included in the range of th
SDF. If one alternative were always excluded from choice, we would have
two-alternative model, or a degenerate, trivial version of the model at han

Now let's turn to the crucial requirement of *nonmanipulability*. How ca
we represent the idea that no person should ever have an incentive to falsel
reveal his preferences? How, in fact, can strategic behavior, manipulatio
or profitable lying, be represented in terms of these figures? We illustra
with an example.

Suppose we know some of the social choices for the preference profiles
•f row one of Table 11-1:

Social Choices

x	x	y	z	?	?

This is just part of one possible SDF.) That is, for the preference profile of
ow one, column one, we know that x wins; for the preference profile of
olumn two, x wins; for the preference profile of column three, y wins; for
he preference profile of column four, z wins, and we know nothing more.
n this case, person two has an opportunity to profitably misrepresent his
•references. Suppose his real preferences are

y
z (column four in Table 11-1).
x

That is, he prefers y to z to x.) If he reports this honestly (and 1 is also hon-
st), the SDF outcome is z. However, if he (falsely) claims his preferences
re

y
x (column three in Table 11-1),
z

he SDF outcome is y, which he (truly) prefers to z. In short, person 2 can
rofitably manipulate the SDF when person 1 prefers x to y to z and he pre-
ers y to z to x (that is, when the preference profile is the one in row one,
olumn four of Table 11-1).

If there is any opportunity for 1 (or 2) to secure a preferred outcome by
•isrepresenting his preferences, the SDF is said to be *manipulable*. If it is
ever possible for 1(or 2) to secure a preferred outcome by misrepresenta-
•on, the SDF is said to be *nonmanipulable,* or *cheatproof.*

Note that the definition of nonmanipulability used here only requires
•at an SDF be immune to lying by single individuals — not that it be im-
•une to lying by arbitrary groups of individuals. In the majority voting
•ith an agenda example of the last section, a group (both of the type 2
oters) profitably misrepresented its preferences. That was group-manipu-
•tion, or *coalition-manipulation.* One might require that an SDF be coali-
•on-nonmanipulable. But we only require individual-nonmanipulability,
nd our version of nonmanipulability is a less stringent requirement.

The SDF partly illustrated above is evidently manipulable. What about the dictatorial SDF of Table 11-2? Clearly 2 cannot manipulate it since his preferences never affect the outcome. Misrepresenting them must be useless. Nor can 1 manipulate it, since he always gets his (true) first choice. He can never secure a preferred outcome by lying. Dictatorship is, therefore, nonmanipulable. However, it is unacceptable. We require that a foolproof SDF be nondictatorial.

Are there any nontrivial, nondictatorial and nonmanipulable SDF's?

Since there are 150 thousand trillion possible SDF's in this simple model, it is obviously impossible to systematically examine all of them to discover which, if any, are universal, nondictatorial, nonmanipulable, and nondegenerate. Nonetheless, an unambiguous negative answer to the question can be reached, in a profound, inescapable "impossibility" theorem much like Arrow's theorem. The theorem, discovered independently by Allan Gibbard and Mark Allen Satterthwaite in the 1970s, says *there are no foolproof social decision functions.*

We shall turn to a formal statement and proof of the theorem below. The proof, however, will depend on an intuitively appealing proposition, which we state here and prove in the Appendix to this chapter:

Proposition 1: Suppose an SDF is nondegenerate and nonmanipulable. Suppose both people prefer one alternative to a second alternative. Then the social choice, the winner, cannot be the second alternative.

Now we can turn to the fundamental result:

The Gibbard-Satterthwaite Impossibility Theorem: Any SDF which satisfies the universality, nondegeneracy, and nonmanipulability requirements must be dictatorial. Therefore, there is no SDF which satisfies all requirements.

Proof: The proposition above implies that any nondegenerate nonmanipulable SDF must be consistent with Table 11-3.

For example, if person 1 prefers x to y to z and person 2 prefers x to z to y (the first row, second column cell of Table 11-1), the proposition says that neither y nor z can be the social choice, since both people prefer x to y, and both people prefer x to z. Therefore, the social choice must be x. Again, for the first row, third column preference profile of Table 11-1, where person 1 prefers x to y to z and person prefers y to x to z, the social choice cannot be z, since both prefer x to z. This line of reasoning is applied to the entirety of Table 11-1, to get Table 11-3.

TABLE 11-3

Social Choices

x	x	not z	not z	not y	
x	x	not z		not y	not y
not z	not z	y	y		not x
not z		y	y	not x	not x
not y	not y		not x	z	z
	not y	not x	not x	z	z

Now let us focus on the first row of Table 11-1:

1	2	1	2	1	2	1	2	1	2	1	2
x	x	x	x	x	y	x	y	x	z	x	z
y	y	y	z	y	x	y	z	y	x	y	y
z	z	z	y	z	z	z	x	z	y	z	x

Thus far, this much is known about the corresponding social choices:

Social Choices

x	x	not z	not z	not y	

To start the machinery cranking, an assumption must be made: Suppose that the social choice for the third column cell (which cannot be z) is x.

It follows that:

Social Choices

x	x	x	not z	not y	

Now if the social choice in column four, five or six were y, person 2 would have an opportunity to manipulate in column three. That is, he could force the choice of y instead of x, when his real preferences are

y
x,
z

by pretending his preferences were as in four, five, or six. Therefore, for any nonmanipulable SDF, we must have:

Social Choices

x	x	x	x	not y	not y

Next, if the social choice in column five or six were z, person 2 would have an opportunity to manipulate in column four. That is, he could force the choice of z instead of x, when his real preferences are

y
z,
x

by pretending his preferences were as in five or six. Therefore, for any nonmanipulable SDF, we must have:

Social Choices

x	x	x	x	x	x

Similarly reasoning forces particular social choices as one drops down and fills in all thirty-six cells in Table 11-3. The rest of the filling in process is left as an exercise. When all thirty-six cells are filled in, the result is a table identical to Table 11-2, and consequently, *person 1 is a dictator*.

This outcome became inevitable when we assumed that the social choice for the first row, third column cell was x. Had we assumed y, person 2 would have been the dictator.

In either case, a nondegenerate nonmanipulable SDF must be dictatorial. Therefore, there is no nondegenerate, nondictatorial cheatproof SDF.   Q.E.D.

Before leaving the theorem we should make some observations about the special case nature of the proof. Here there are two individuals, three alternatives and no indifference. Using more sophisticated tools the theorem is generalizable to two or more individuals, three or more alternatives, and indifference permissible. Proofs are in the articles referred to at the end of this chapter.

SIGNIFICANCE OF THE
GIBBARD-SATTERTHWAITE THEOREM

It is worthwhile to briefly discuss the significance of the Gibbard-Satterthwaite Theorem. What does the theorem say, and what doesn't it say? First of all, it doesn't say that there are no useful social decision functions. Obviously we can and do live with imperfect decision rules. Majority voting, with an agenda to make cycles impossible, is for many people an acceptable SDF, in spite of the fact that it is not foolproof. It is certainly superior to dictatorship. Demand-revealing tax schemes may in some cases provide acceptable SDF's, although the assumption of separability for utility functions violates our universality requirement. Nor does the theorem say that no decision will be reached in a given situation. Some alternative is always chosen.

However, the Gibbard-Satterthwaite Theorem does raise questions about how people will behave in making social decisions. For example, what sorts of strategies will they adopt when they are all acting dishonestly? It does raise questions about the dynamics of decision making: How do people react to one another's preferences? How do 1's misstatements of preferences affect 2's? And how do 2's affect 1's? Through what process of feint and counterfeint is an equilibrium reached?

It also raises questions about the optimality of any social decision. The rules we generally use are manipulable, so we cannot rely on Proposition 1 above to guarantee Pareto optimality. There is no a priori reason to believe that non-Pareto optimal choices won't be made. What choices are ultimately made depends on assumptions about strategic behavior, and optimality of the final equilibrium depends on these assumptions as well.

The Gibbard-Satterthwaite Theorem does raise questions about political legitimacy: In a world in which many, or all voters are misrepresenting their preferences, it is difficult to say that an outcome is "right" or "correct" or "proper" or "legitimate." Suppose for instance, that candidate A wins an election process in which there were several other candidates, and suppose that some people voted "as if" their preferences were other than what they really are. It is then slightly naive to maintain that A is the "people's choice," the "legitimate" winner, since it is quite possible that if other people had misrepresented their preferences B might have won, or, if everyone had voted honestly, C might have won!

Finally, in the economic sphere, the Gibbard-Satterthwaite theorem raises questions about the provision of public goods like bridges, parks, schools, roads, national defense, and so on. How narrow are the circumstances under which one can truly say: this project should be carried through; this bridge should be built?

In short, if people vote strategically, or report their preferences for public goods strategically, the final outcome produced by an SDF falls under a more or less dark cloud of suspicion. And the Gibbard-Satterthwaite Theorem says that cloud covers a lot of territory.

EXERCISES

1. For the bridge example of this chapter, suppose T_i is defined as follows:

$$T_i = \begin{cases} \dfrac{1}{n-1} \sum_{j \neq i} v_j + [C - \sum_{j \neq i} v_j], & \text{if } \sum_{j \neq i} v_j < C \leq \sum_{i=1}^{n} v_i \\[2em] \dfrac{1}{n-1} \sum_{j \neq i} v_j, & \text{otherwise} \end{cases}$$

It is assumed here that the

$$\frac{1}{n-1} \sum_{j \neq i} v_j$$

is always collected, whether or not the bridge is built!

Show that no individual can profitably misrepresent his preferences, given this tax rule. Show that the Bridge Board will have enough revenue if it does build the bridge.

2. For the bridge example, can you find a tax scheme that satisfies all the following requirements?
   a. No one ever gains by misrepresenting v_i.
   b. If the bridge is built, that is, if

$$\sum_{i=1}^{n} v_i \geq C$$

   the Bridge Board has sufficient revenue, that is

$$\sum_{i=1}^{n} T_i \geq C$$

   c. If the bridge is not built, that is, if

$$\sum_{i=1}^{n} v_i < C,$$

   then all the T_i's are zero
   (Warning: Actually it cannot be done!)
3. Plurality rule is an SDF that works as follows. There are n candidates. Each person ranks the candidates in his order of preference (assuming no one is indifferent between two candidates). The Election Board collects the rankings, and, for each candidate, counts the number of times he is ranked first. Barring ties, the candidate with the highest number of firsts is the winner.
   Construct an example to show how plurality rule might be manipulated.
4. The Reverend C. L. Dodgeson (better known as Lewis Carroll, and author of *Alice's Adventures in Wonderland*) wrote several pamphlets on voting rules. (These pamphlets are reproduced in part in Duncan Black's *Theory of Committee and Elections*.) One of Dodgeson's rules is called the "method of marks," and it works as follows. Each voter gets a certain fixed number of points, or "marks," which he may distribute among the various candidates as he chooses. For instance, if a voter gets 10 points, he might assign 3.5 points to candidate A, 4.5 points to candidate B, 2 points to candidate C, and zero to all the rest.
   Construct an example with three candidates and three voters, where each voter gets 10 points to distribute, to show that Dodgeson's method of marks is liable to strategic voting.
5. A multistage procedure called exhaustive voting works as follows. There are n candidates for a position. In the first stage of the voting,

each voter assigns one vote to each of the $n - 1$ candidates he likes best — and assigns no vote to the candidate he likes worst. The votes are counted, and the candidate with the smallest total is dropped from the field. In the second stage, each voter assigns one vote to each of the $n - 2$ candidates he likes best — and assigns no vote to the candidate he likes worst. Again, the votes are counted, and the candidate with the smallest total in this stage is dropped from the field. The process continues through stages 3, 4, . . ., until only one candidate remains. He is the winner. Consider the following preferences:

Type 1	Type 2	Type 3
A	B	C
B	C	A
C	A	B
(3 people)	(2 people)	(2 people).

Carefully show how the exhaustive voting procedure can be manipulated, if voters have the preferences indicated above.

6. In the proof of the Gibbard-Satterthwaite Theorem, the nondegeneracy and nonmanipulability assumptions were used to fill the six cells of row one of Table 11-3. Continue the filling in process in the remainder of the thirty-six cells.

APPENDIX

We now turn to the proof of Proposition 1. We will, in fact, present a more general result than the one given above. We suppose that there are n people and many alternatives. The notation here is also slightly more complicated than what was used above. We let the function F represent an SDF, and $(P_1, P_2, \ldots, P_n)$ a preference profile for the n people. Alternatives will be denoted with X's and Y's. XP_iY then means person i prefers X to Y. F transforms preference profiles into winning alternatives, we can write, for example, $F(P_1, P_2, \ldots, P_n) = X$. If this is the case for some preference profile, alternative X is said to be in the range of F.

Proposition. Suppose the SDF F is nonmanipulable, and X is in the range of F. If XP_iY for all i, then, $F(P_1, P_2, \ldots, P_n) \neq Y$.

Proof. Define P_i' from P_i by moving $\{X, Y\}$ to the top of i's list, preserving the $\{X, Y\}$ ordering ($XP_i'Y$ for all i), and preserving the ordering among all elements other than X and Y.

First, we claim that $F(P_1', P_2', \ldots, P_n') = X$. Suppose to the contrary that $F(P', P_2' \ldots, P_n') \neq X$, and let $(P_1'', P_2'', \ldots, P_n'')$ be a preference profile which does give rise to the choice of X.

Define $X_0 = F(P_1'', P_2'', \ldots, P_n'')$ $\quad (= X)$
$X_1 = F(P_1', P_2'', \ldots, P_n'')$
$X_2 = F(P_1', P_2', \ldots, P_n'')$

.

.

.

$X_n = F(P_1', P_2', \ldots, P_n')$ $\quad (\neq X)$.

Let j be the smallest number for which $X_j \neq X$. Then

$$F(P_1', \ldots, P_{j-1}', P_j'', \ldots, P_n'') = X$$

but

$$F(P_2', \ldots, P_{j-1}', P_j', \ldots, P_n'') = X_j \neq X$$

By the construction of P_j', $XP_j'X_j$. This implies F is manipulable by j at $(P_1'_j, \ldots, P_{j-1}', P_j', \ldots, P_n'')$, a contradiction. Therefore, $F(P_1', \ldots, P_n') = X$, as claimed.

Next, suppose that $F(P_1, P_2, \ldots, P_n) = Y$. Define

$Y_0 = F(P_1', P_2', \ldots, P_n')$ $\quad (= X)$
$Y_1 = F(P_1, P_2', \ldots, P_n')$
$Y_2 = F(P_1, P_2, \ldots, P_n')$

.

.

.

$Y_n = F(P_1, P_2, \ldots, P_n)$ $\quad (= Y)$

Let k be the largest number for which $Y_k \neq Y$. Then

$$F(P_1, \ldots, P_k, P_{k+1}', \ldots, P_n') = Y_k \neq Y$$

and

$$F(P_1, \ldots, P_k, P_{k+1}, \ldots, P_n') = Y$$

There are two cases to consider. (i) If $Y_k = X$, then $XP_{k+1}Y$ by assumption, and F is manipulable by $k+1$ at $(P_1, \ldots, P_k, P_{k-1}, \ldots, P_n')$, a contradiction. (ii) If $Y_k \neq X$, then $YP_{k+1}'Y_k$ by the construction of P_{k+1}', and F is manipulable by $k+1$ at $(P_1, \ldots, P_k, P_{k+1}', \ldots, P_n')$, again a contradiction. In either case the supposition that $F(P_1, \ldots, P_n) = Y$ is untenable, which completes the proof of the proposition.

Q.E.D.

SELECTED REFERENCES

(Items marked with an asterisk (*) are mathematically difficult.)

1. D. Black, *The Theory of Committees and Elections,* Cambridge University Press, London, 1958.

    See the Chapter 9 References section.

2. R. Farquharson, "Theory of Voting," Yale University Press, New Haven, 1969.

    This remarkable short book was written a decade before it was published, and so it ranks as one of the earliest serious treatments of strategic voting. Farquharson writes in his preface that he studied the works of Kenneth Arrow and Duncan Black, but "found, however, that they both assumed that voters used neither strategy nor skill, while Von Neumann and Morgenstern, to whom their footnotes referred me, had not applied the theory of games to actual voting procedures." So Farquharson proceeded to do just that.

    The interesting and readable monograph develops several of the notions later used by Gibbard and Satterthwaite: particularly sincere voting, and straightforward (dominant) strategies.

*3. P. Gärdenfors, "A Concise Proof of a Theorem on Manipulation of Social Choice Functions," Public Choice, 1977.

    Gärdenfors provides a relatively clear version of the proof of the Gibbard-Satterthwaite Theorem in the general, many person, many alternative case.

4. P. Gärdenfors, "On Definitions of Manipulation of Social Choice Functions," in J. J. Laffont, ed., *Aggregation and Revelation of Preferences,* North-Holland Publishing Co., 1979.

    In this clearly written paper, Gärdenfors surveys possible definitions of manipulation for social decision functions that produce multiple winners, or multiple best alternatives. (One example is an election procedure that allows ties. Another is a rule that generates a whole set of good alternatives, like the rule that defines the set of Pareto optima.) When there are multivalued choice sets, manipulation has many possible interpretations, since there are many senses in which an individual might prefer one set of alternatives to another set.

5. T. Groves and J. Ledyard, "Some Limitations of Demand Revealing Processes," *Public Choice,* V. XXIX-2, 1977, pp. 107–124.

    See the Chapter 6 References section.

*6. A. Gibbard, "Manipulation of Voting Schemes: A General Result," *Econometrica,* V. 41, 1973, pp. 587–601.

    This paper has the first published version of the Gibbard-Satterthwaite Theorem. Actually, Gibbard proves something more general. A game form is a rule that transforms strategies of all the players into outcomes, so an SDF is a special type of game form, in which the only playable strategies are preference relations. And a game form is straightforward if each player always has a dominant strategy, that is, a strategy that will produce a best outcome for him no matter what the other players do.

Gibbard proves that no nontrivial game form is straightforward. The result on what we have called SDF's and what Gibbard calls voting schemes follows immediately.

The first half of the paper is nonmathematical and very clear.

*7. A. Gibbard, "Manipulation of Schemes that Mix Voting with Chance," *Econometrica*, V. 45, 1977, pp. 665–681.

Some SDF's (or voting schemes, in Gibbard's terms) mix voting and lotteries. For instance, a two-way tie for first place might be broken by the flip of a coin. Or, voting might work this way. Everyone might write down the name of his favorite candidate. Let p_A = the proportion of ballots with A's name, p_B = the proportion of ballots with B's name, and so on. All the ballots might be mixed together, and the winner might be drawn at random from the mixed ballots. Then A's probability of winning would be p_A, etc.

Gibbard characterizes nonmanipulable mixed schemes in this paper.

*8. M. A. Satterthwaite, "Strategy-Proofness and Arrow's Conditions: Existence and Correspondence Theorems for Voting Procedures and Social Welfare Functions," *Journal of Economic Theory*, V. 10, 1975, pp. 187–217.

This is Satterthwaite's original version of the Gibbard-Satterthwaite Theorem. Unlike Gibbard's, Satterthwaite's version of the proof does not rely on the Arrow Impossibility Theorem. In fact, Satterthwaite shows that his theorem can be used to provide a new proof of Arrow's Theorem.

9. T. Nicolaus Tideman, ed., *Public Choice,* V. XXIX-2, Special Supplement to Spring, 1977.

See the Chapter 6 References section.

12 EPILOGUE

Welfare economics and social choice theory are about the "goodness" or "badness" of economic arrangements in particular, and social choices in general. They offer partial answers to questions like these: Does a competitive economic system produce good results? Is there a necessary connection between market competition and optimality? Are there criteria for judging among distributions of goods, or wealth, other then market criteria? For example, is fairness an appropriate criterion for deciding when our distribution of goods is superior to another? Are traditional nonmarket decision methods, like voting, able to show us what social choices are good and what are bad? Are there intrinsic logical limitations to all methods, market and nonmarket, for deciding what social alternatives are good and what are bad?

In this book we were guided by the principals that any judgment about social welfare, or about what is good or bad for society, had to be directly based on the welfare of the individuals involved. And the best judge of a particular individual's welfare is that individual himself. This means that we took individuals' preferences as given, as the foundation upon which all the analysis rests. It also means, for example, that if a group of people do some-

216

thing which a consumer advocate, or an energy official, or a religious leader, considers awful, they are nonetheless best off doing the awful thing. What is good for society depends fundamentally on what individuals consider to be good for themselves.

Since individual preferences were viewed as fundamental here, Chapter 1 began with an analysis of individual preferences. An individual was characterized by a preference relation defined over an abstract set of alternatives. We saw that if a preference relation is complete and transitive, or even only complete and acyclic, it is possible to use it to find best alternatives. We also saw that if the preference relation is complete and transitive, it can be used to derive a utility function. These preference relations, or equivalently, these utility functions, provide the basic givens throughout all the subsequent analysis.

With utilities or preferences in hand, in Chapters 2 and 3 we analyzed barter exchange, and market (or price governed) exchange. Chapter 2 developed elementary analytical tools, such as the Edgeworth box diagram, and also developed modern game-theoretic exchange notions, in particular, blocking and the core. Roughly speaking, a group of traders can block a proposed allocation if it can achieve with its own resources a distribution of goods that its members prefer to the proposed one. The core is the set of unblocked allocations. This is the set of allocations of goods that would evolve in a world with costless, frictionless, bargining. It is the set of solutions in a perfect exchange economy, and it clearly has significance for welfare economists. An allocation in the core is good in the sense that no group can oppose it on the grounds that it can do better by itself. Conversely, an allocation outside of the core is bad in the sense that some group can oppose it on these grounds. Any allocation in the core must be Pareto optimal; the concept of the core is a refinement of the concept of Pareto optimality.

Chapter 3 introduced prices into the barter model. It developed a market model of exchange. Traders chose what to buy and sell according to market-clearing prices. A competitive equilibrium was defined as a situation in which every person chooses the bundle of goods that maximizes his utility, subject to his budget constraint, and in which supply equals demand for every good. In this chapter the two fundamental theorems of welfare economics were introduced, discussed, and in one case proved. The First Fundamental Theorem traces its roots to Adam Smith. It says, roughly, that the free market will bring a society to a good economic organization. Competitive buying and selling among selfish and possibly greedy traders leads to a social optimum. In Chapter 3, the theorem took this form: Any competitive equilibrium allocation of goods must be a core allocation, and must be Pareto optimal.

The Second Fundamental Theorem is almost a converse of the first. It says, roughly, that any Pareto optimal allocation must be achievable through the competitive mechanism, given an appropriate cash transfer system. The theorem implies that any economy, even a socialist economy, can turn to the market mechanism to achieve its ends. If a planner in a socialist state, for example, wants to bring about a particular egalitarian and Pareto optimal distribution of goods, he need not rely on a gigantic bureaucracy to distribute all goods to all people. He can instead use a relatively simple cash transfer program, and let the market work by itself.

The thrust of Chapter 3, in short, was this: in an exchange economy, the market mechanism leads to distributions of goods that are Pareto optimal, and in this sense good for society, and the market mechanism, suitably modified, can be used to get to any particular Pareto optimal distribution of goods.

In Chapter 4 we developed a model of production. This model starts with production sets, defines optimality for production plans, and then relates production to the market mechanism. The production versions of the two fundamental theorems of welfare economics were discussed and proved.

The main thrust of Chapters 3 and 4 was that the competitive mechanism produces results that are good for society. However, there are two basic shortcomings in all this. The first is that unregulated competition has mischievous properties assumed away in the classical theorems. For instance, there might be external or spillover effects. One person's price-governed consumption, or one firm's price-governed production, might directly affect another person's utility level, or another firms' production set. These effects might not be reflected properly in market prices, and consequently a competitive equilibrium might not be optimal after all. Or there might be public goods, which ought to be provided and paid for by a government; that is, there might be goods whose use is nonexclusive, and which would, if provided privately, break the link between the competitive market mechanism and optimality.

The second shortcoming of the competitive mechanism is its neglect of equity: even if it leads to a Pareto optimal allocation, that allocation might be quite unequal, or quite unfair. The Second Fundamental Theorem does say that any equitable Pareto optimal allocation can be reached via a modified competitive mechanism. But how do we judge among allocations to find the one that is not only Pareto optimal, but also best for society? What are the criteria for judging among Pareto optima? How do we choose the best from among the optimal? The market provides no clue.

Chapter 5 provided a brief treatment of externalities, and, with examples, sketched how the competitive mechanism might be modified to correct spillover effects. The basic principal there was the idea of a Pigouvian tax or subsidy. A person or firm which is imposing external costs (or benefits) on others ought to be taxed (or subsidized) at a rate equal to marginal external cost (or marginal external benefit).

Chapter 6 provided a lengthy treatment of public goods. The crucial question there was: What system of public decision making and taxation will bring about the optimal output of a public good? The Wicksell-Lindahl tax scheme satisfies Samuelson's optimality condition, and it links a person's tax to his marginal utility from the public good. However, its disadvantage is its extreme susceptibility to abuse by free riders, people who claim a low marginal utility and consequently pay a low tax, even though they get substantial benefits from the public good. The fixed tax shares majority voting scheme is not so vulnerable to free rides, but it will generally lead to levels of output for the public good that do not satisfy the Samuelson optimality condition. The demand-revealing tax scheme solves the free rider problem since it provides no incentives for people to misrepresent their preferences. And it lead to an optimal level of output for the public good. However, it might collect more taxes than necessary to produce the public goods, and, because of the special logic of this tax system, it might be necessary to waste this budget surplus. Consequently, the demand-revealing tax scheme might lead to a situation that is overall not Pareto optimal, even though it involves an optimal level of output for the public good. The Groves-Ledyard tax scheme also leads to an optimal level of output for the public good, and, unlike the demand revealing tax scheme, it produces no wasteful budget surplus. However, it does not solve the free rider problem so much as it sidesteps it, and, unfortunately, it depends on an iterative process whose convergence is an open question. In short, the public goods problem is complicated and not yet completely solved, but there are decentralized ways to bring about optimality in the provision of these goods. The market mechanism should not be abandoned because of the existence of public goods.

Chapter 7 and the subsequent chapters addressed the second shortcoming of the competitive mechanism: How do we judge among allocations to find one that is not only Pareto optimal, but also socially best? Chapter 7 reviewed the compensation criteria or social improvement criteria traditionally used in applied fields of microeconomics. These criteria were first developed by Nicholas Kaldor, Tibor Scitovsky, and Paul Samuelson, in order to refine the economist's ability to judge among social alternatives; in order to allow the economist to say "*A* is better for society than *B*," even when either *A* or *B* might come about through the market mechanism. The underlying theme here is something like this. *A* is better than *B* if the gainers in a move from B to A gain so much that they could, in theory, compensate the losers for their losses in the move from B to A. We saw that this criterion, and the more sophisticated ones derived from it, all had logical drawbacks. For instance, neither the Kaldor, the Scitovsky, nor the Samuelson criterion can successfully distinguish between alternative Pareto optimal allocations in an Edgeworth box diagram.

Chapter 8 jumped straight away from the traditional compensation criteria, and away from the usual welfare-competition analysis. It examined the idea of fairness in the non-envy sense, and the Rawls criterion, as ways to judge when one distribution of goods is better for society than another. But again there are problems. Fairness is not in fact a criterion that one can join to the market mechanism, or to the Pareto criterion, in order to find out what is really best for society. For it turns out that the criterion of fairness might conflict with the other usual economic criteria, and that fairness might not survive trade. Fairness and either barter or market exchange, do not mix well. The Rawls criterion, the idea of maximizing the welfare of the worst off person, has the serious disadvantage of being overly biased toward the poor. It implies a social preference for a state in which everyone is poor, to a state in which one person is very poor but thousands of others are very rich. In short, if we want to narrow down the range of good social alternatives, if we want to decide among Pareto optima, we ought to look beyond these two egalitarian criteria.

Chapter 9 and the subsequent chapters looked at other (mostly) nonmarket choice mechanisms. The market mechanism generally cannot tell us when alternative A is better for society than alternative B. What about voting rules? Can they serve this purpose? Can the "will of the people" be discovered in election procedures, rather than in the market? Can voting rules answer the questions about what is socially best that the market mechanisms leave unanswered? Chapter 9 examined the most common voting procedure, majority rule. The voting paradox of Condorcet was presented, and the paradox was "solved" for the special case of single-peaked preferences, first analyzed by Duncan Black. The significance of Black's Theorems is that for particular types of individual preferences, majority voting provides a logically ideal way to decide when alternative A is socially preferable to alternative B, and, in fact to decide what alternatives are socially best. Unfortunately, single-peakedness is a rather stringent condition, and it cannot be easily generalized to multidimensional alternative sets. Since the distribution of goods or income is inherently a multidimensional problem, majority voting fails as a logically satisfactory way to decide when a distribution A is socially preferable to another distribution B.

The search for means to judge among social alternatives continued in Chapter 10.

There we presented the general question raised by Kenneth Arrow: Does there exist a method to judge between social alternatives that has no serious flaws? The Pareto criterion is flawed by its inability to judge among the many Pareto noncomparable states. The majority voting rule is flawed by its possible inconsistencies, its paradoxes. The criterion of fairness is flawed by its possible incompatibility with voluntary, utility-increasing trades. Is there any foolproof way to discover which alternatives are socially better than which? Chapter 10 presented a simple model in which the question is answered with Arrow's Impossibility Theorem. This theorem says that there is no completely satisfactory way to aggregate individual preference relations. There is no completely satisfactory collective choice rule. Every mechanism for deciding whether A is socially "better" than B has, inevitably, serious shortcomings.

This negative answer was carried further in Chapter 11. There we examined social decision functions (SDF's), or rules that produced unique socially best alternatives, rather than the collective choice rules. In Chapter 11, we picked up a criterion for foolproof that first appeared in Chapter 6, on public goods: We required that a social decision function be immune to strategic misrepresentation of preferences, in order to be considered foolproof. The idea is that if people misrepresent their true feelings, and the outcome of (say) a voting process is alternative A, it is implausible to argue that A is really socially "best"!

Does there then exist a foolproof SDF, an SDF that is not liable to manipulation, and that is also nondictatorial and nontrivial? The negative answer is given in the Gibbard-Satterthwaite Impossibility Theorem. This theorem says that every procedure will in some circumstances induce people to misrepresent their preferences. Consequently, the decisions of any social choice procedure, any voting procedure, any rule to decide what is socially best, are suspect.

To sum up, this book had a positive half and a negative half. The positive half was in the analysis of the market mechanism. There the major result was that there is a fundamental tendency for the market to produce Pareto optimal distribution of goods. A competitive equilibrium allocation is likely to be Pareto optimal. It might not be equal, it might not be fair, but it is apt to be Pareto optimal. The negative half was in the analysis of nonmarket mechanisms. If one wants to make fine judgments about what is best and what isn't best for society, if one wants to judge among Pareto optimal distributions of goods, then problems appear. And the theorems of the last two chapters indicate these problems are inescapable. We know that the market gives good results. But if we insist on finding the best among the good by invoking nonmarket rules, then we are in trouble.

SUBJECT INDEX

AUTHOR INDEX